THAT CAN BE ARRANGED

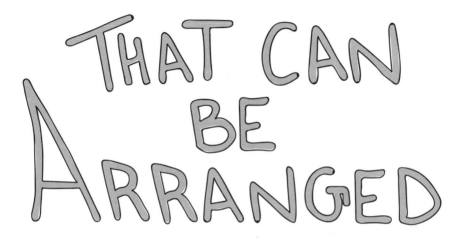

THAT CAN BE ARRANGED

A Muslim Love Story

Huda Fahmy

Andrews McMeel
PUBLISHING®

To Gehad.

From His signs is that amongst yourselves He
created spouses for you to find tranquility in them;
and He put affection and mercy between you.

(Quran 30:21)

Dear Reader,

I can't wait for you to get into this not so "once upon a time" tale of love, life, and low self-esteem. In case the cover didn't give it away, I am a Muslim woman who wears the hijab. That means I cover my hair in public and also wear long, loose clothing to cover the shape of my body.

Because I consider my character an extension of myself, I have made the personal choice to never draw her without hijab. I bring this up because I don't want you to be confused when you see my character sleeping or going to the salon in her hijab and mistakenly assume that it's normal hijabi behavior. SO, for the record:

I **do not** shower with it on.
I **do not** sleep with it on.
I **do** take it off to get my hair done.
I **do** take it off at "ladies only" weddings.
I **do not** cover when I'm at home.
I **do not** cover in front of my husband.

I also want to mention that arranged marriages come in many shapes and sizes. Some couples meet before they wed, while others might not see their betrothed until the day of. Arranged marriages are not to be confused with forced marriages. Contrary to popular belief, forced marriages are not allowed in Islam.

And, this really should go without saying, but say it I shall: this book is specifically about *my* life experiences and should not be used to make assumptions or generalizations about Muslims as a whole. We are not a monolith. Please remember that, just like with anything else, experiences vary from person to person and culture to culture.

Thank you for reading! And if you're like me and usually skip the preface of a book, enjoy being confused about Huda wearing a hijab to bed.

Sincerely,

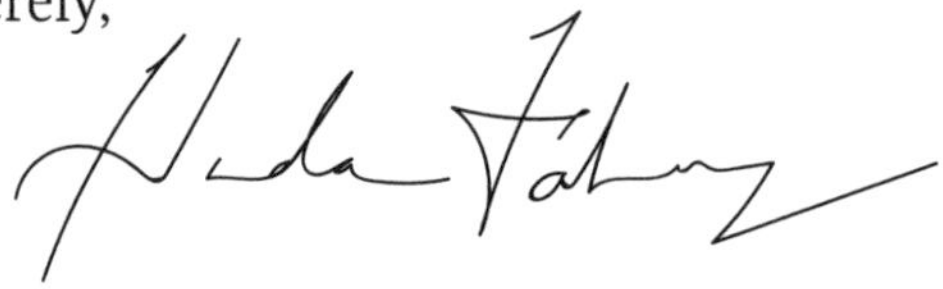

Helpful Terms

Abaya: Arabic word that refers to the long, loose-fitting dress worn by some Muslim women.

Allah: the Arabic word for God; the One who created everything and deserves all worship

Aunty: a woman who is middle-aged or older who offers unsolicited advice to anyone in a five-mile radius. Most powerful around other aunties. *Will* ask you to marry her son upon first meeting you.

Bint: Arabic word meaning "daughter of"

Ilm: Arabic word used to describe religious pursuits of knowledge

Islam: a monotheistic faith; the religion of Muslims. The Arabic root of the word means "submission to God."

Muslim: a follower of the religion of Islam. Arabic word meaning "one who submits to God."

the Prophet (peace be upon him): Prophet Mohammed (pbuh) was the last and final messenger sent by God as a guide for all mankind and to whom the holy Quran was revealed.

Qadr: destiny that was decreed for us before we were even born but can sometimes be changed by appealing to God through worship, prayer, and good deeds

Quran: the words of God revealed to His prophet, Mohammed (pbuh). The central religious text of Islam.

Salam: the shortened greeting Muslims give each other either coming or going. It is an Arabic word meaning "peace." The full greeting is "assalamu alaikum," meaning "peace be upon you."

Shay: Arabic word meaning "tea"

Sheikh: a leader in a Muslim community usually known for their knowledge of the religion. Slang: can be used ironically to refer to anyone with vast amounts of knowledge: *ex., Sheikh Google.*

Shik Shak Shook: popular song by Hassan Abou El Seoud played on repeat at weddings

Yallah: slang Arabic word meaning "come on" or "hurry up"

Zagharit (zaghrouta): celebratory ululations, usually high-pitched and shrill (the more shrill the better)

Introduction

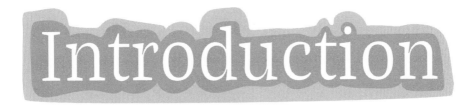

It is a truth universally acknowledged, that a single woman of 25 will probably never get married. Well . . . that was the truth in my community anyway.

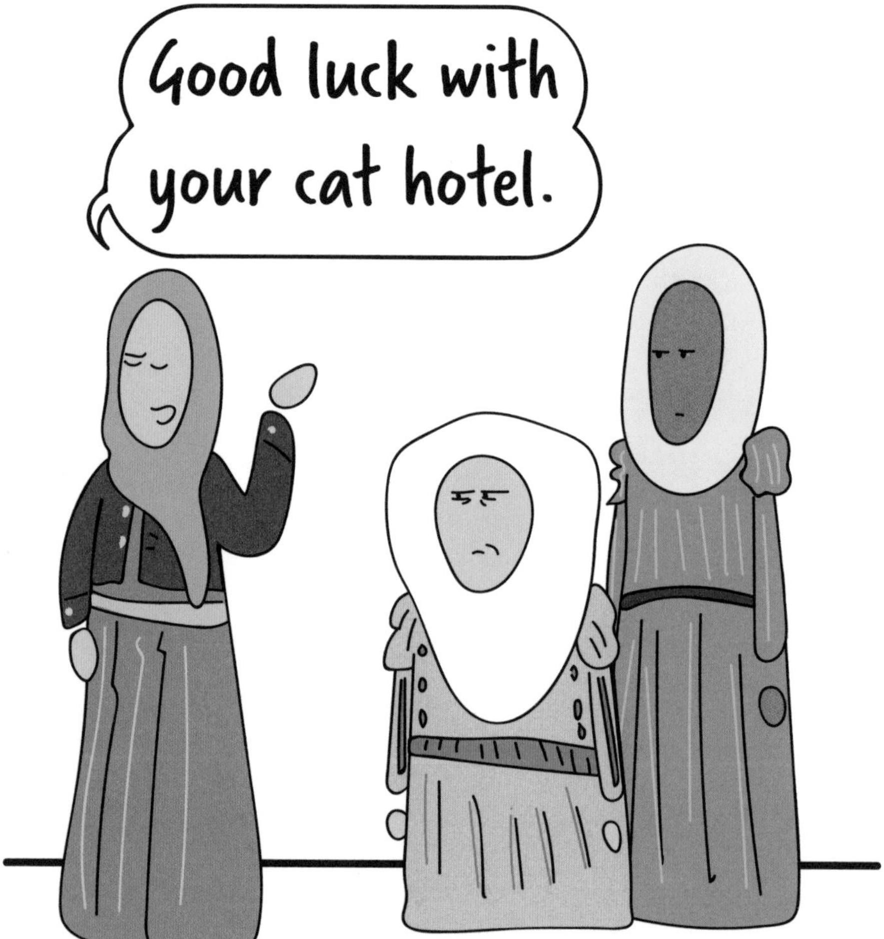
Good luck with your cat hotel.

As fate would have it, I would actually meet my future husband a few months after I turned 25.

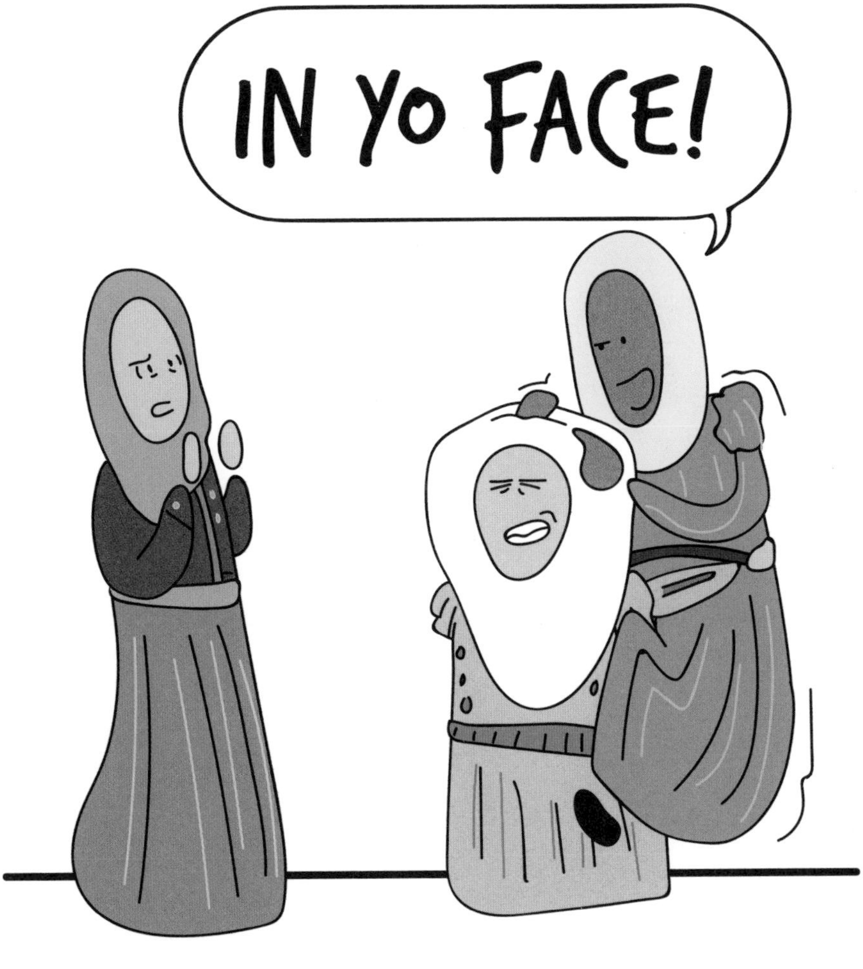
IN YO FACE!

I don't know if I believe in "love at first sight," but I do know that when I first saw my future husband onstage that day about to introduce the next speaker at the weeklong conference we both happened to be attending, I thought one thing:

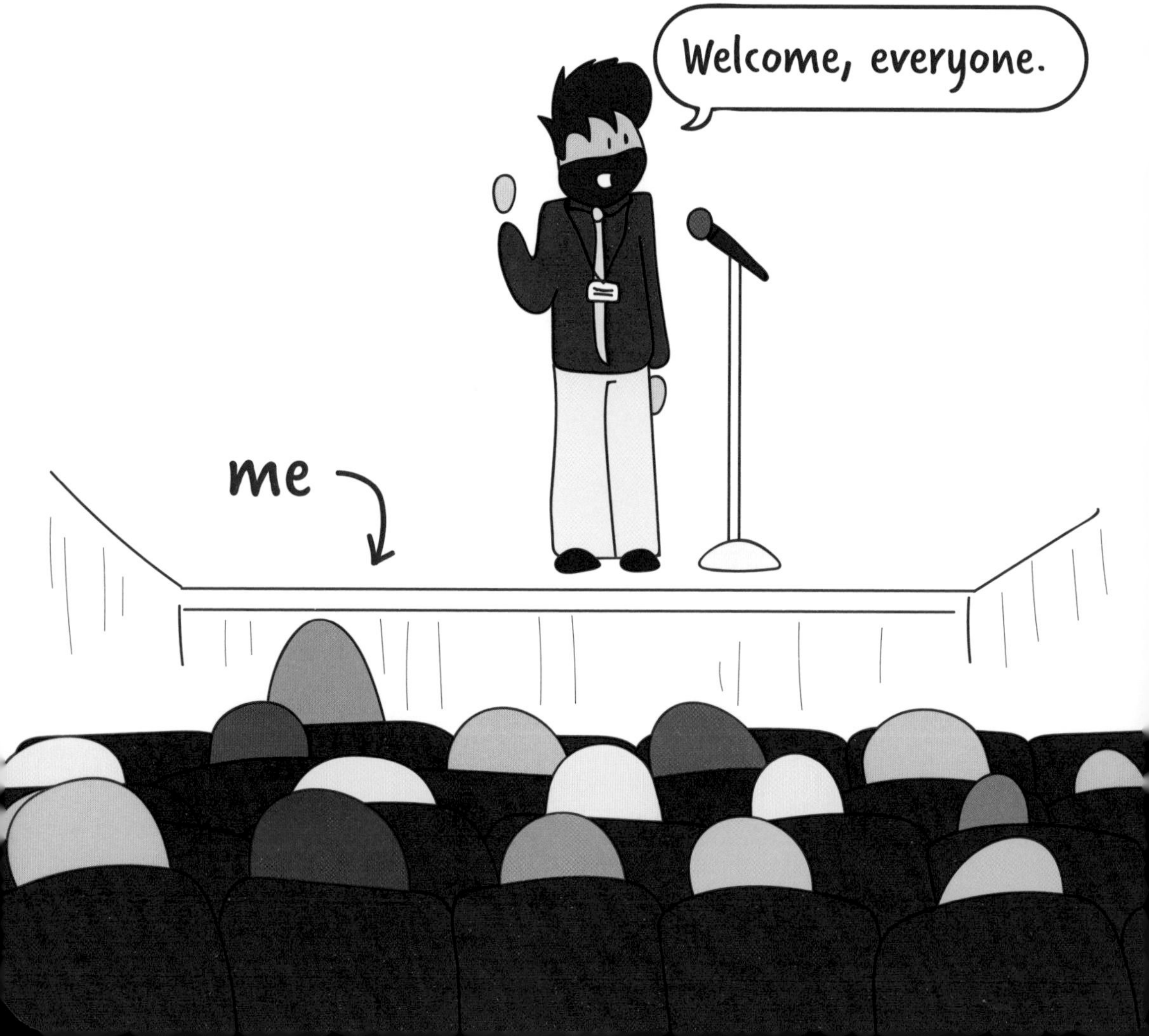
Welcome, everyone.
me

Daaang.

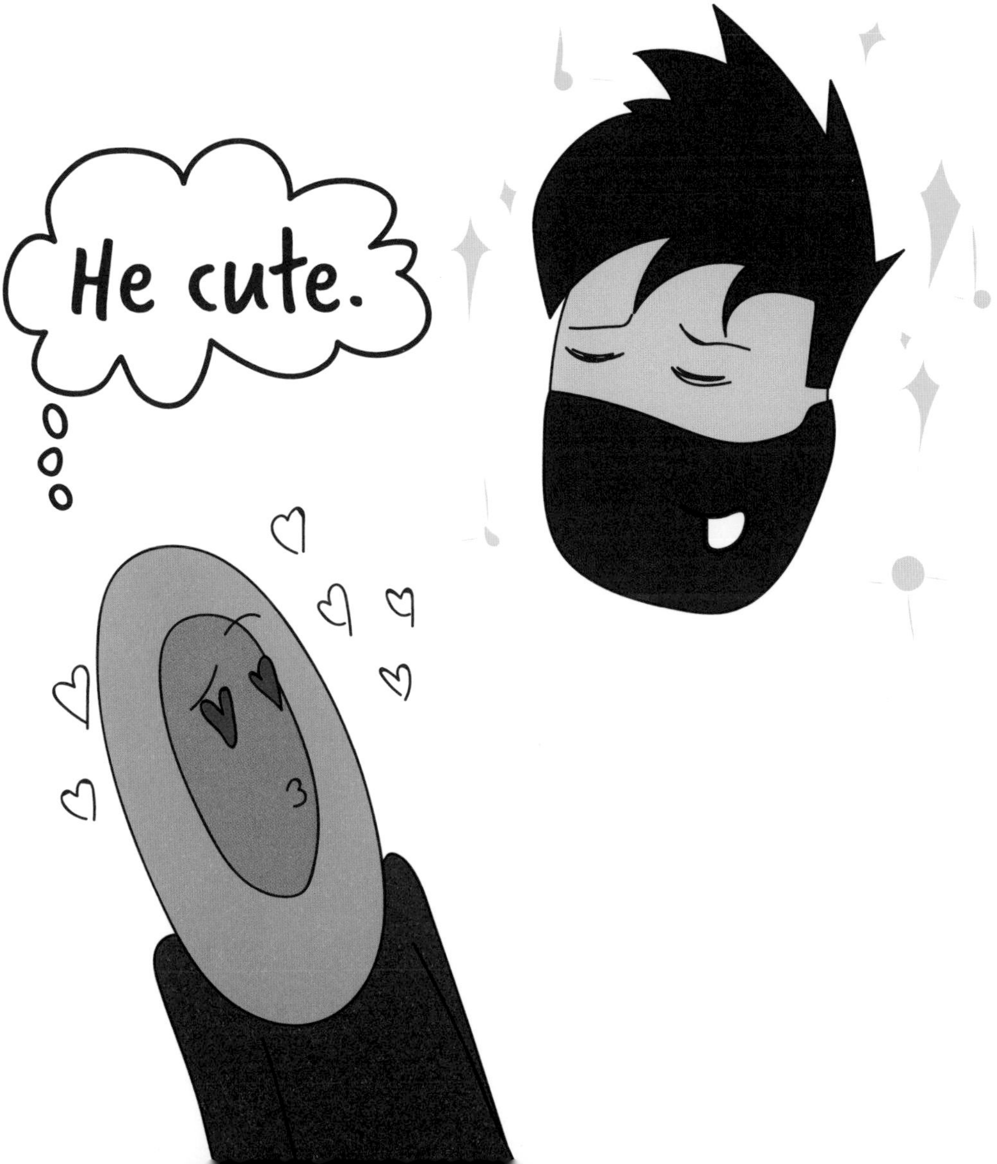
He cute.

He was calm under pressure, too.

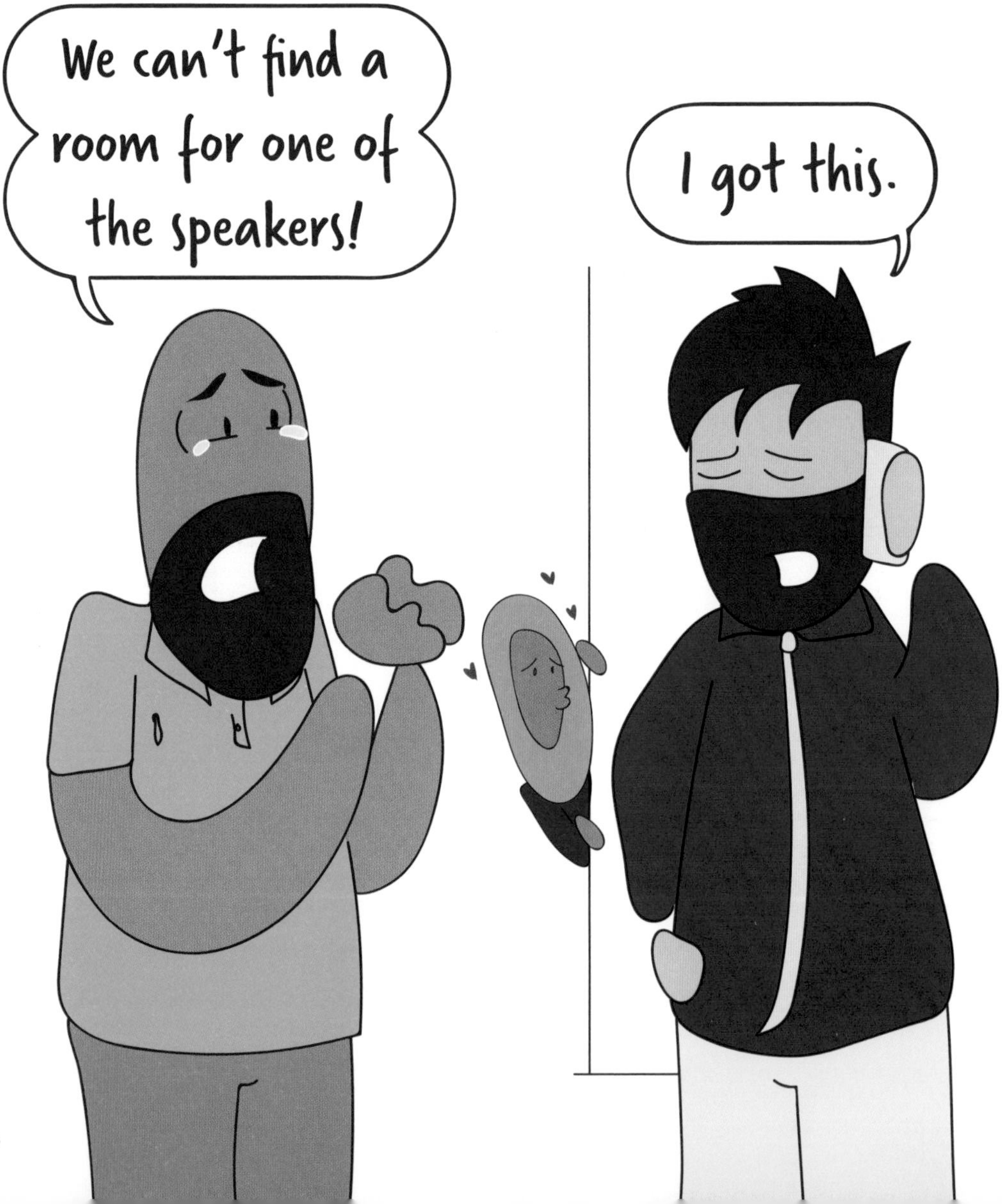
We can't find a room for one of the speakers!
I got this.

I wouldn't say I was head over heels. I mean, I barely knew the guy. But, somehow, I had this feeling that he was going to be the one. Or at least I really, really hoped he was.

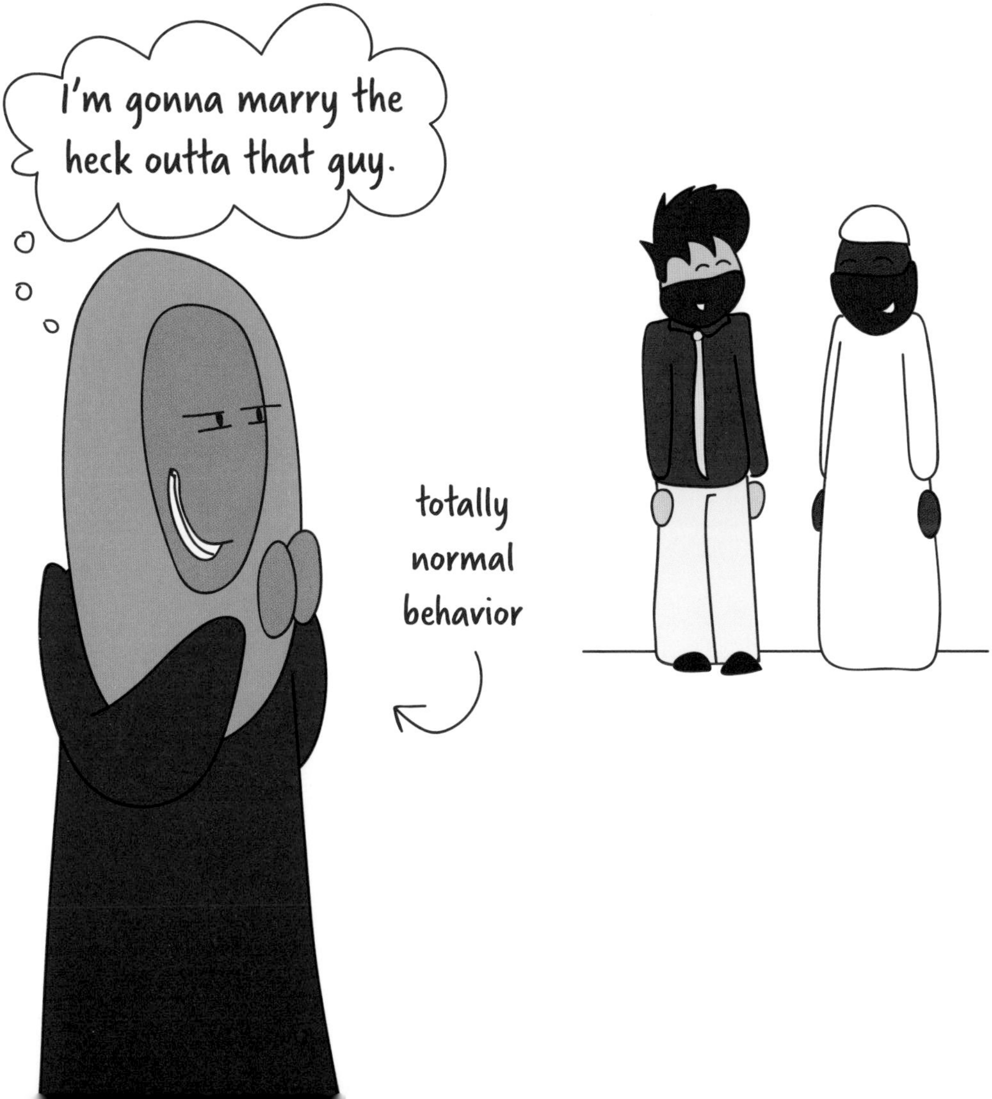

I'm gonna marry the heck outta that guy.
totally normal behavior

But look at me! I've gotten far too ahead of myself. Let's rewind.

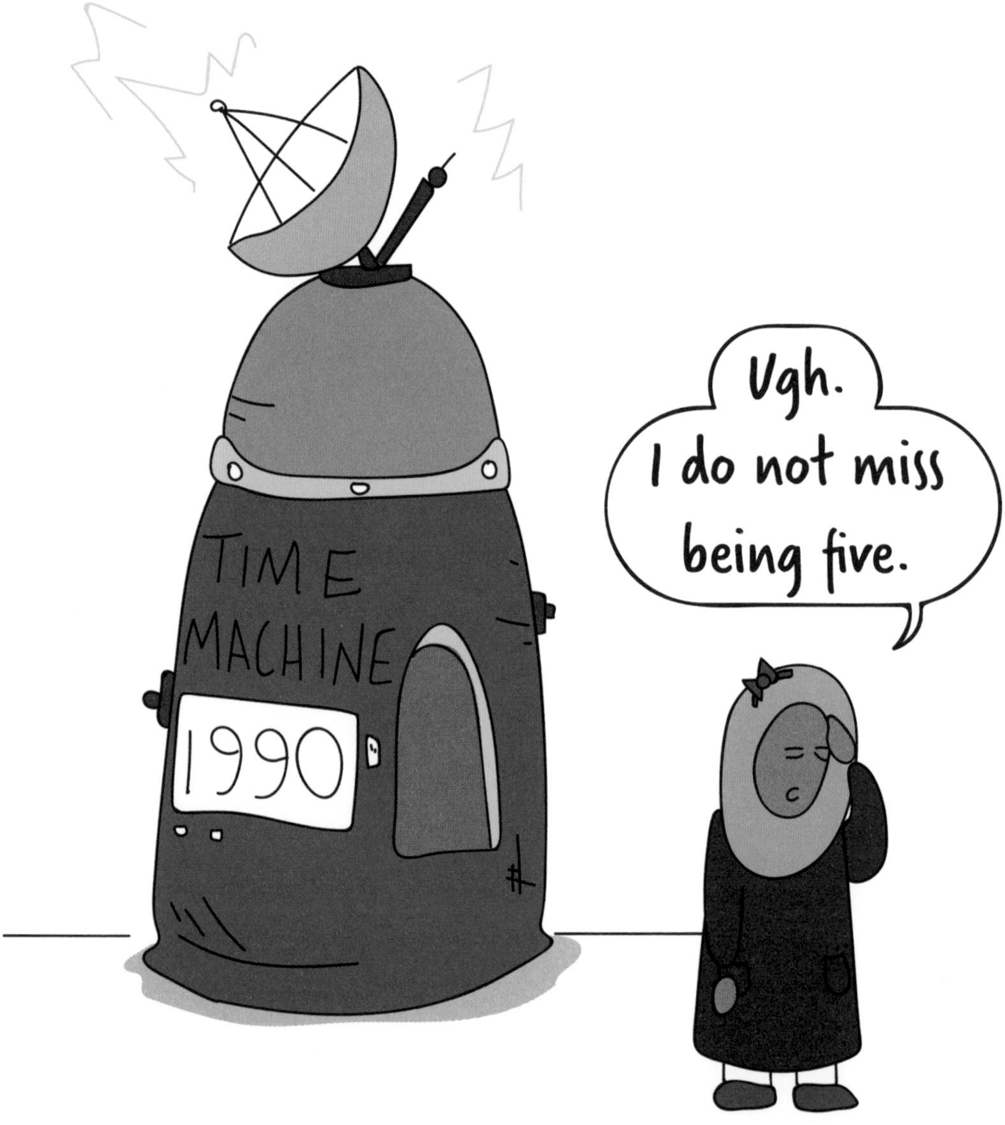
TIME MACHINE
1990
Ugh. I do not miss being five.

The Rules

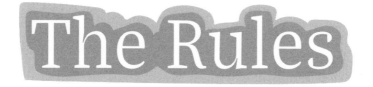

I had my first ever crush at five years old.

He laughed at my jokes and made me feel less like the weirdo I always thought I was.

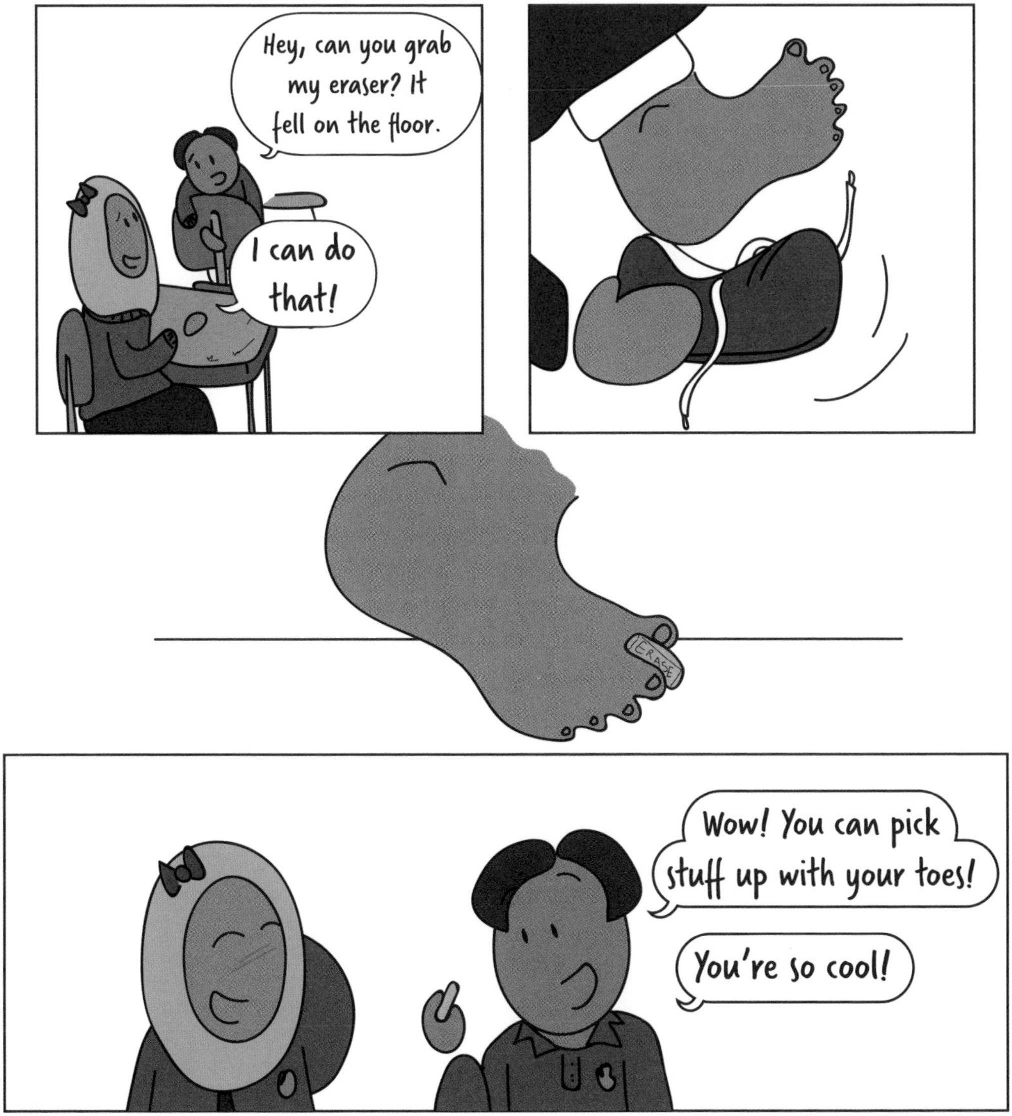
Hey, can you grab my eraser? It fell on the floor.
I can do that!
ERASE
Wow! You can pick stuff up with your toes!
You're so cool!

My God, what simpler times.

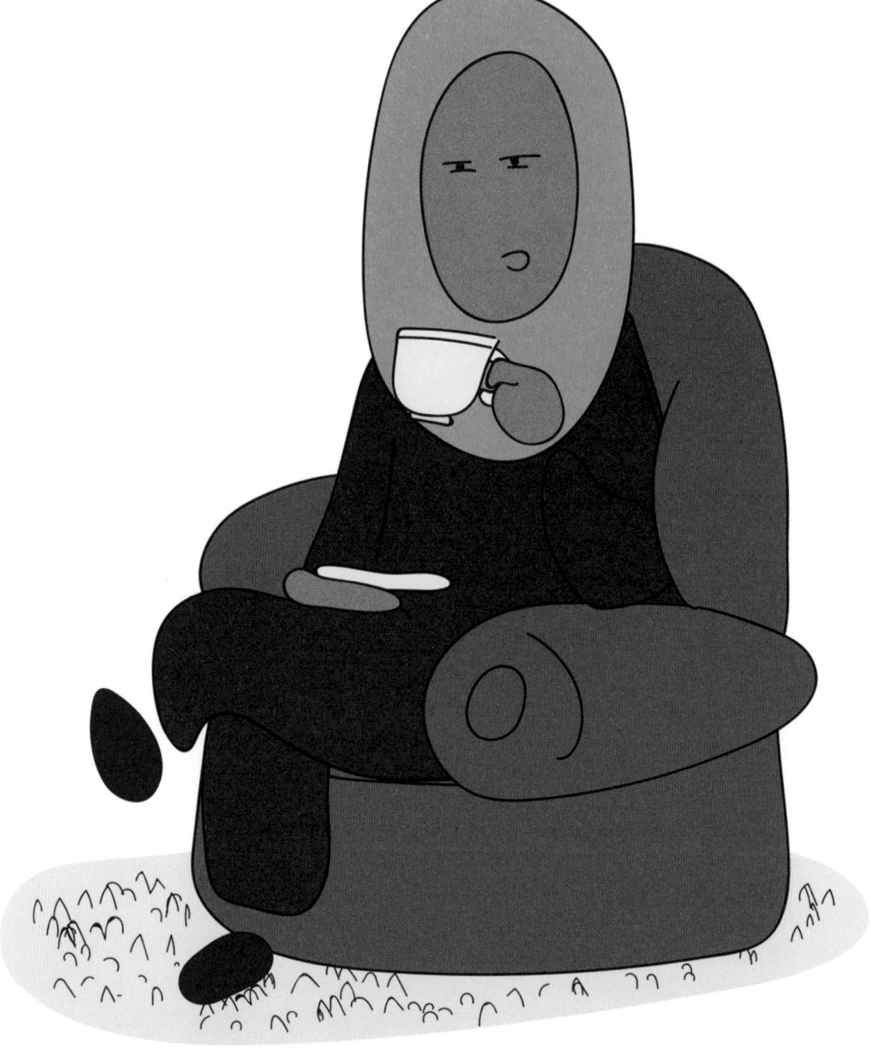

I was convinced we were going to be together forever. I couldn't believe I was lucky enough to have found my soul mate at only five years old!

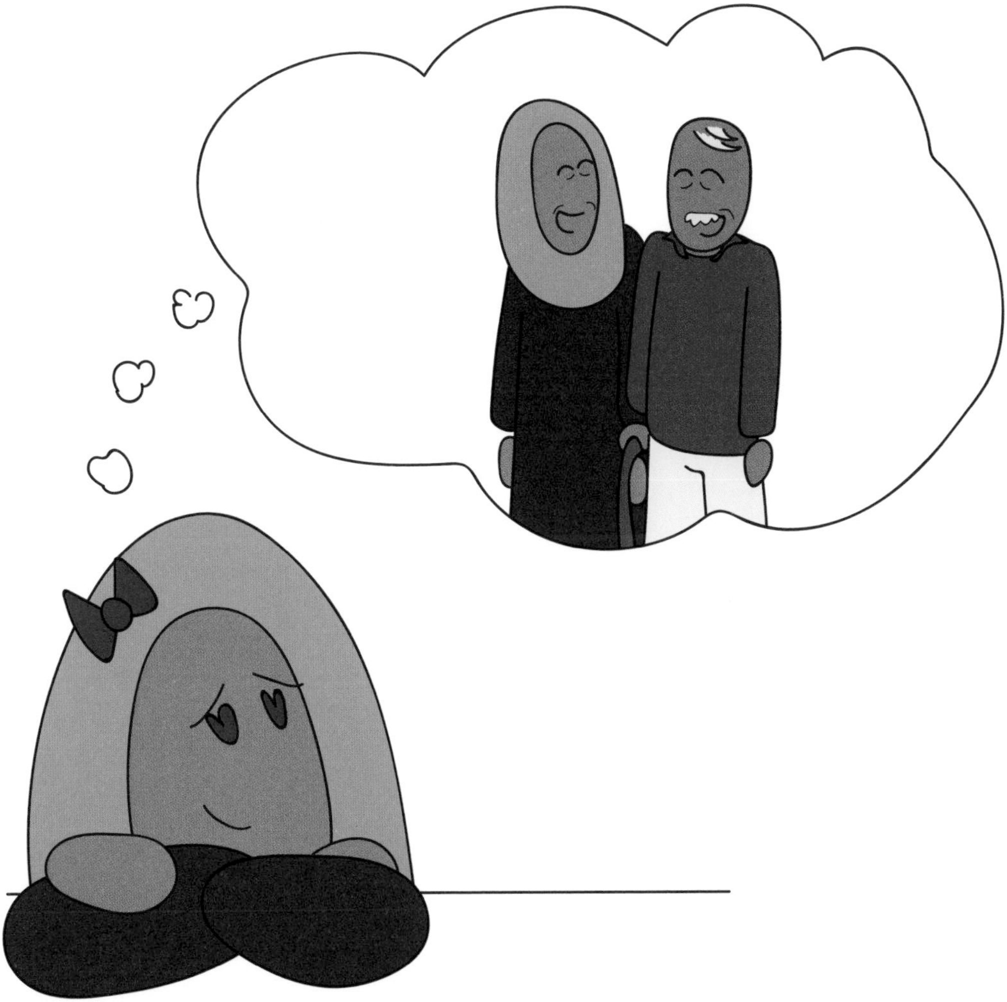

And then he came over one day for lunch and beat up my favorite doll, Penny, so badly he broke her voice box.

My crush didn't know this, but Penny wasn't just any doll. She was my best friend. And now, she would never be able to tell me if she wanted her hair brushed ever again.

Crush crushed.

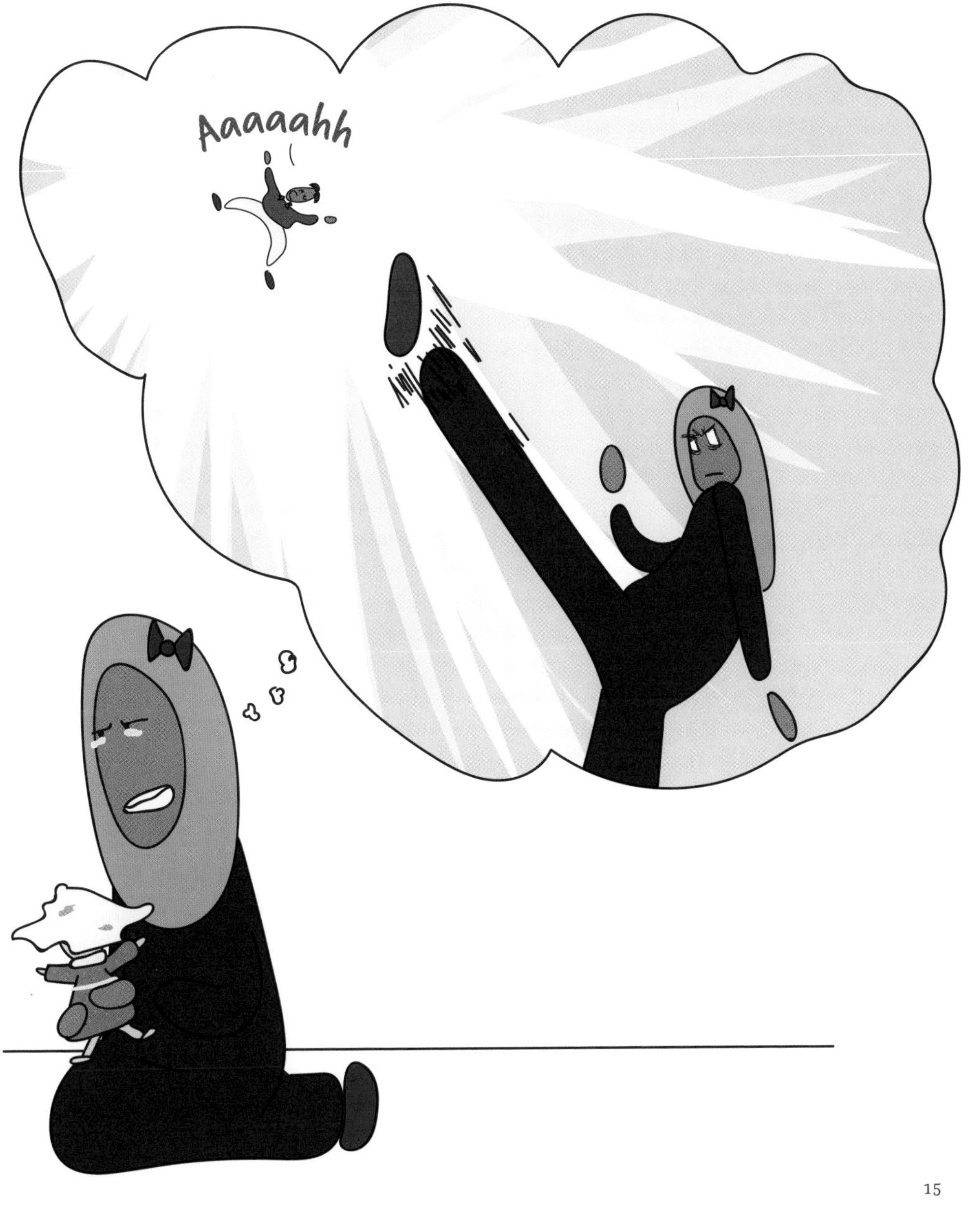
Aaaaahh

It was for the best anyway. Why, you may ask? Well, because of the rules of course! I was taught from a young age that Muslims followed very clear rules about gender relations.

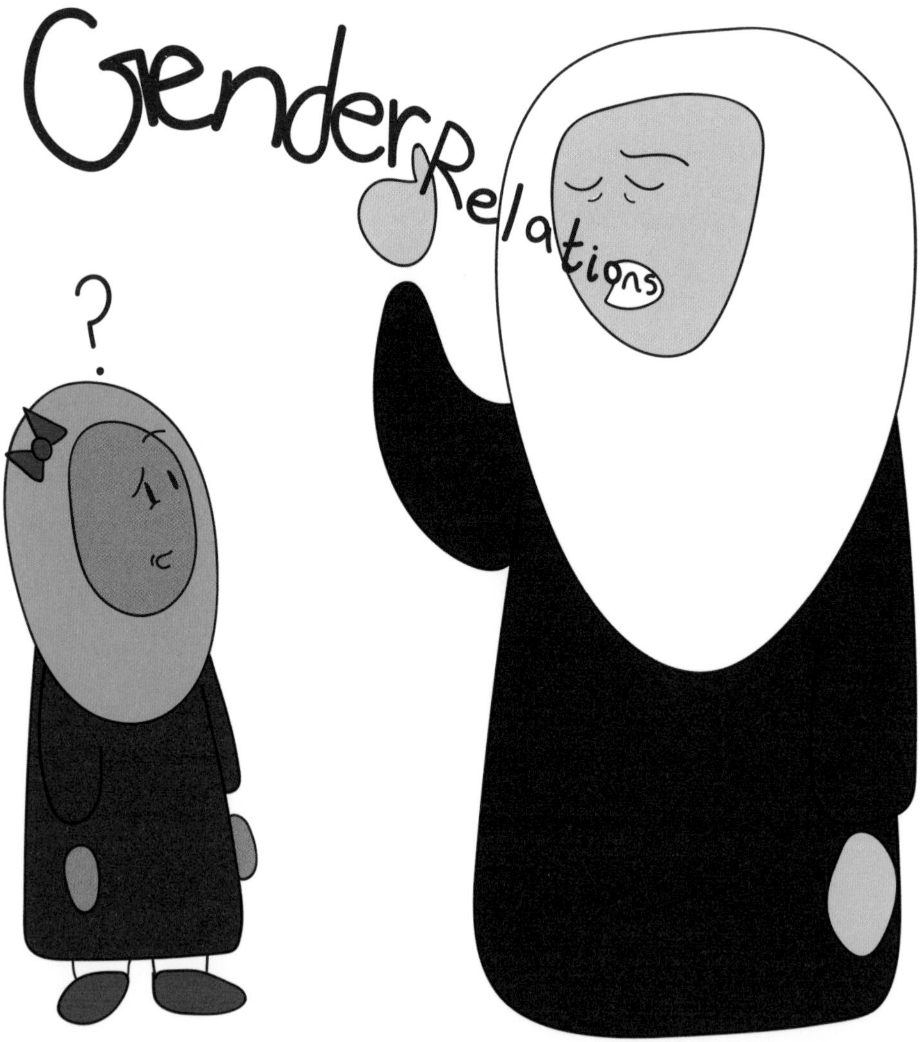
GenderRelations
?

These rules would govern any and all conduct I had with the opposite gender.

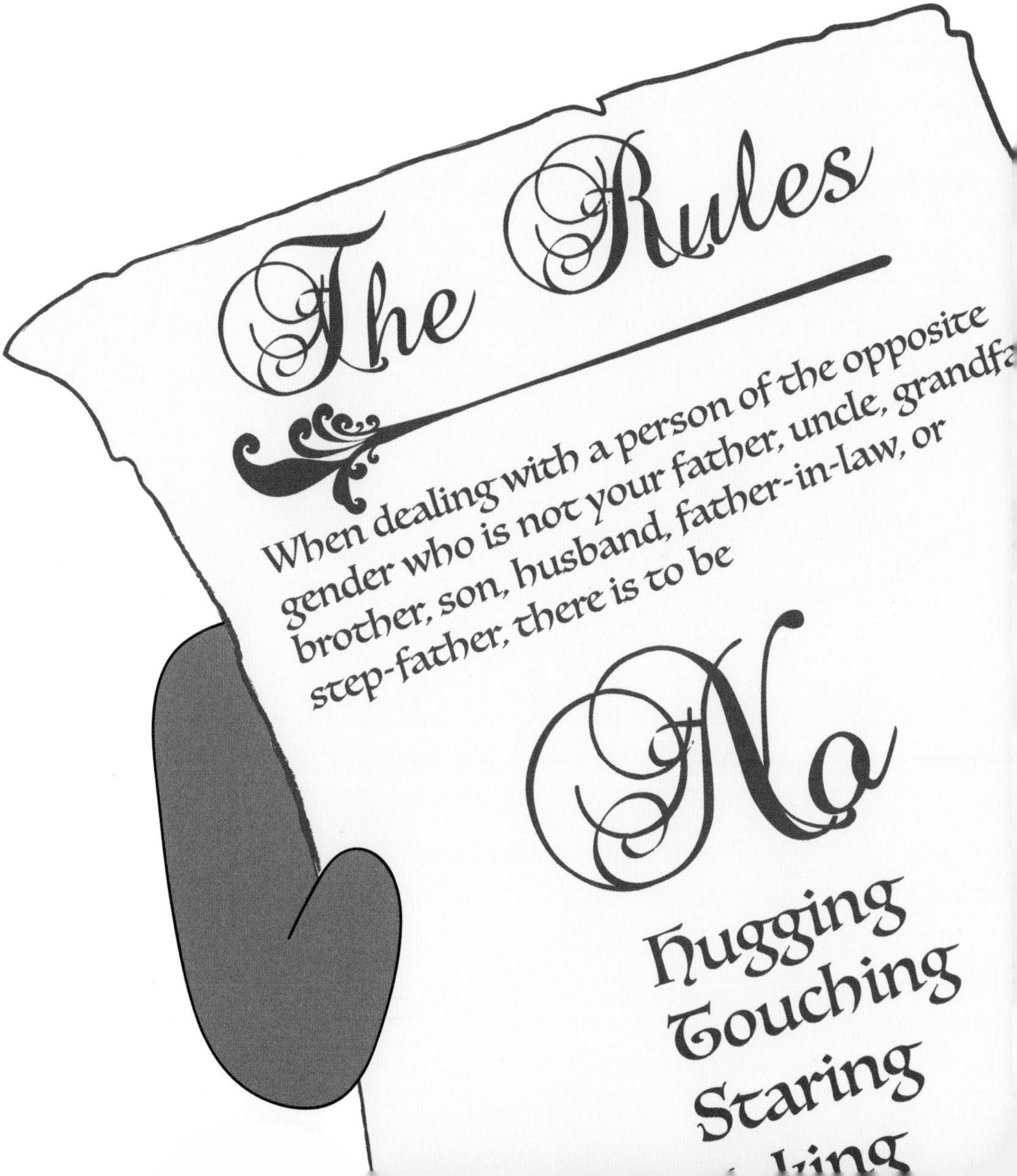
The Rules
When dealing with a person of the opposite gender who is not your father, uncle, grandfa
brother, son, husband, father-in-law, or step-father, there is to be
No
Hugging
Touching
Staring

RULE: Never be alone with a boy

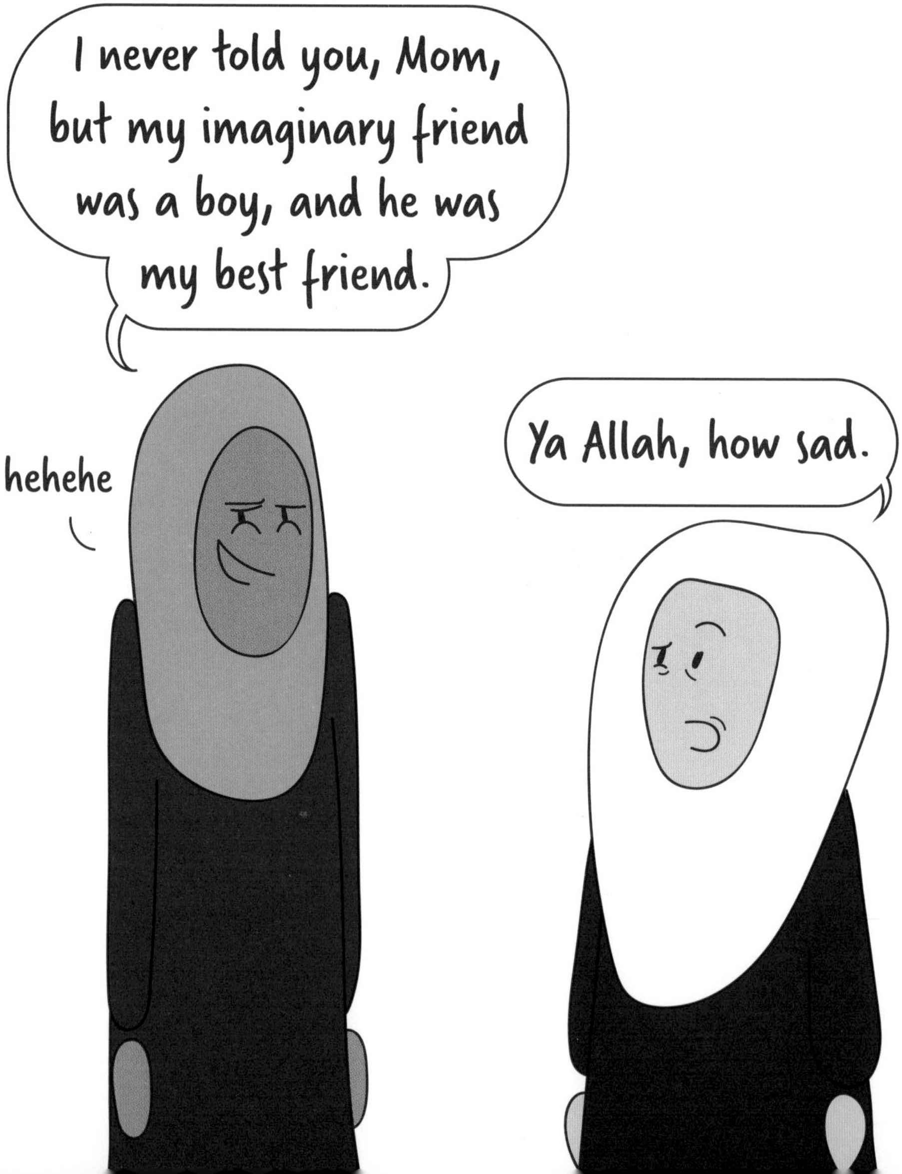
I never told you, Mom, but my imaginary friend was a boy, and he was my best friend.
hehehe
Ya Allah, how sad.

RULE: No shaking hands/touching/or physical contact of any kind

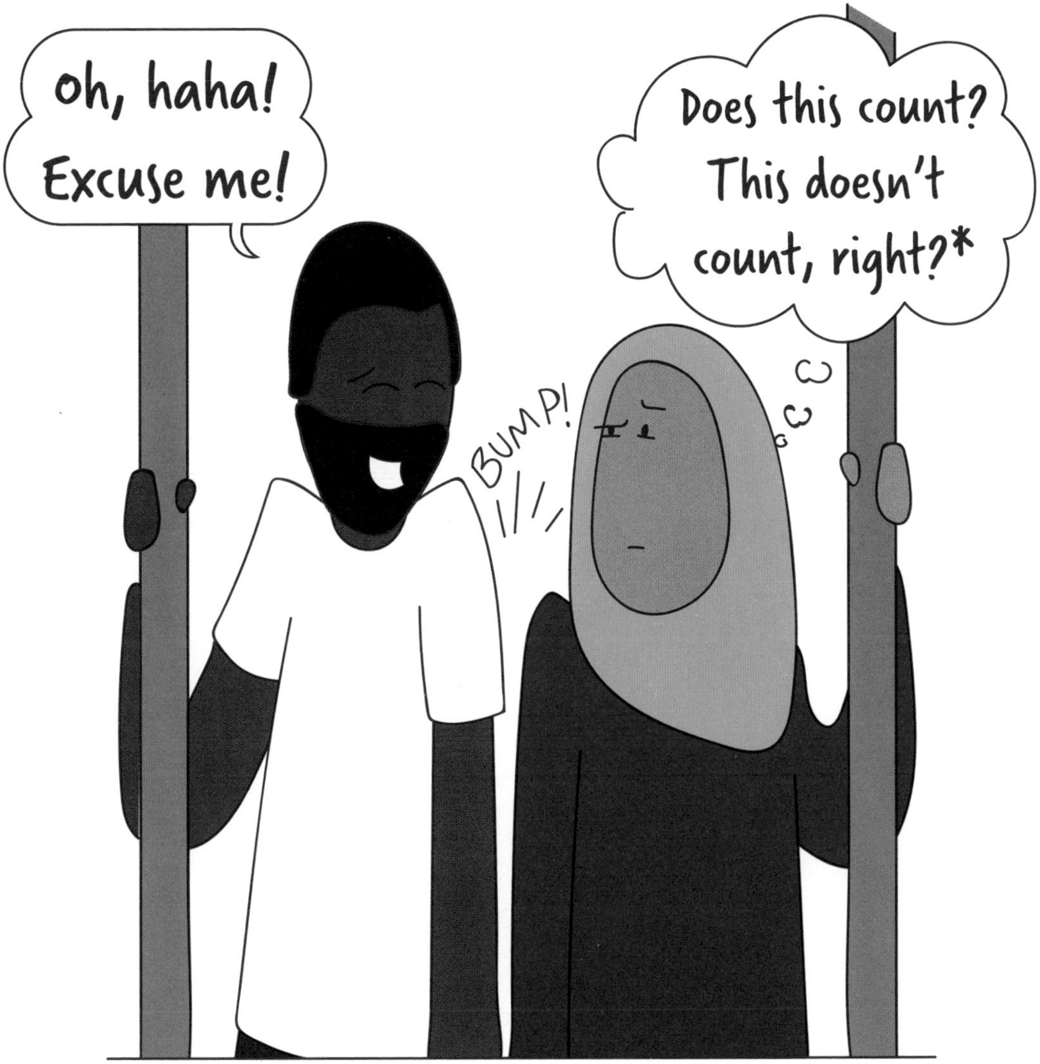
Oh, haha! Excuse me!
Does this count? This doesn't count, right?*
BUMP!

*accidental contact does not count.

RULE: No staring

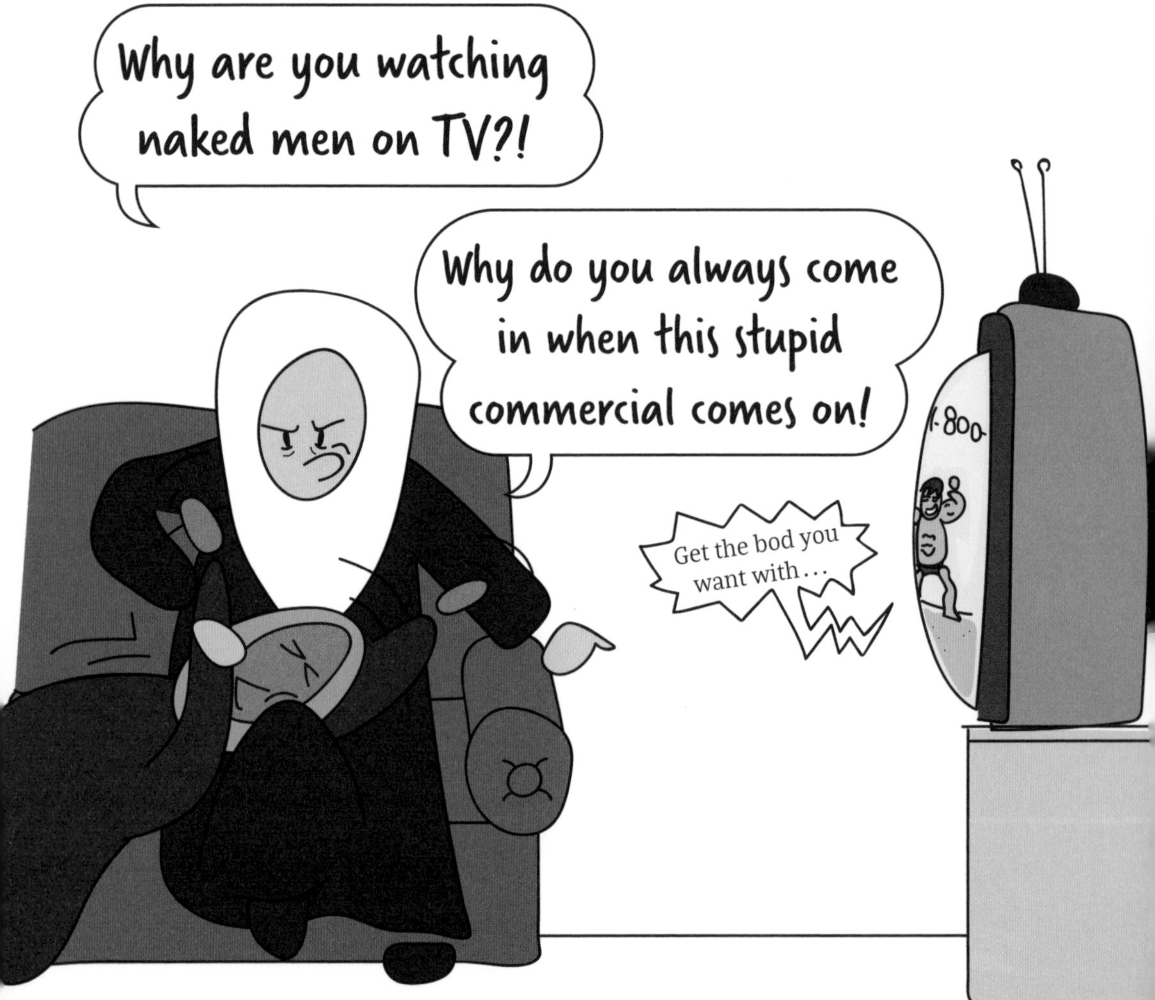
Why are you watching naked men on TV?!
Why do you always come in when this stupid commercial comes on!
Get the bod you want with . . .
1-800-

RULE: No mingling/joking/or laughing

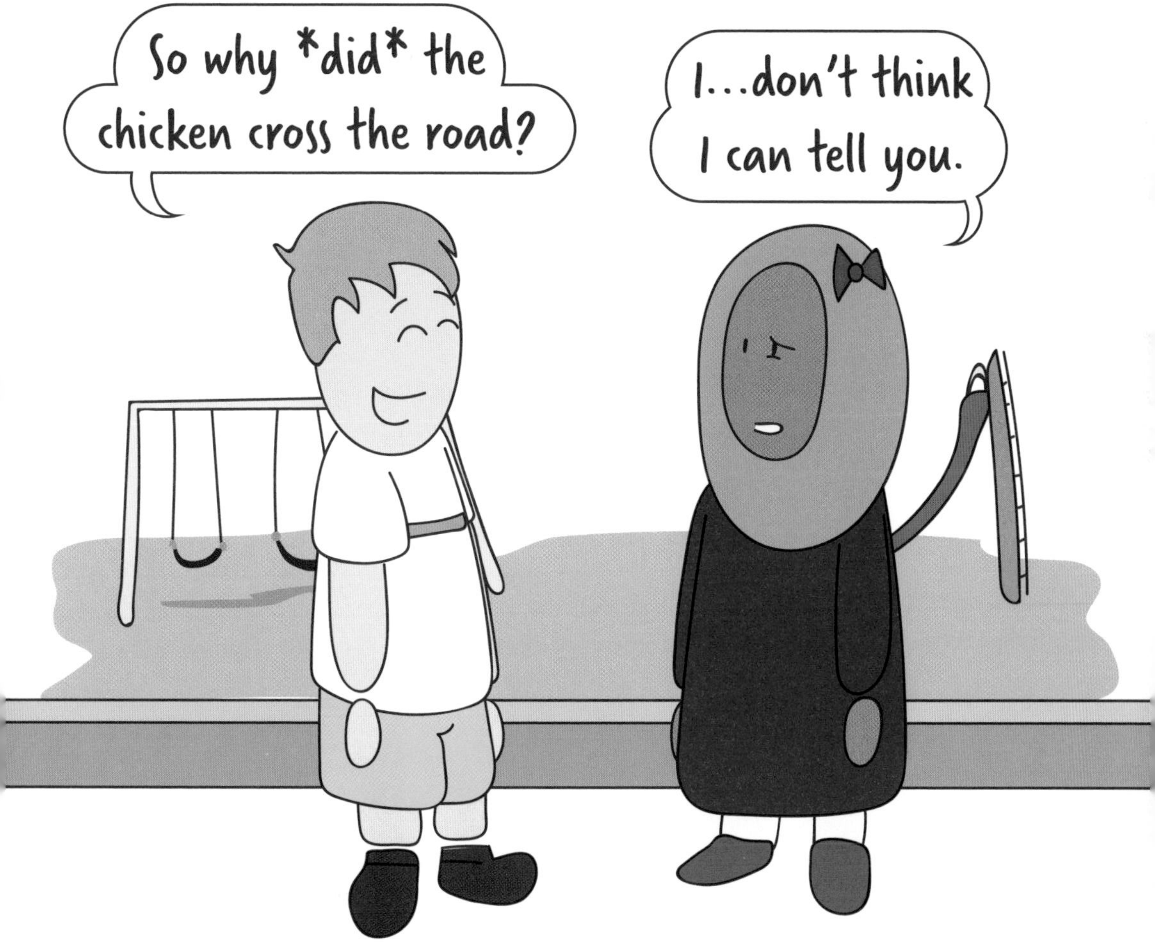
So why *did* the chicken cross the road?
I...don't think I can tell you.

RULE: NO DATING!

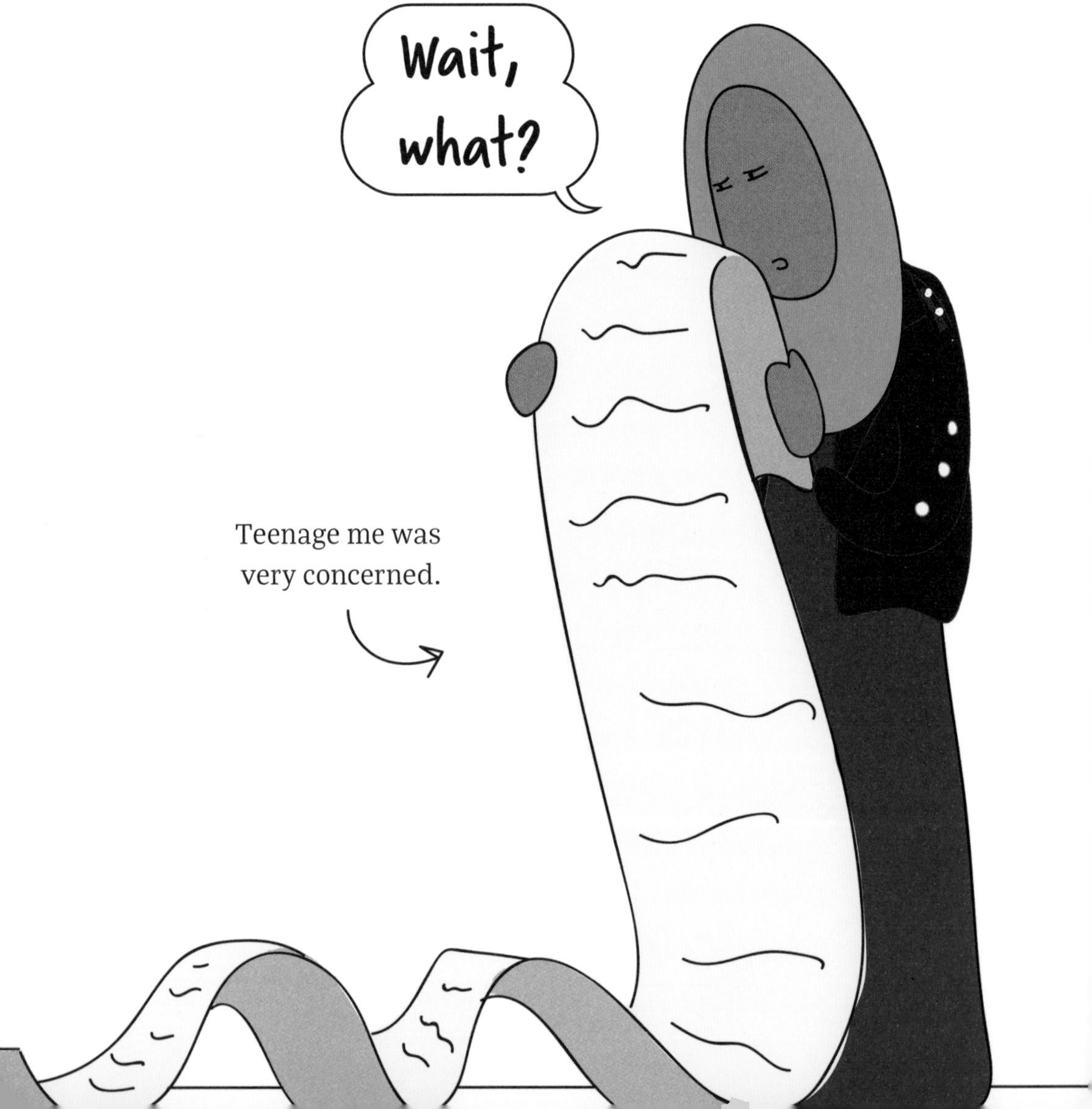
Wait, what?
Teenage me was very concerned.

No dating? I guess I was gonna die alone.

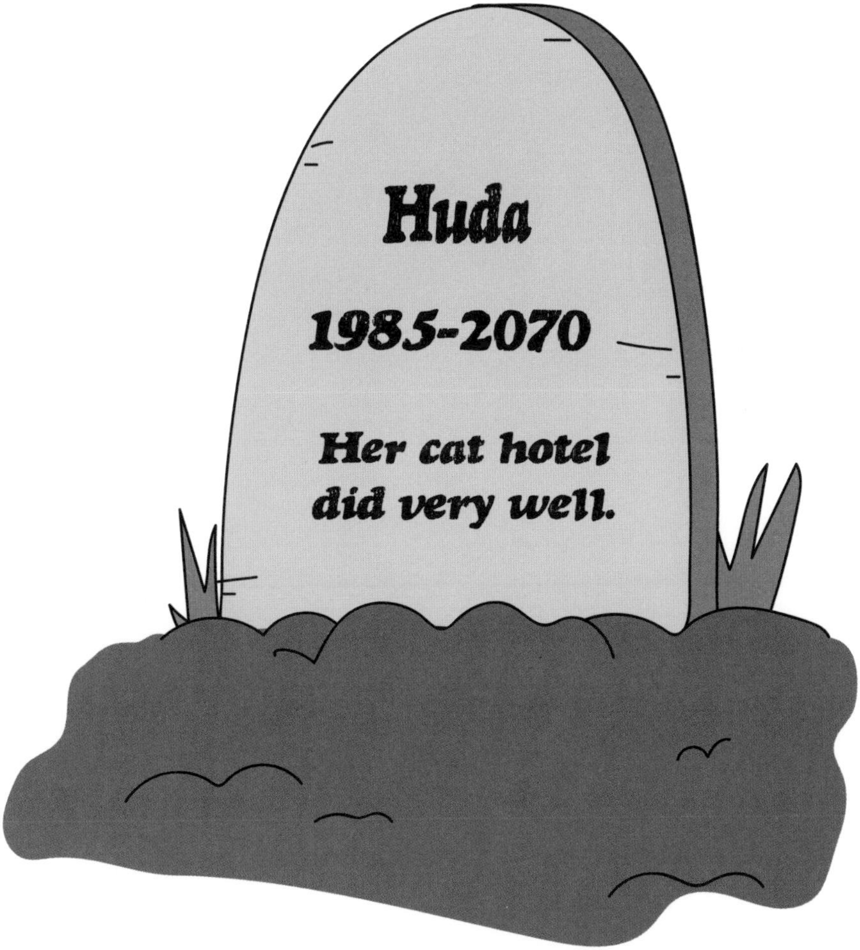
Huda
1985-2070
Her cat hotel did very well.

Ok, so maybe I was being dramatic. After all, there were thousands of people who never dated who were happily married!

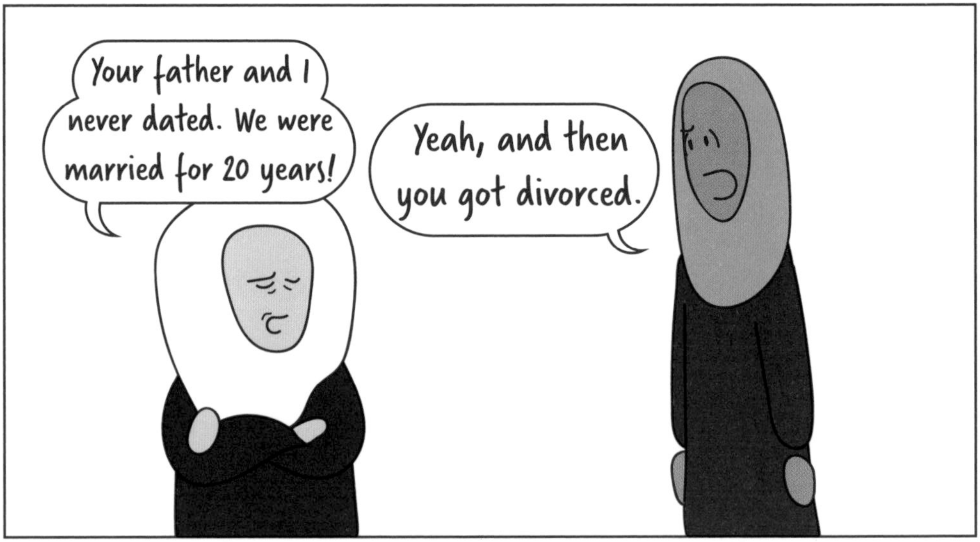
Your father and I never dated. We were married for 20 years!
Yeah, and then you got divorced.

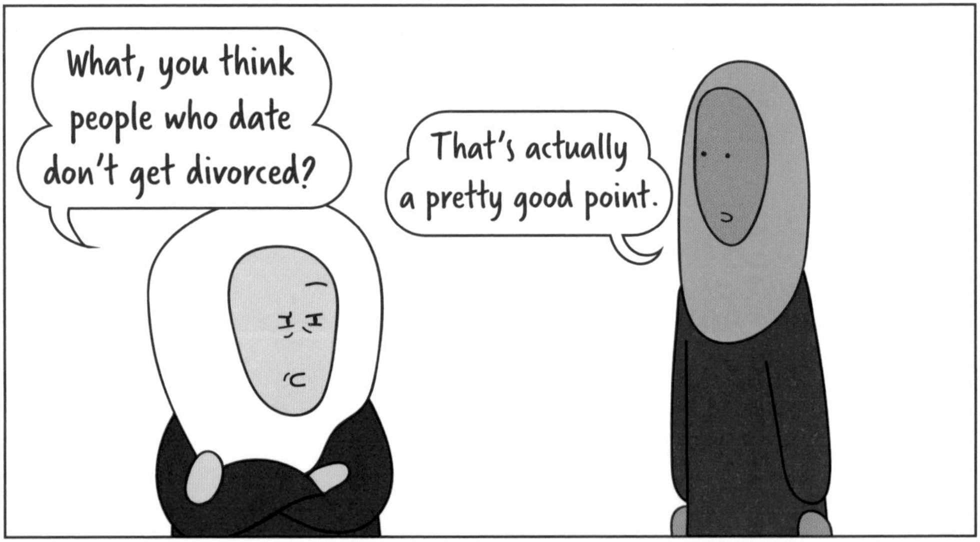
What, you think people who date don't get divorced?
That's actually a pretty good point.

If it was meant to be, I *would* find my soul mate. And if it wasn't, well, I told myself and anyone who would listen that I'd rather be single for the rest of my life than be stuck in a horrible marriage.

The Suitors

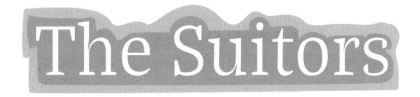

My parents didn't date. They met for the very first time, and a week later, they were married.

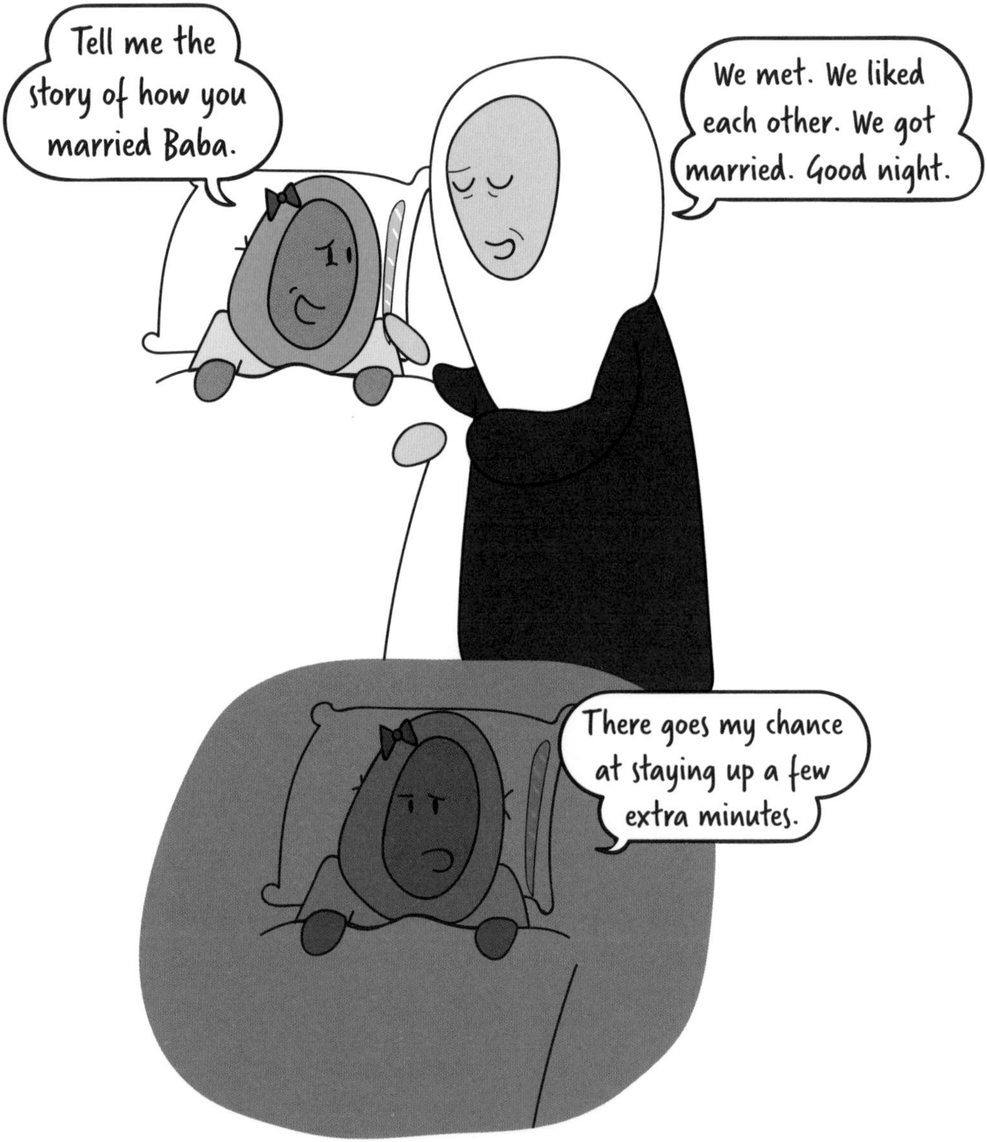
Tell me the story of how you married Baba.
We met. We liked each other. We got married. Good night.
There goes my chance at staying up a few extra minutes.

That may have been all fine and dandy back then, but times have changed! By 15, I was sure: there was no way I would ever agree to marrying a virtual stranger.

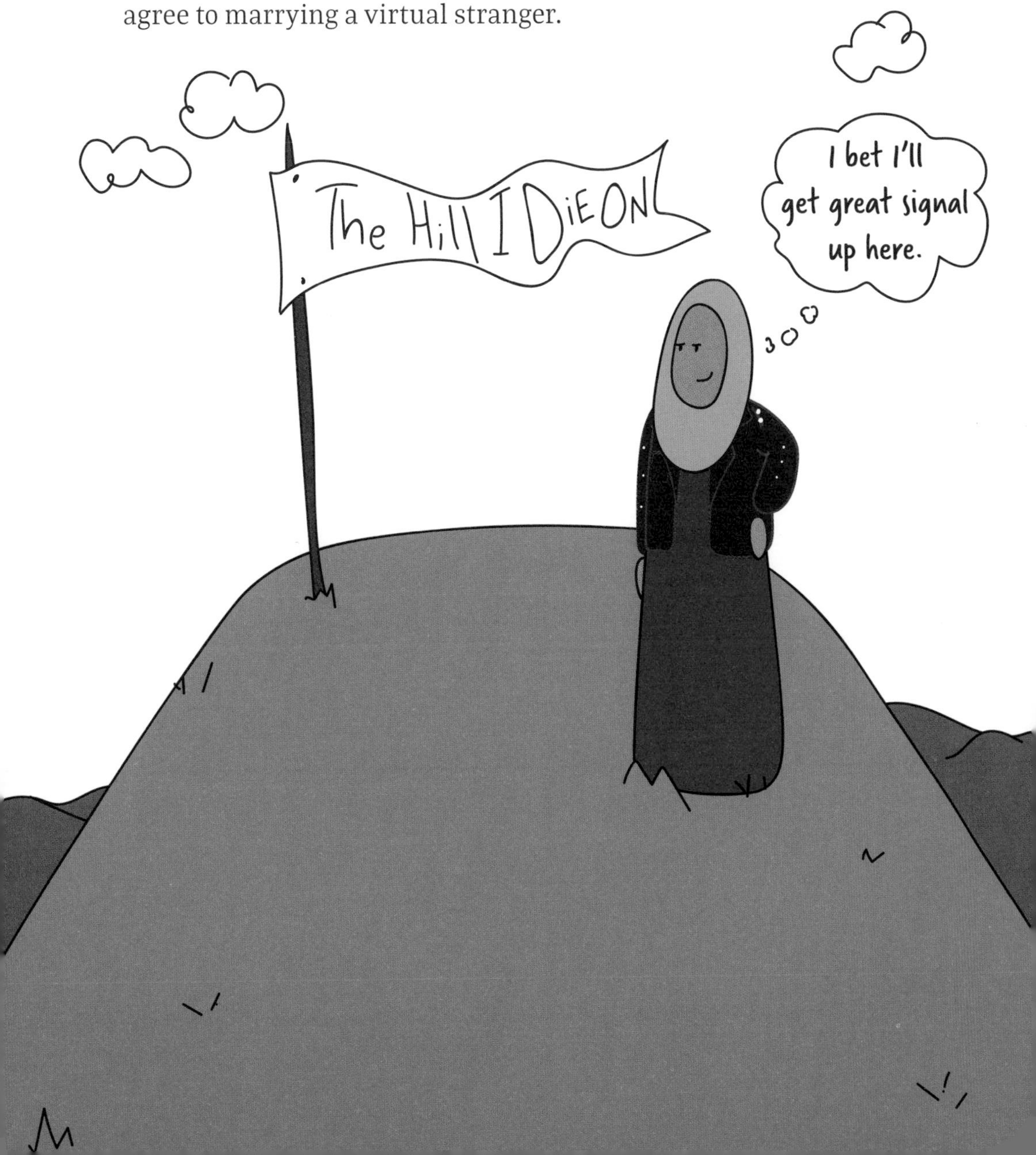
The Hill I Die On
I bet I'll get great signal up here.

But, that's pretty much what the girls in my community were doing. Their parents would arrange for them to meet a dude–*excusez-moi,* a suitor–and if they liked each other . . .

Wedding bells.

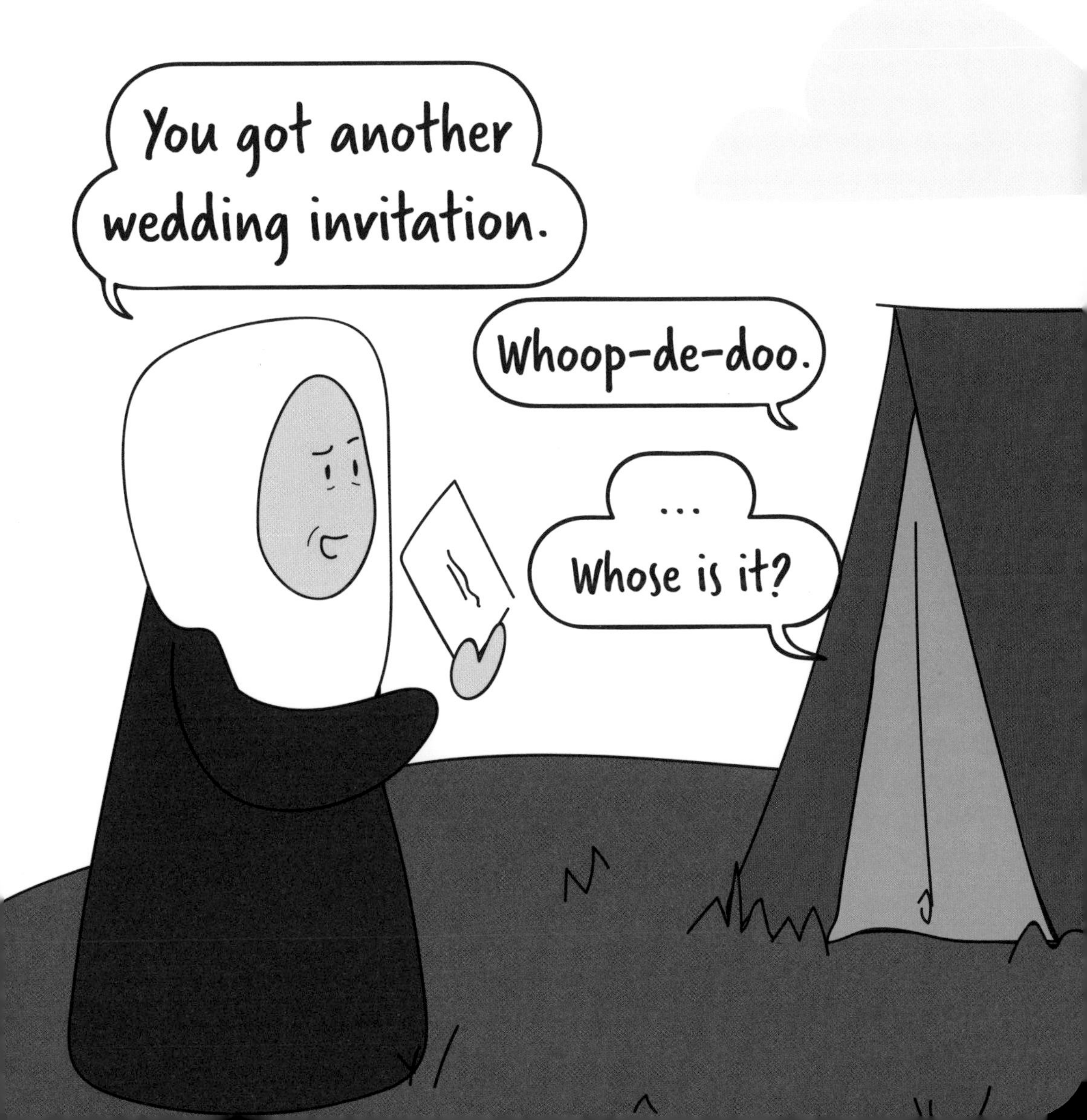
You got another wedding invitation.
Whoop-de-doo.
...
Whose is it?

By unspoken community standards, if you weren't married by 21, you were old news. Something must be wrong with you. At 25, you were declared broken.

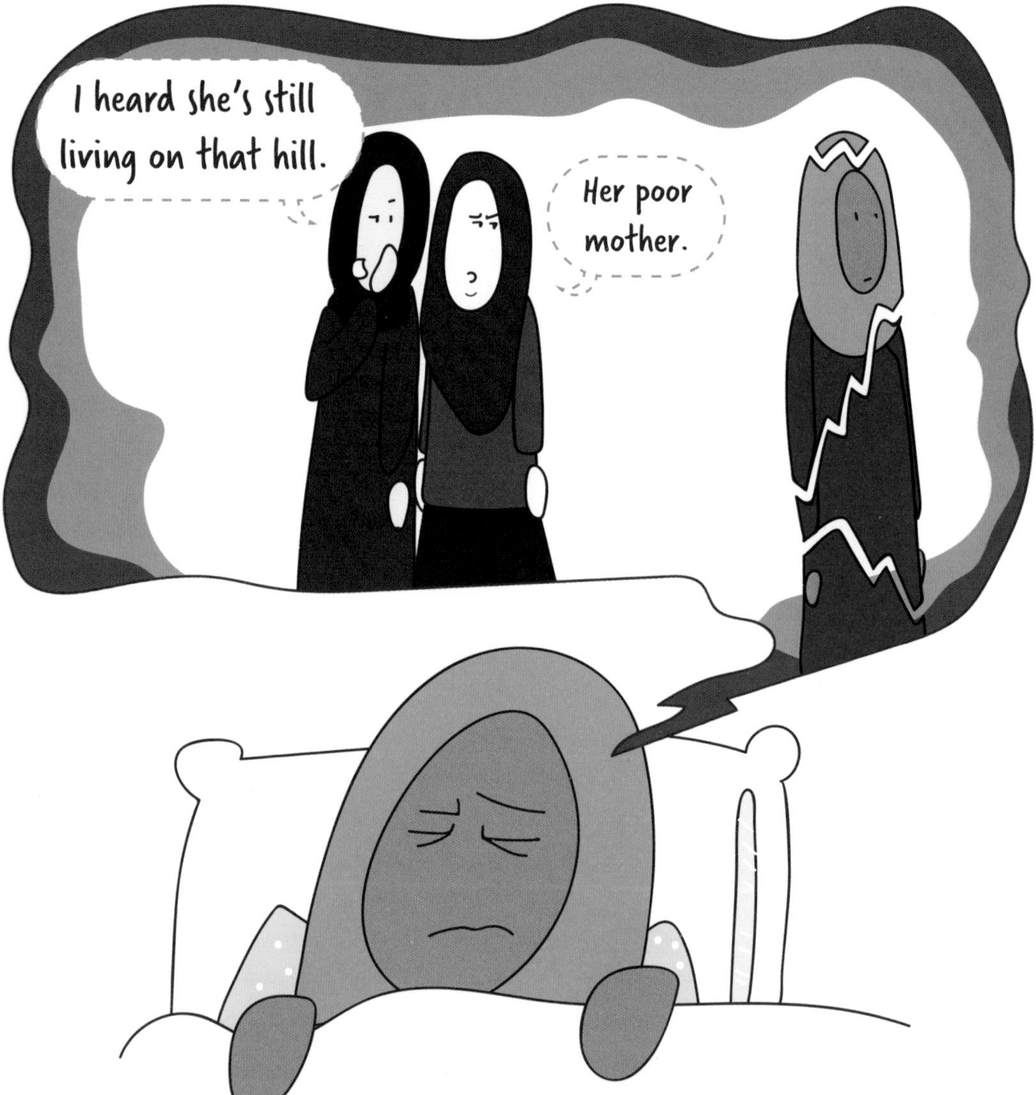
I heard she's still living on that hill.
Her poor mother.

No pressure. It wasn't like every time we went to the grocery store, my mom would browse wedding gown magazines at the checkout line and make me guess her favorite dresses.

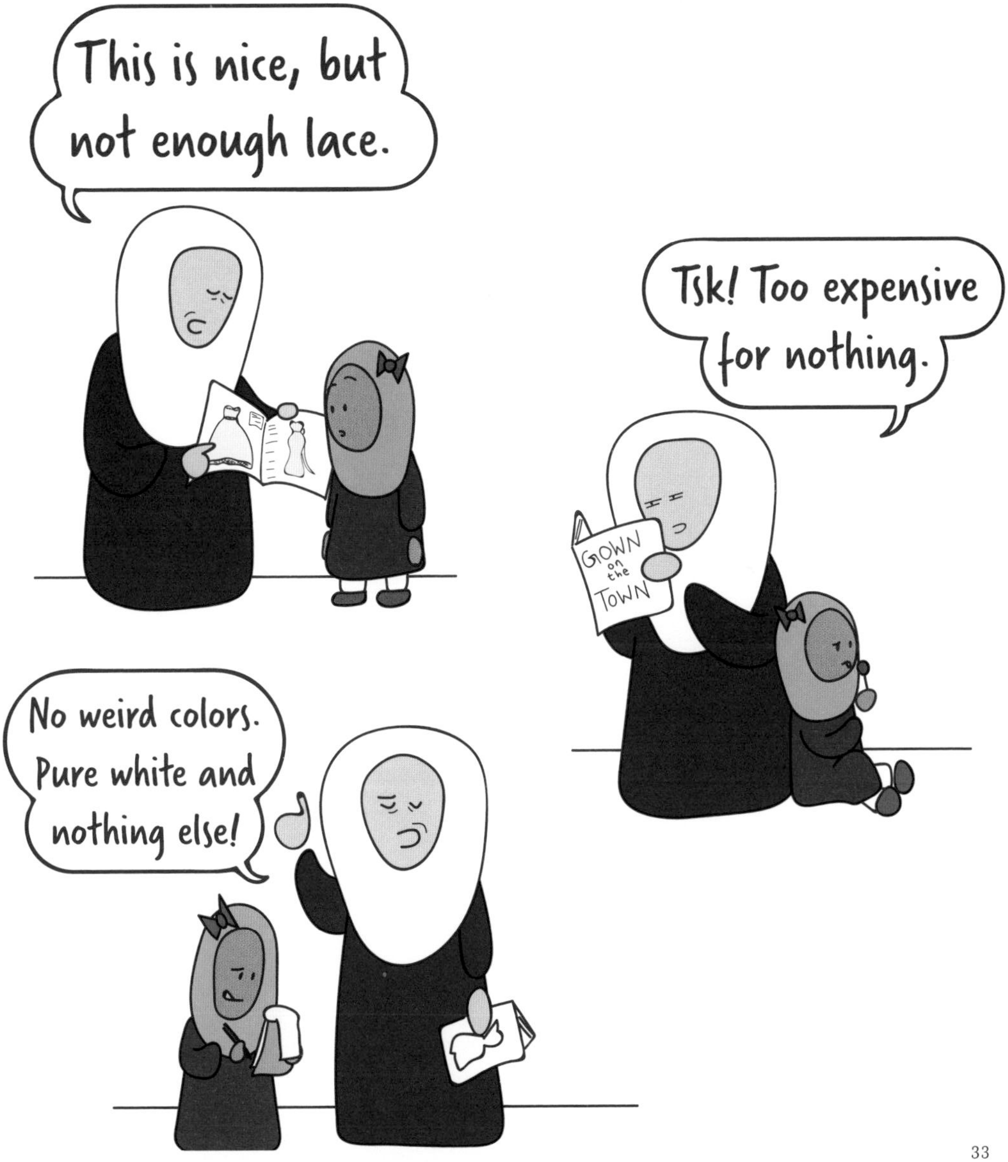

This is nice, but not enough lace.
Tsk! Too expensive for nothing.
GOWN on the TOWN
No weird colors. Pure white and nothing else!

This was fun when I was a little girl. I got to look at pretty dresses and imagined myself wearing one someday. But, the fantasy eventually wore off when I hit puberty and hated the way I looked in dresses.

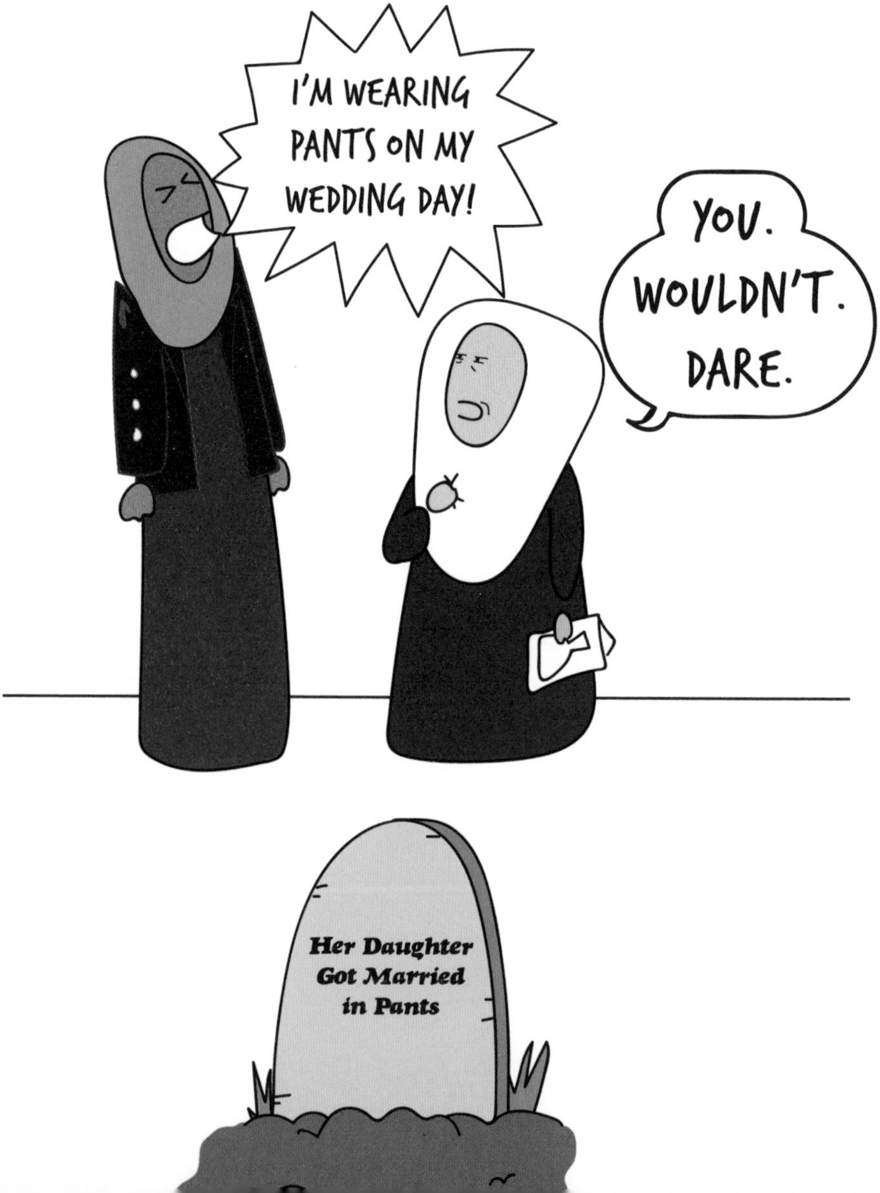
I'M WEARING PANTS ON MY WEDDING DAY!
YOU. WOULDN'T. DARE.
Her Daughter Got Married in Pants

It definitely felt like the clock was ticking.

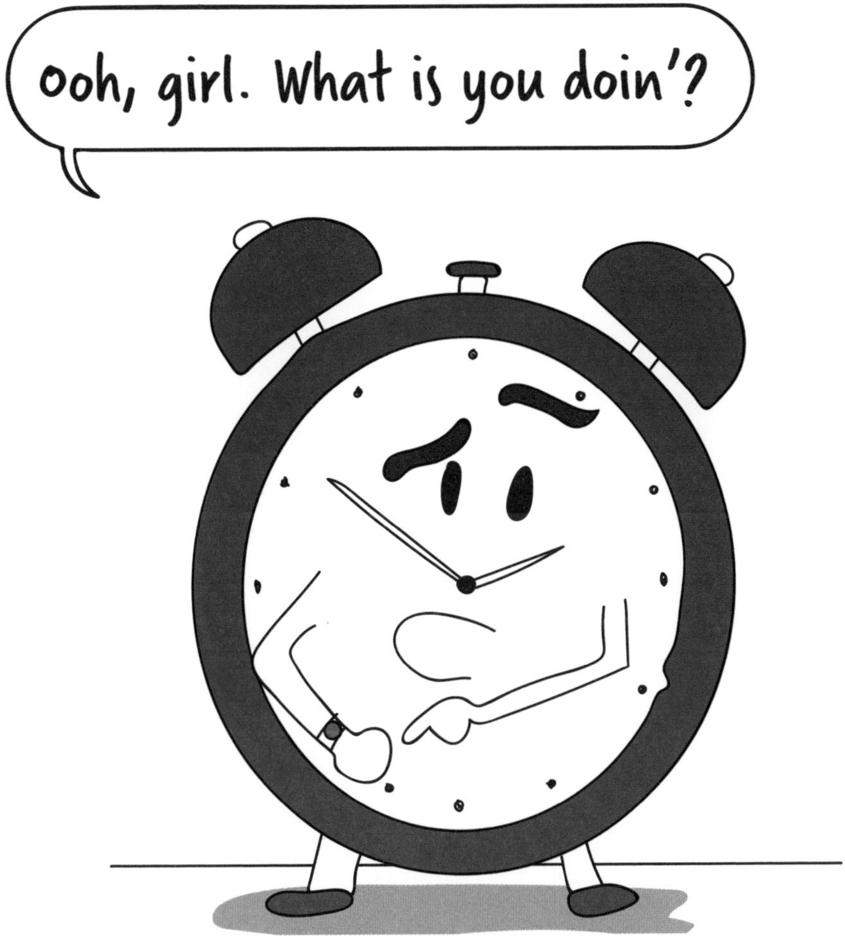
Ooh, girl. What is you doin'?

It started ticking even faster when my friend, and fellow 16-year-old, announced she was getting married. I was over here worrying about AP Lit, and she was planning a friggin' wedding. All of a sudden, marrying a virtual stranger didn't sound too bad. AP Lit can do that to ya.

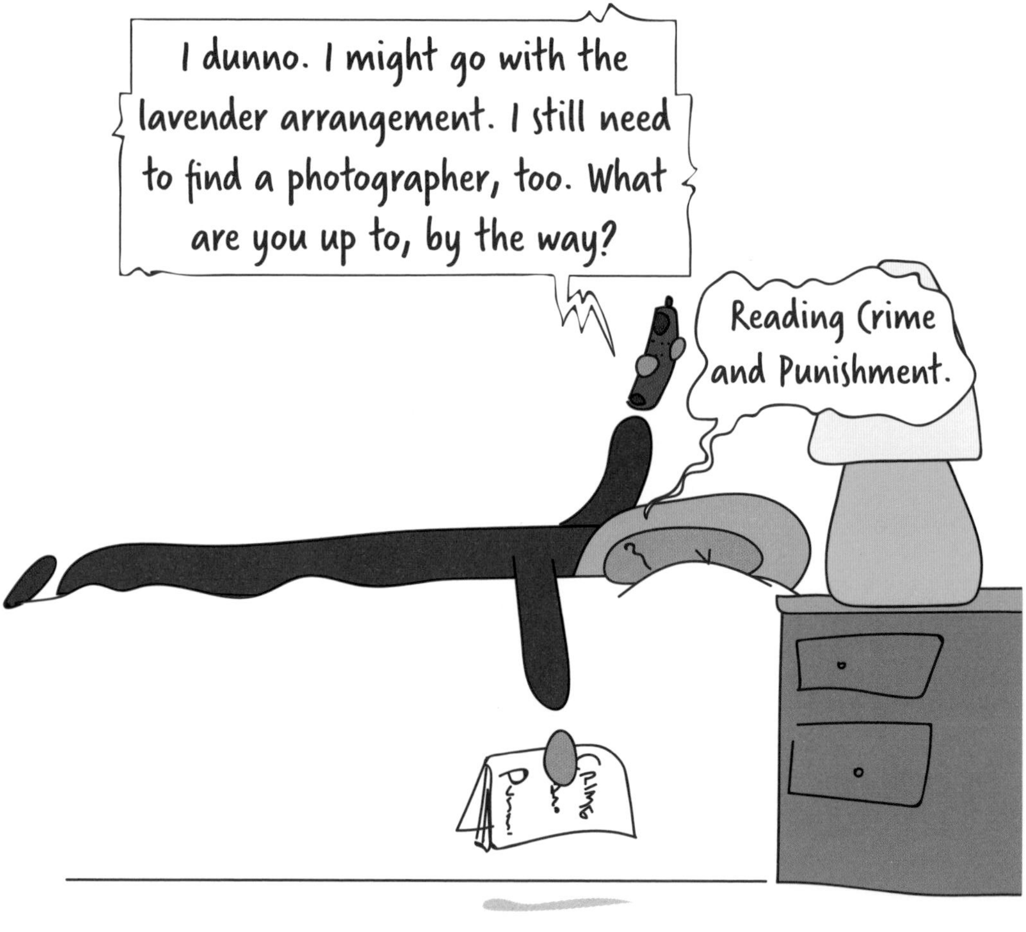
I dunno. I might go with the lavender arrangement. I still need to find a photographer, too. What are you up to, by the way?
Reading Crime and Punishment.

Suitor *(noun)*: a man who pursues a relationship with a woman for the purpose of marriage.

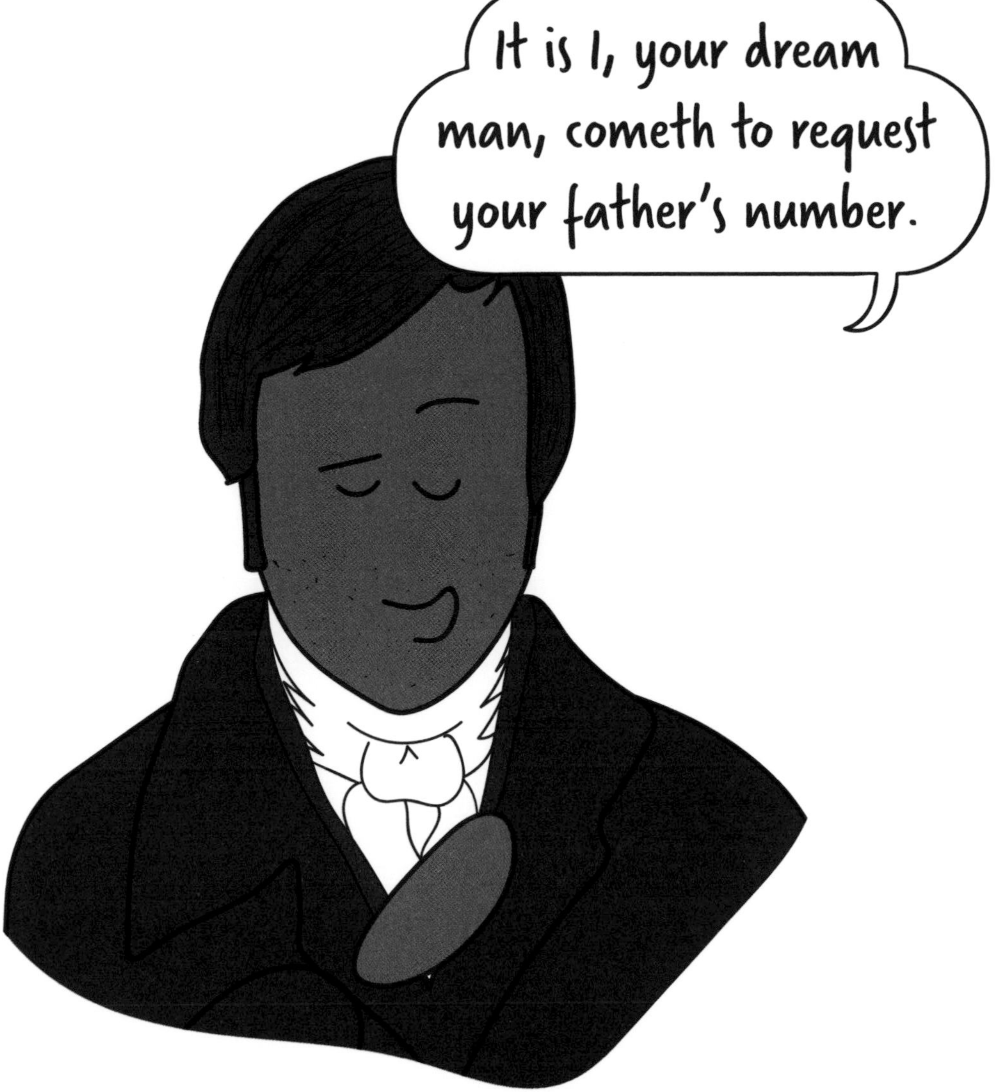
It is I, your dream man, cometh to request your father's number.

There were many types.

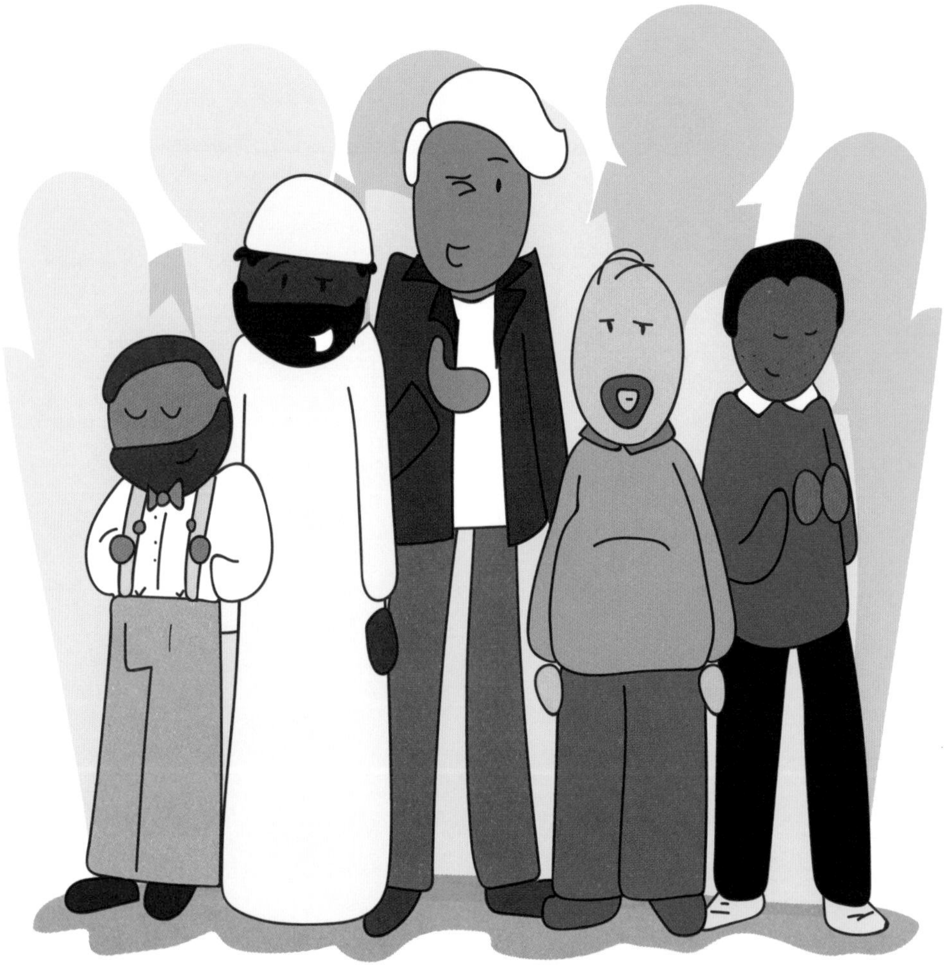

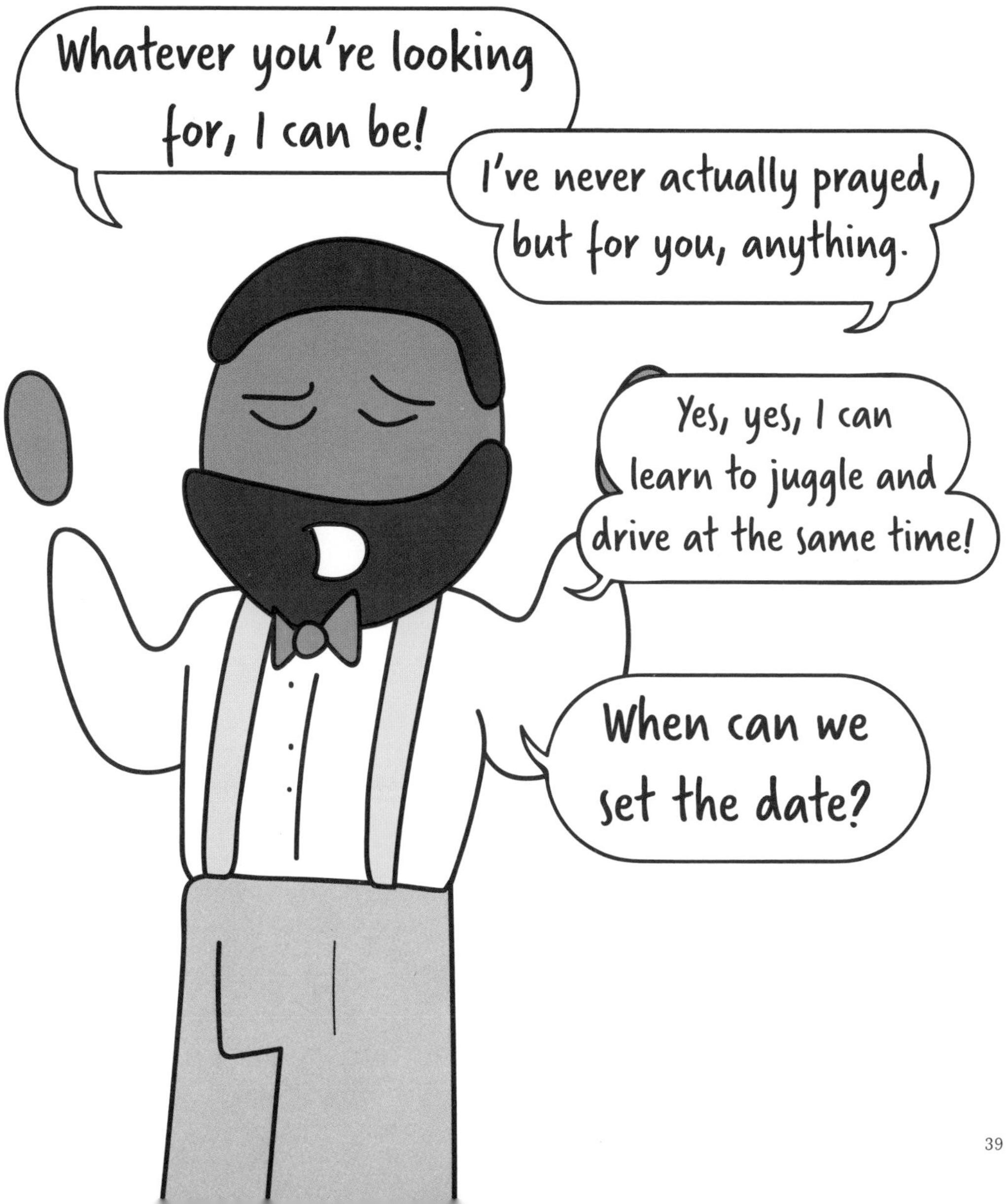
Whatever you're looking for, I can be!
I've never actually prayed, but for you, anything.
Yes, yes, I can learn to juggle and drive at the same time!
When can we set the date?

The Shopper

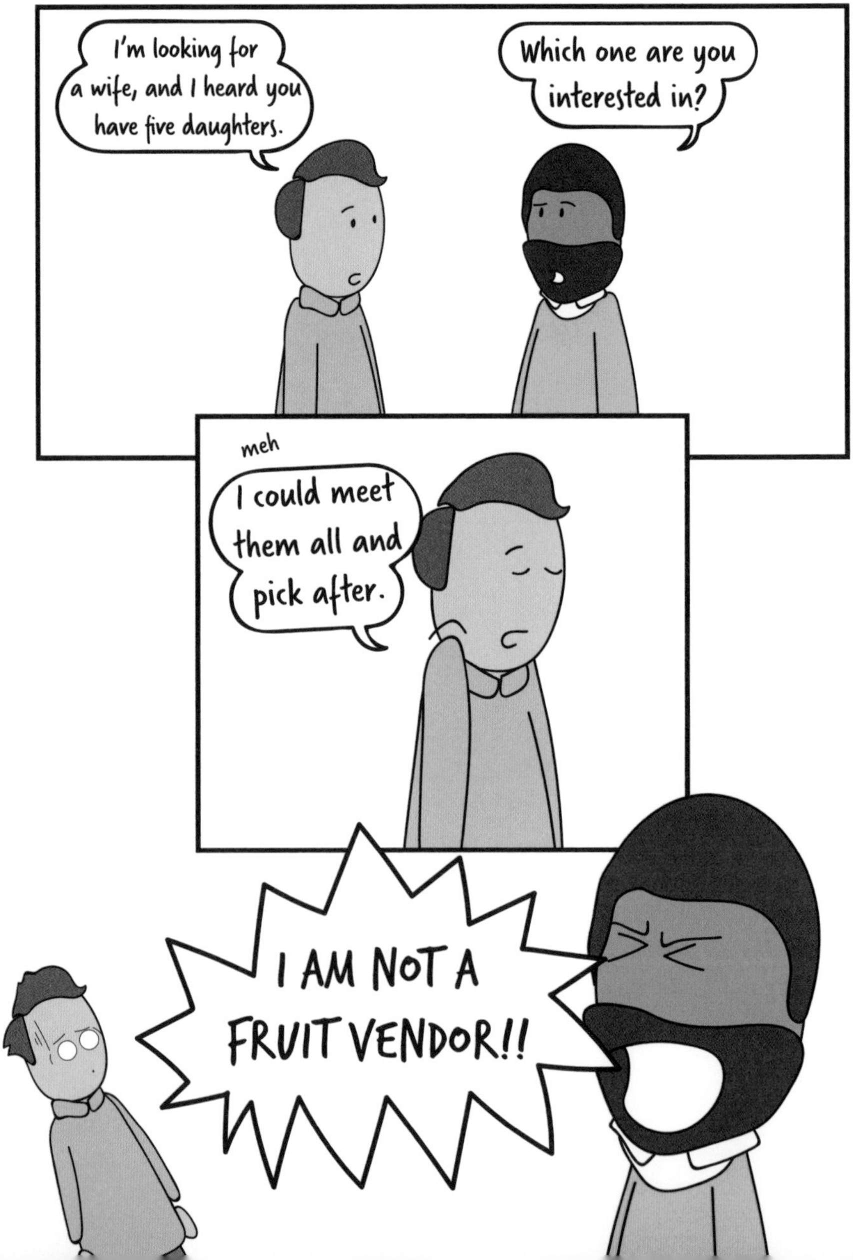
I'm looking for a wife, and I heard you have five daughters.
Which one are you interested in?
meh
I could meet them all and pick after.
I AM NOT A FRUIT VENDOR!!

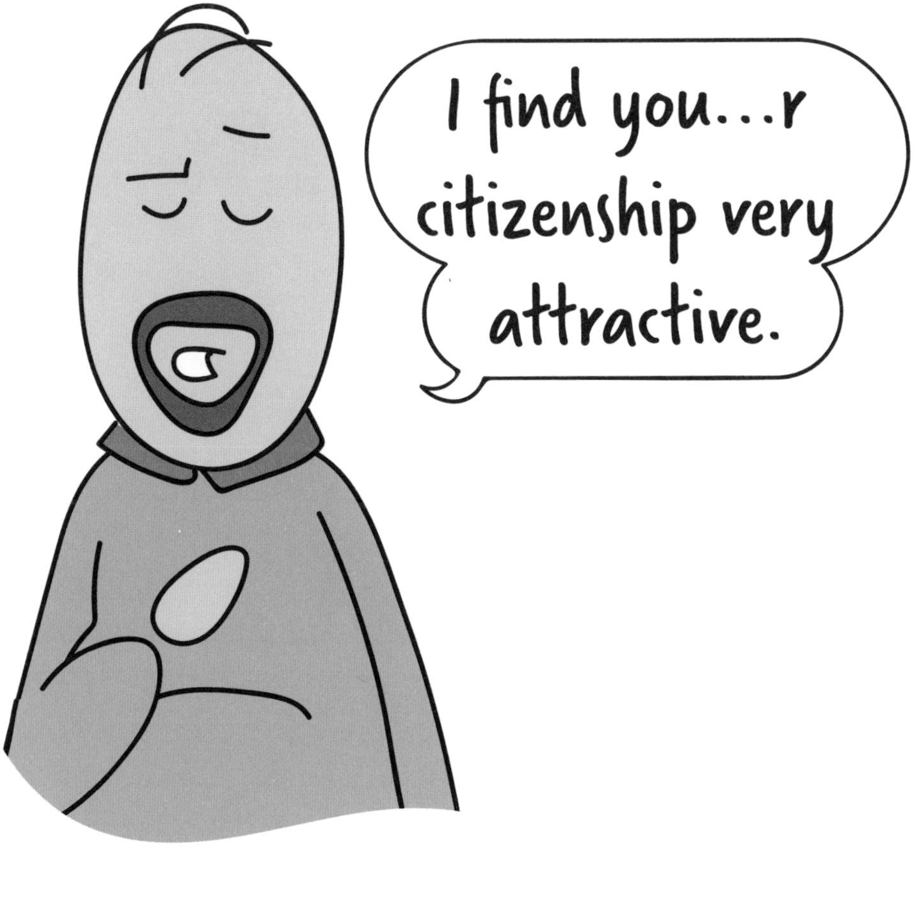
I find you...r citizenship very attractive.

The Simply Incompatible

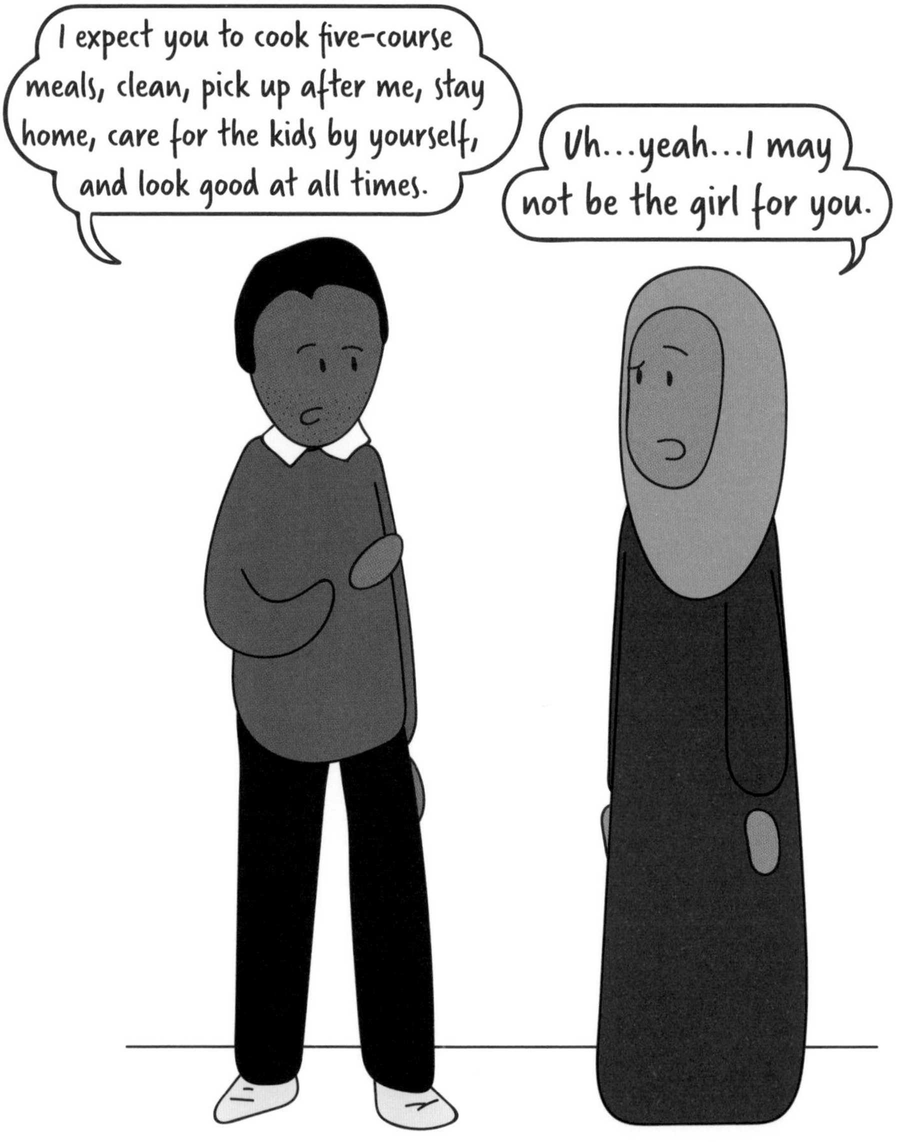
I expect you to cook five-course meals, clean, pick up after me, stay home, care for the kids by yourself, and look good at all times.
Uh...yeah...I may not be the girl for you.

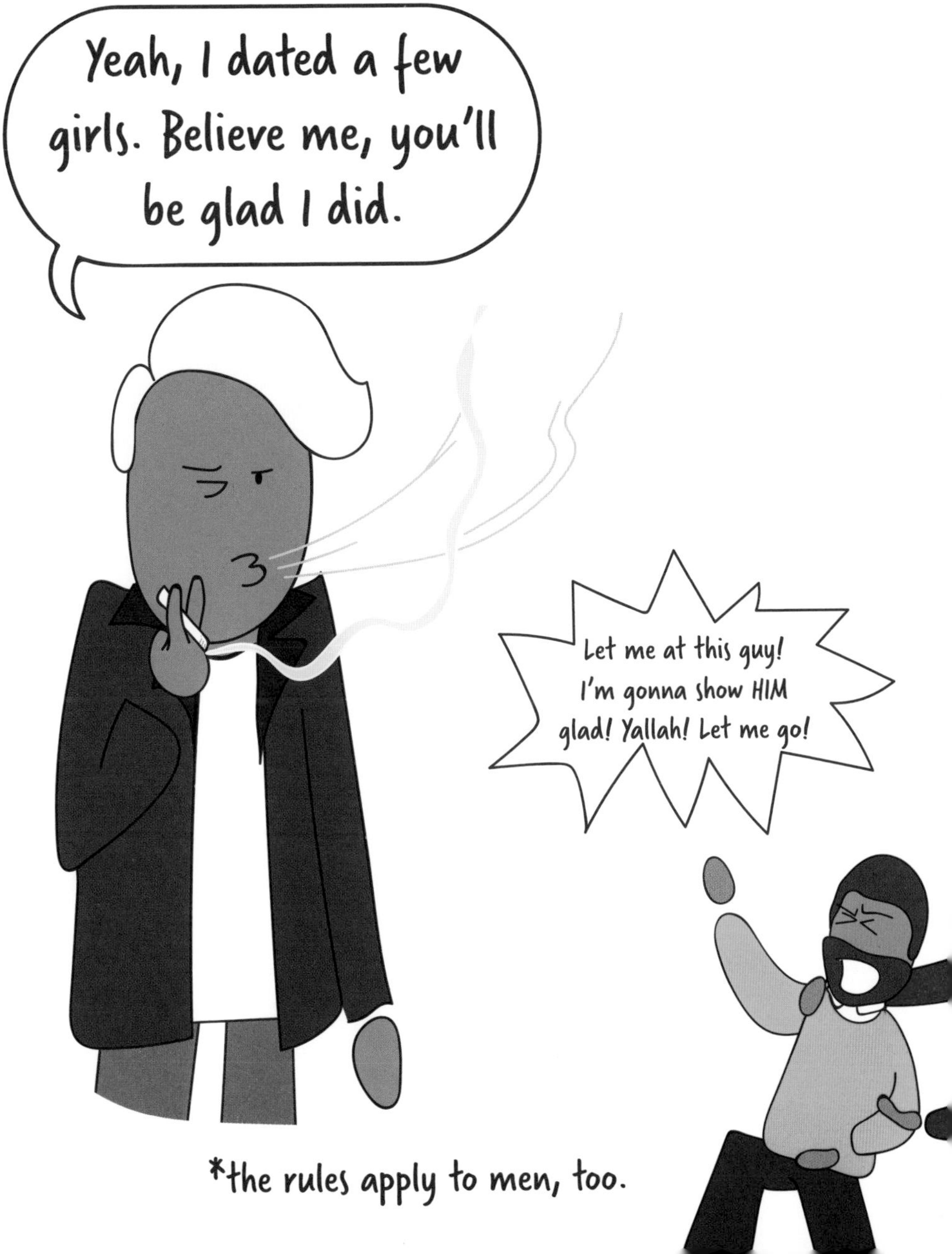
Yeah, I dated a few girls. Believe me, you'll be glad I did.
Let me at this guy! I'm gonna show HIM glad! Yallah! Let me go!
*the rules apply to men, too.

The Home Country

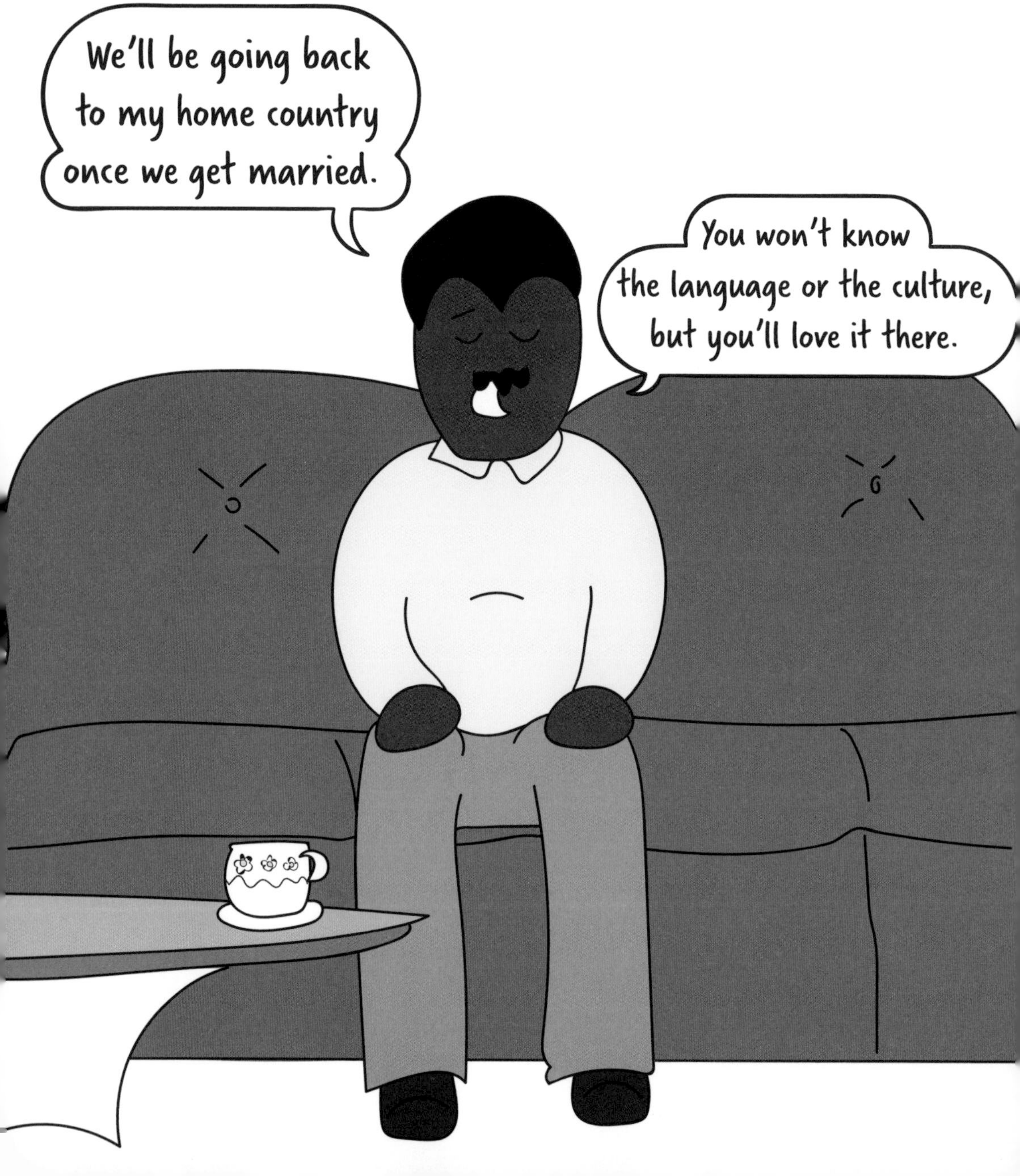
We'll be going back to my home country once we get married.
You won't know the language or the culture, but you'll love it there.

At 17, all my friends had already met a handful of suitors each. I began to worry. I begged my parents to arrange something for me. They did *not* think I was ready.

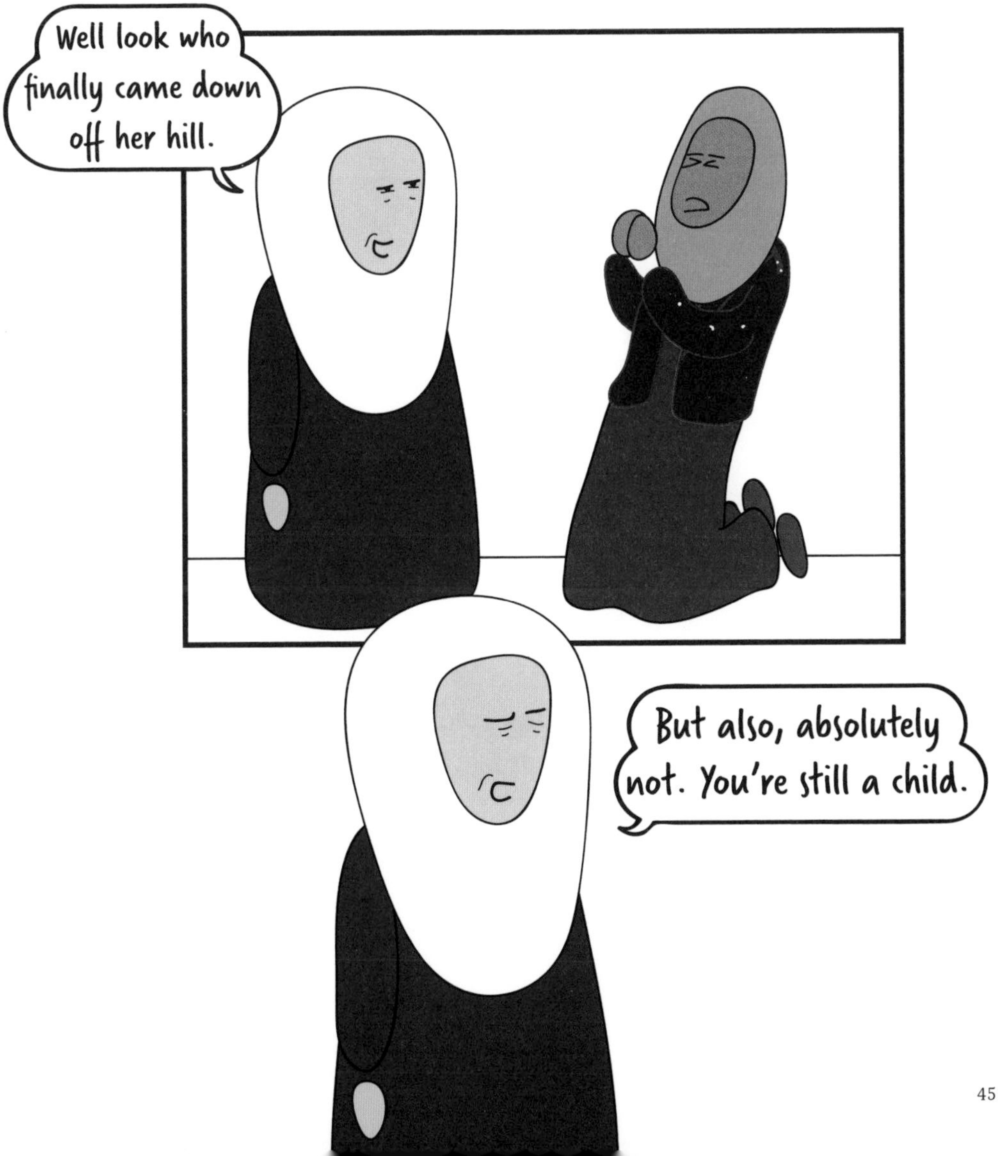
Well look who finally came down off her hill.
But also, absolutely not. You're still a child.

So, I started telling my mom about all the boys I had crushes on. That seemed to do the trick.

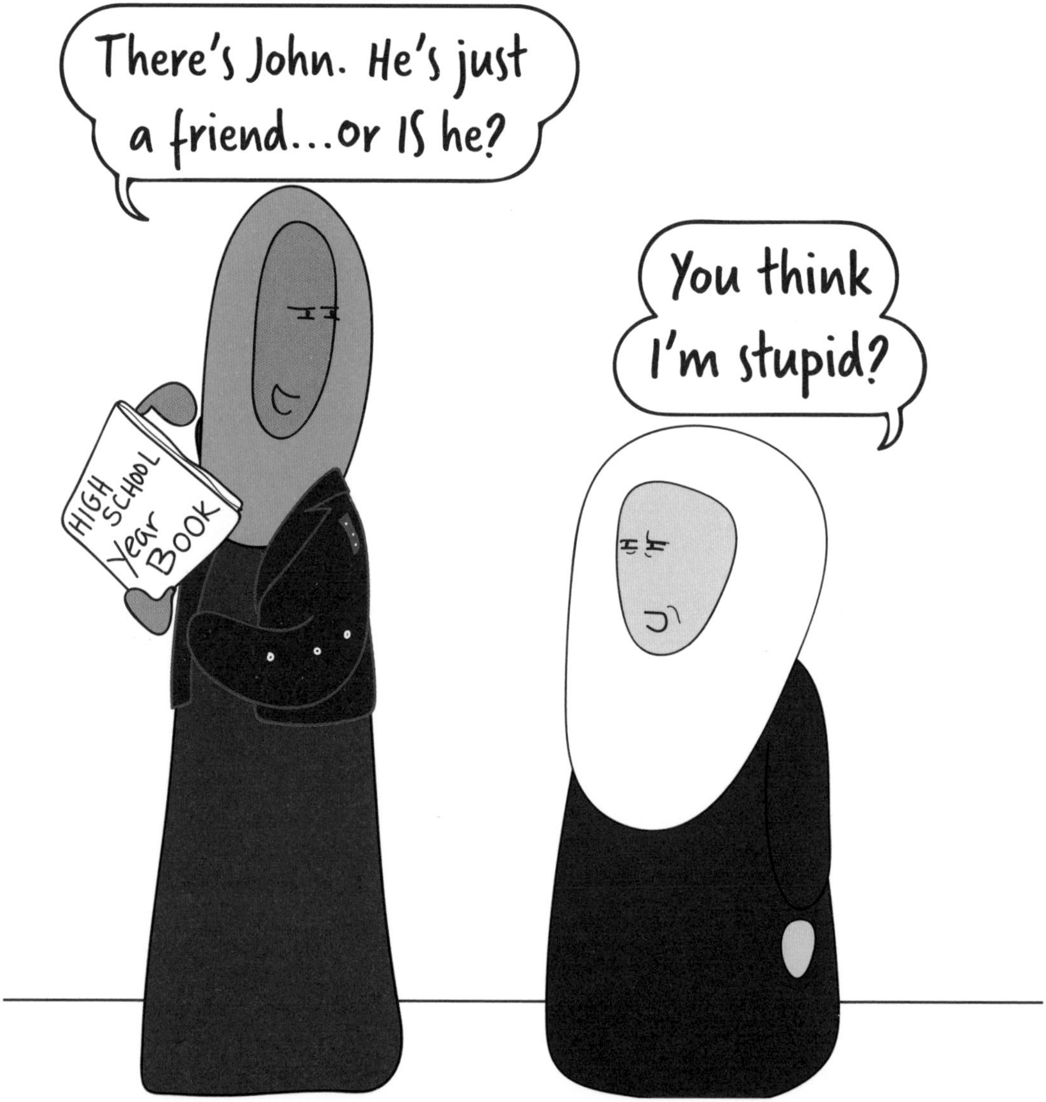
There's John. He's just a friend...or IS he?
You think I'm stupid?
HIGH SCHOOL Year BOOK

I met my first suitor shortly after, and God bless 'em, my parents were right.

I was not ready.

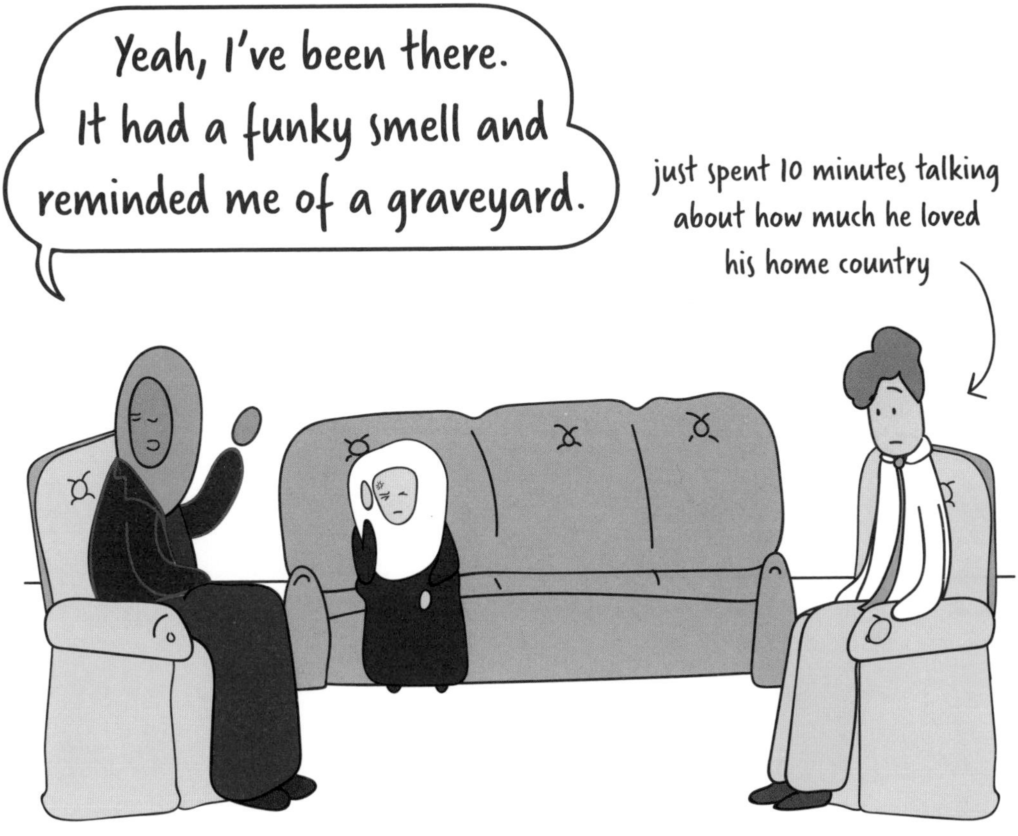
Yeah, I've been there. It had a funky smell and reminded me of a graveyard.
just spent 10 minutes talking about how much he loved his home country

He didn’t call back. Whatever, he wasn’t my type anyway.

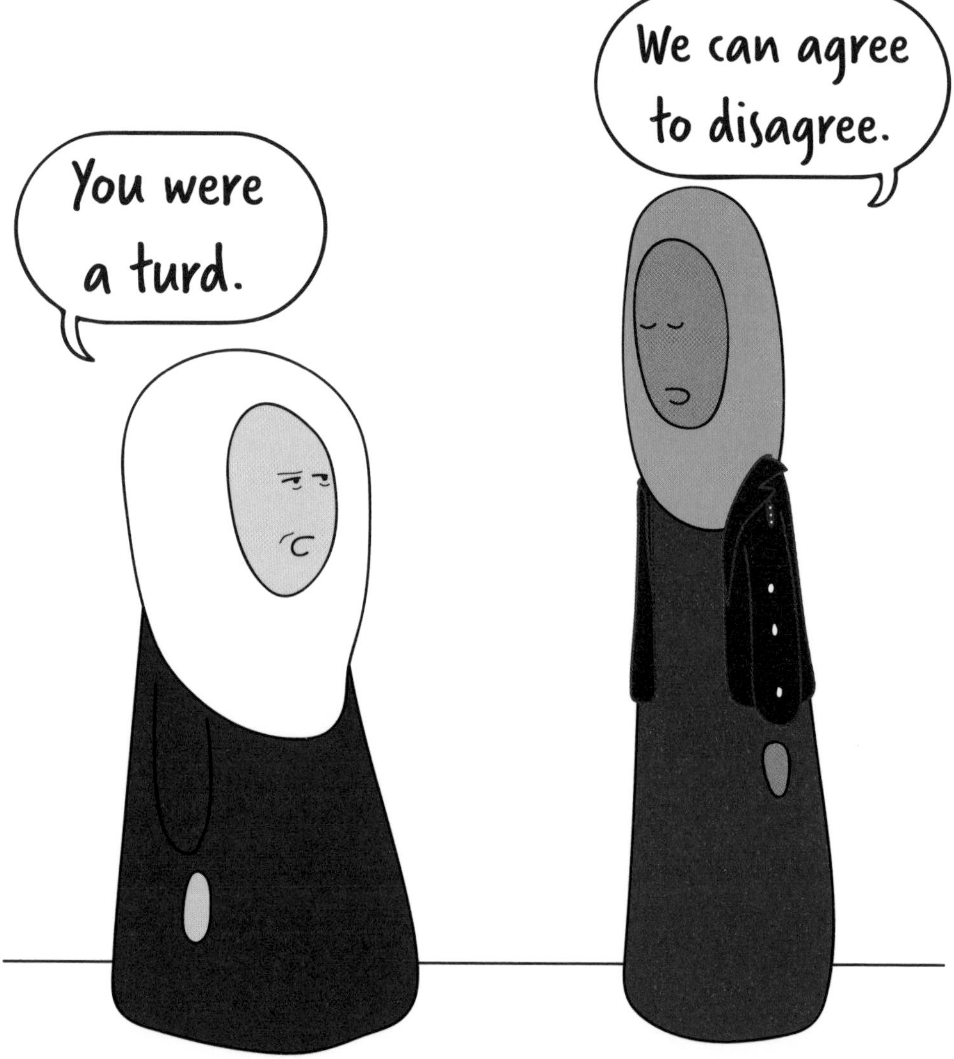
You were a turd.
We can agree to disagree.

*I was indeed a turd.

Courtship

I wouldn't meet someone again for a long time. Not for lack of wanting. It was just that no one wanted . . . me.

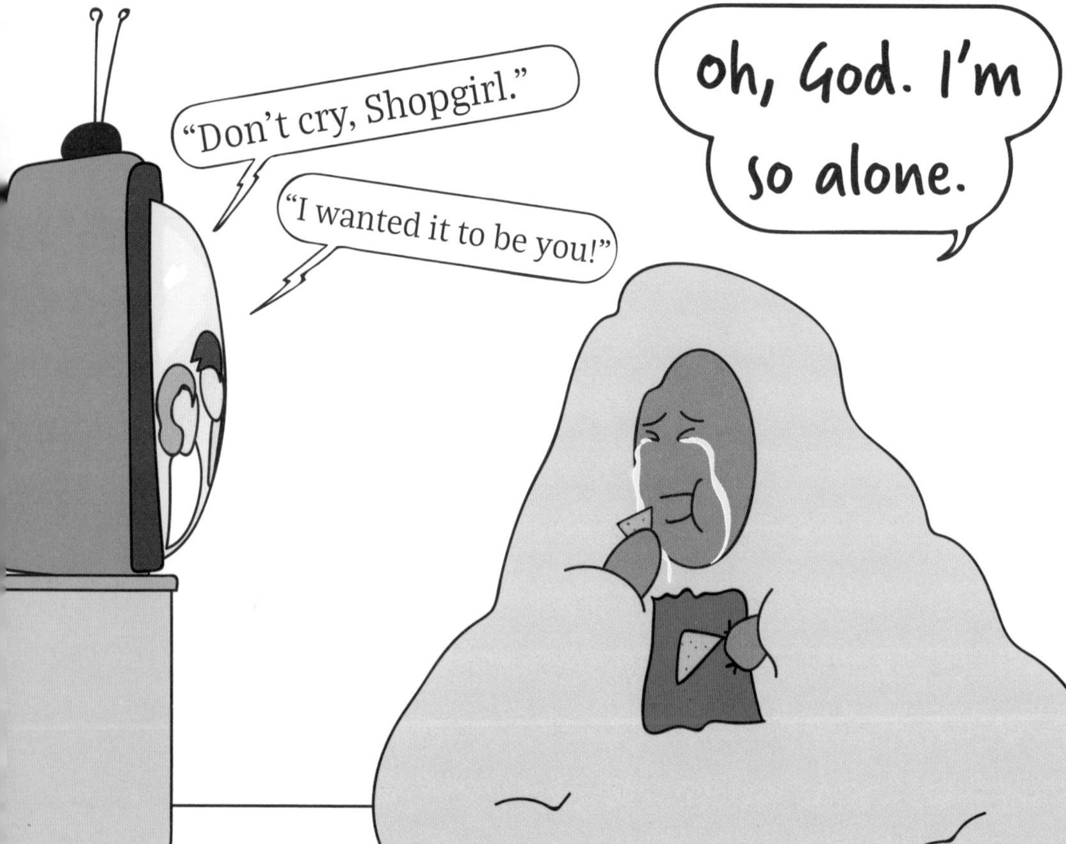
"Don't cry, Shopgirl."
"I wanted it to be you!"
Oh, God. I'm so alone.

I focused on college, majored in English, and read A LOT of Jane Austen.

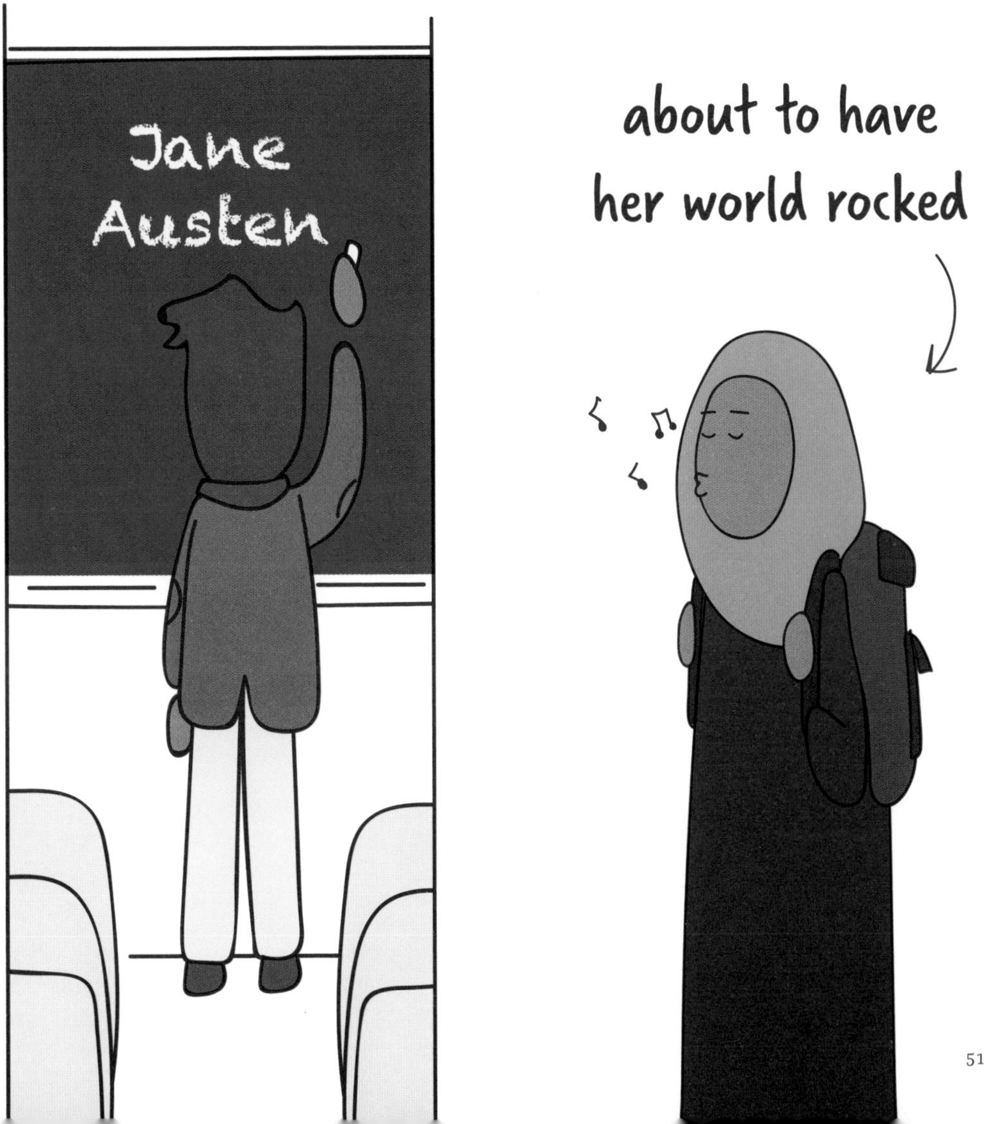
Jane Austen
about to have her world rocked

And let me tell you, I related HARD to the rules of courtship in Austen's novels.

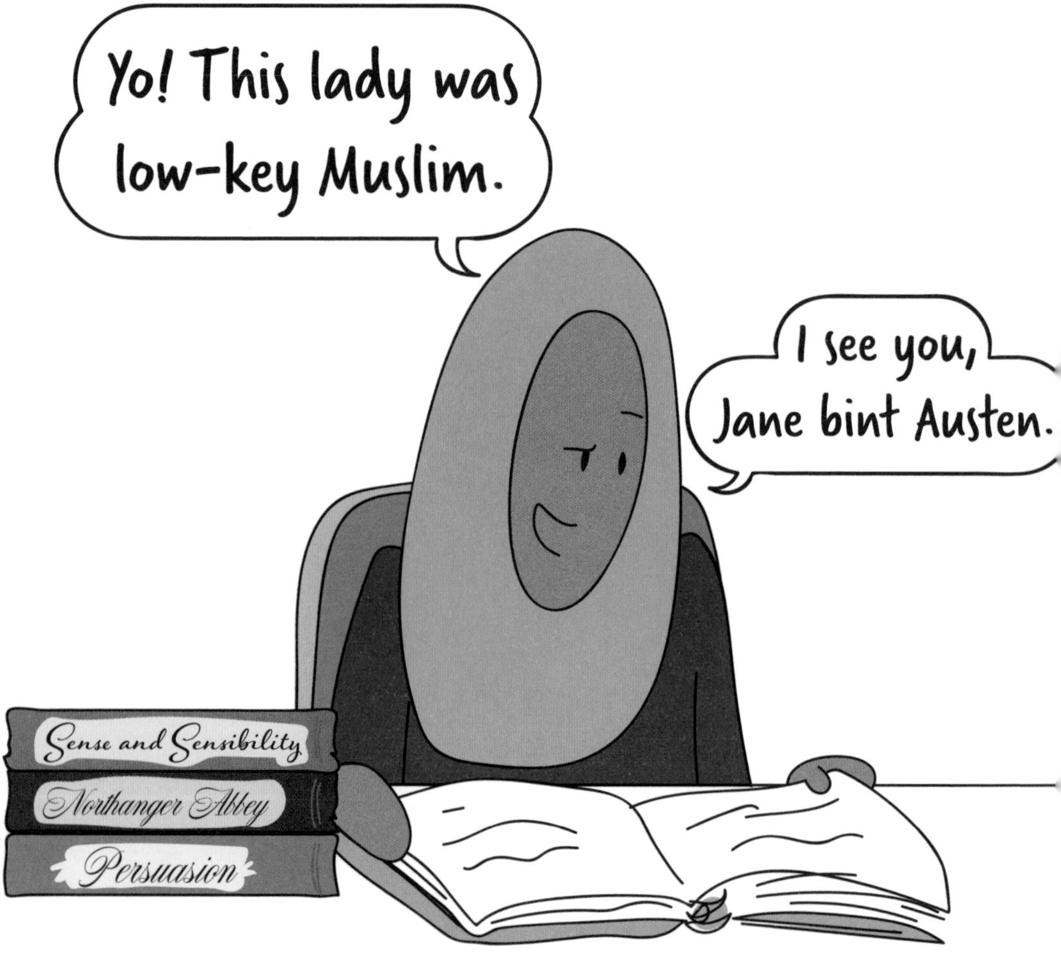
Yo! This lady was low-key Muslim.
I see you, Jane bint Austen.
Sense and Sensibility
Northanger Abbey
Persuasion

The Nosy Moms

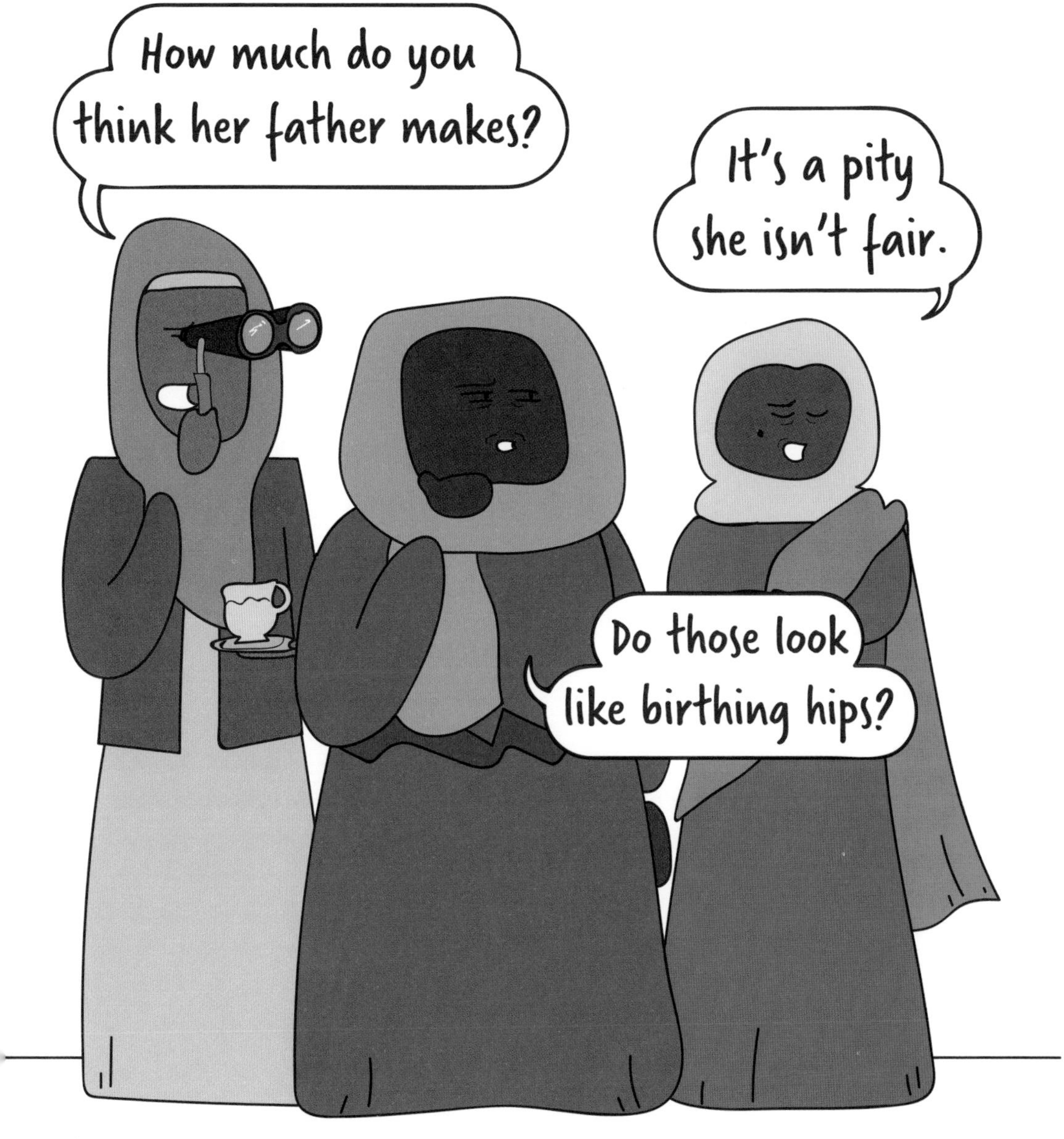
How much do you think her father makes?
It's a pity she isn't fair.
Do those look like birthing hips?

The Balls

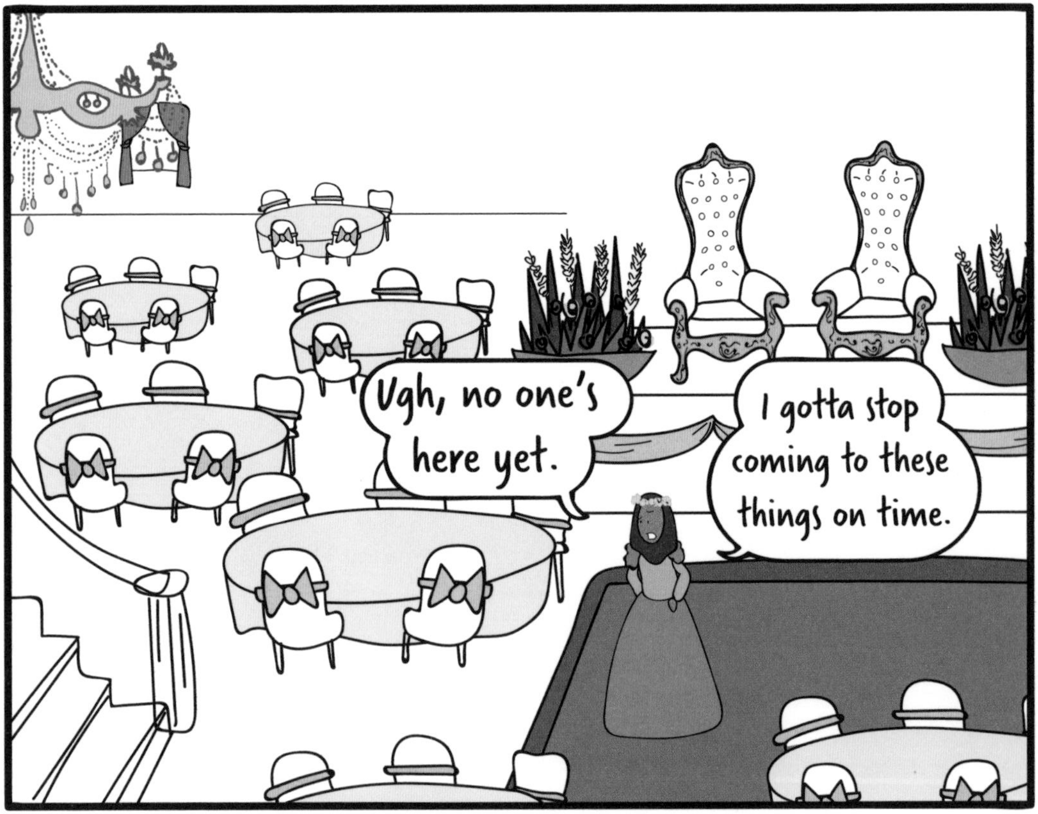
Ugh, no one's here yet.
I gotta stop coming to these things on time.

The Chaperones

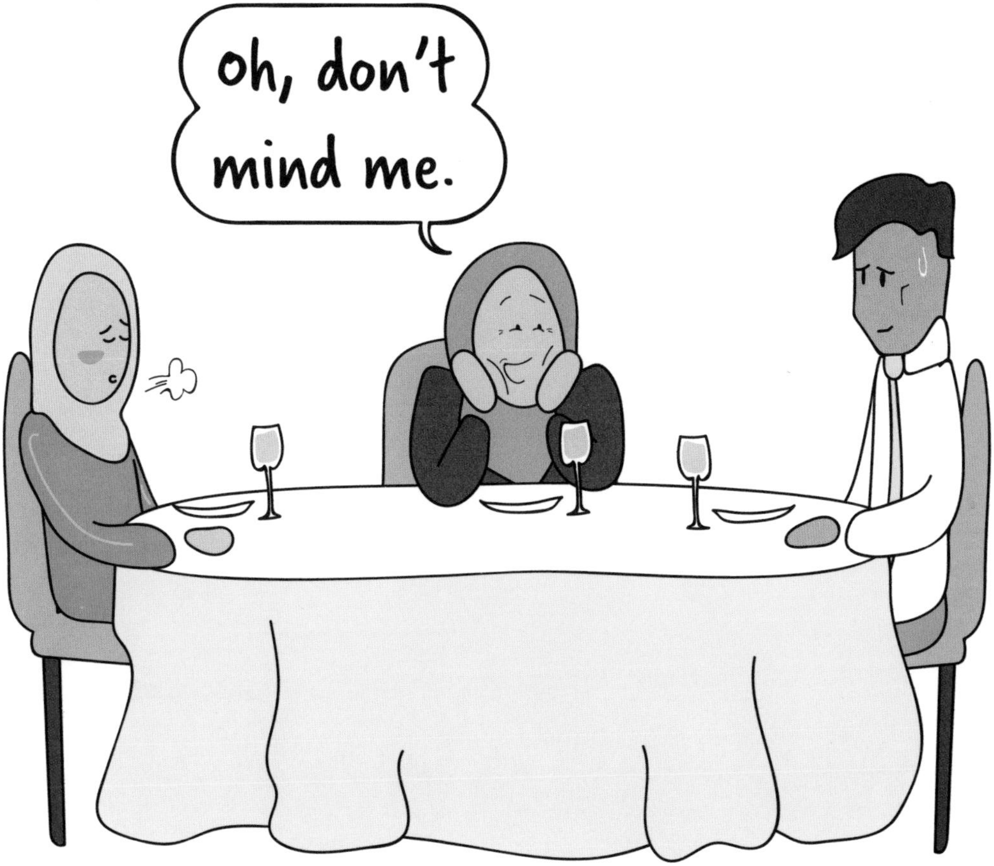
oh, don't mind me.

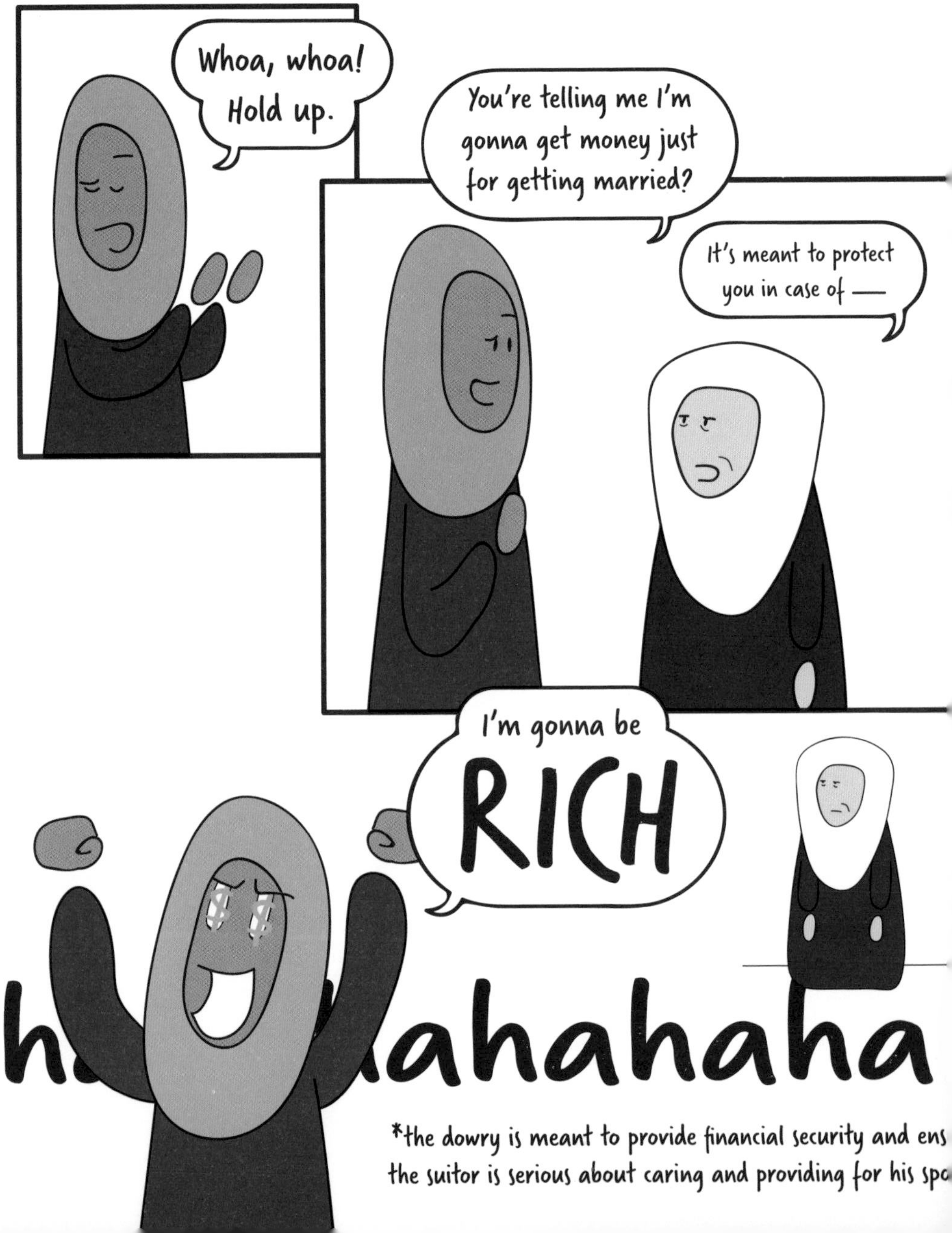
Whoa, whoa! Hold up.
You're telling me I'm gonna get money just for getting married?
It's meant to protect you in case of —
I'm gonna be RICH
ahahahaha
*the dowry is meant to provide financial security and ens
the suitor is serious about caring and providing for his sp

I saw myself in Austen's world.

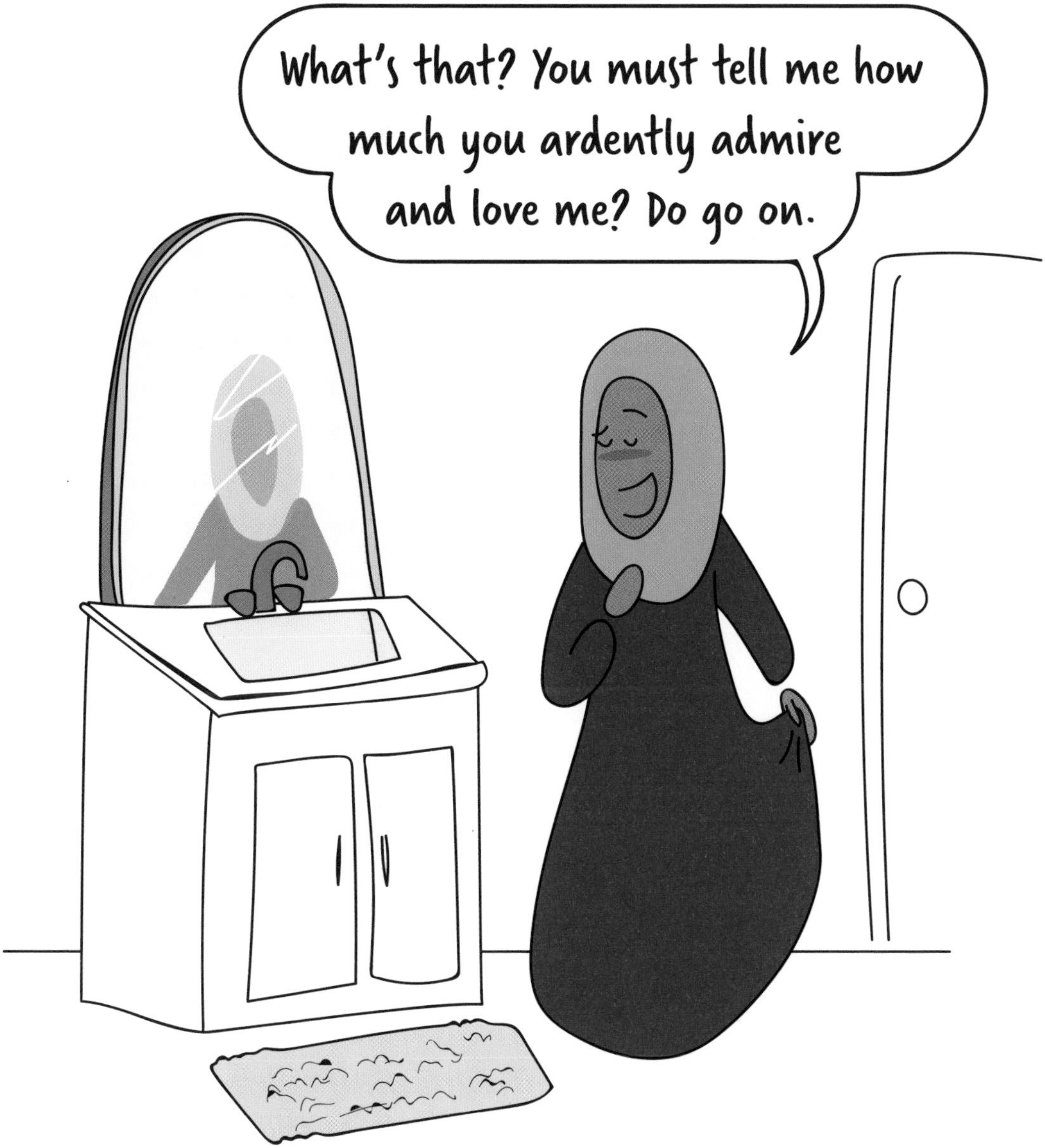
What's that? You must tell me how much you ardently admire and love me? Do go on.

Especially come Wedding Season. Going to a wedding for the first time as a young woman felt like I was entering Society.

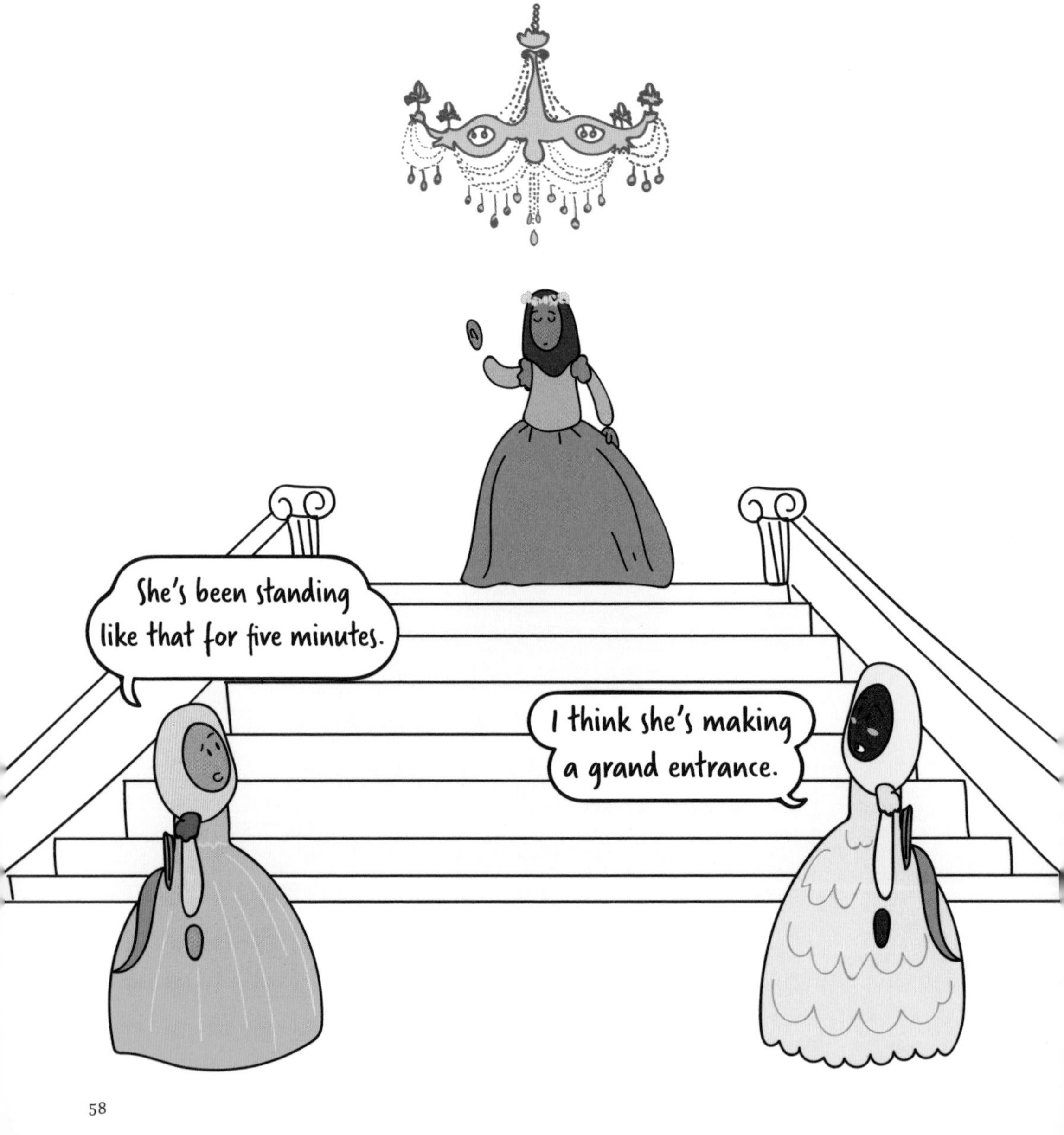
She's been standing like that for five minutes.
I think she's making a grand entrance.

I won't lie; it was a lot of fun. I got to wear ball gowns, get my hair done, dance the night way, and, of course, dodge nosy mothers.

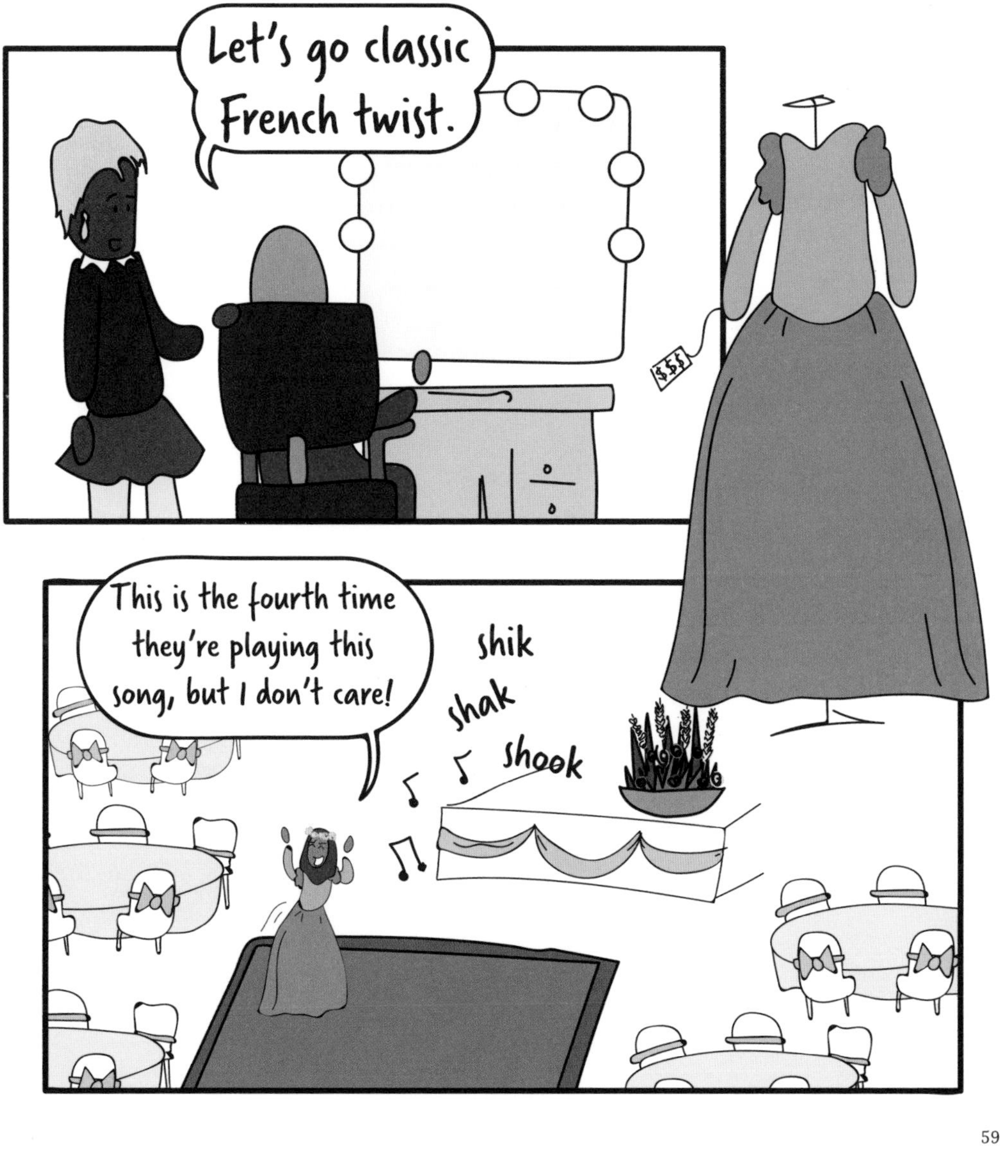

Let's go classic French twist.
$$$
This is the fourth time they're playing this song, but I don't care!
shik
shak
shook

À la Austen's balls, nosy mothers were ever present. They came to gossip, make snide remarks, show off their daughters, and scope out potential wives for their sons.

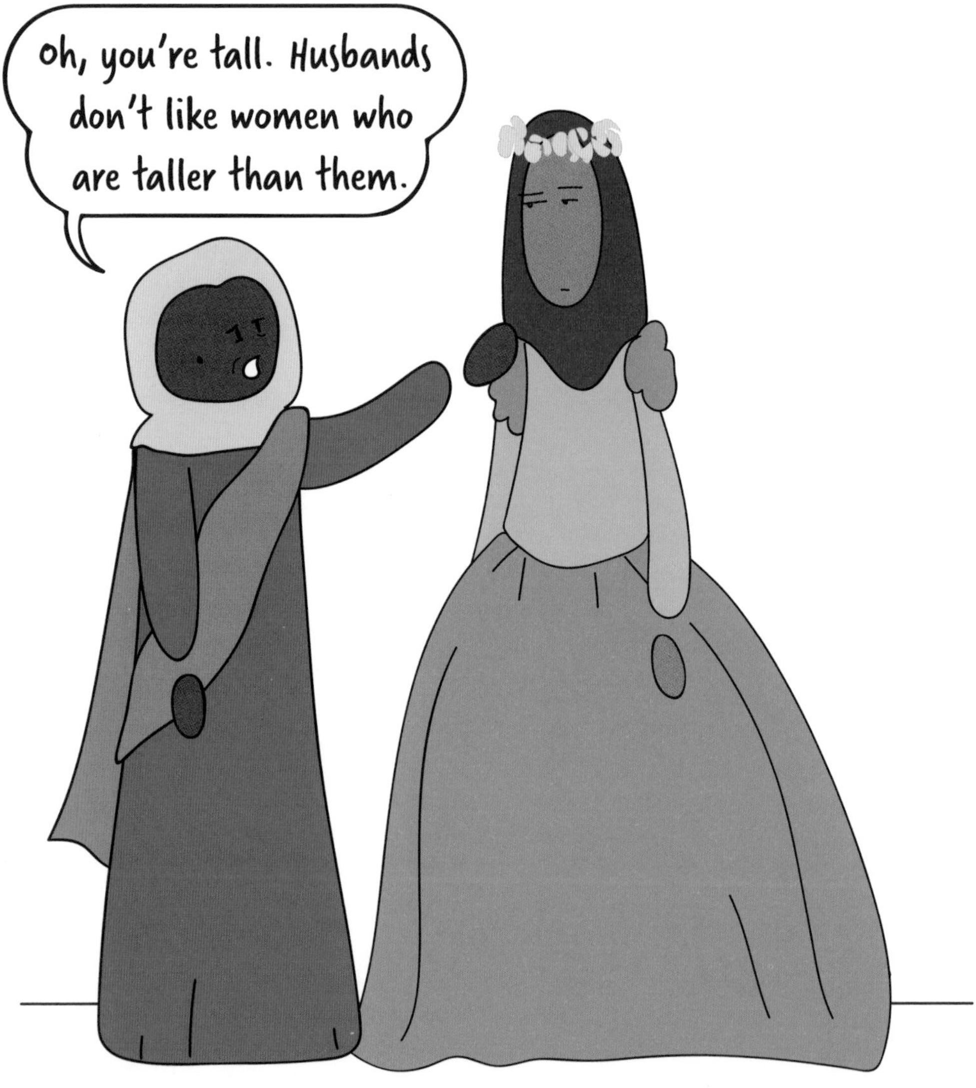
Oh, you're tall. Husbands don't like women who are taller than them.

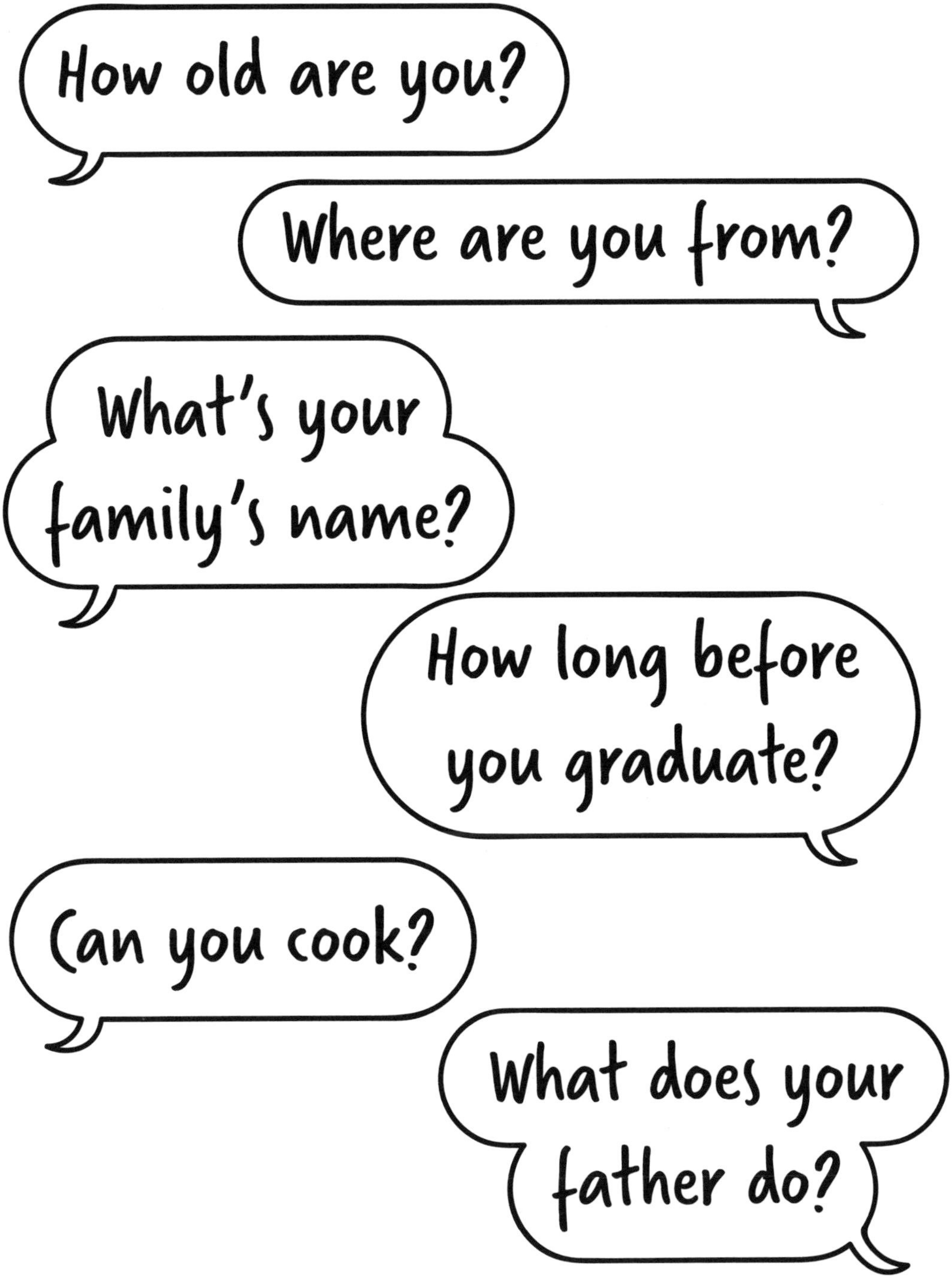
How old are you?
Where are you from?
What's your family's name?
How long before you graduate?
Can you cook?
What does your father do?

If one of these moms liked what she saw, she would either ask for my father's phone number so that her son could call directly, OR she'd ask for my biodata.

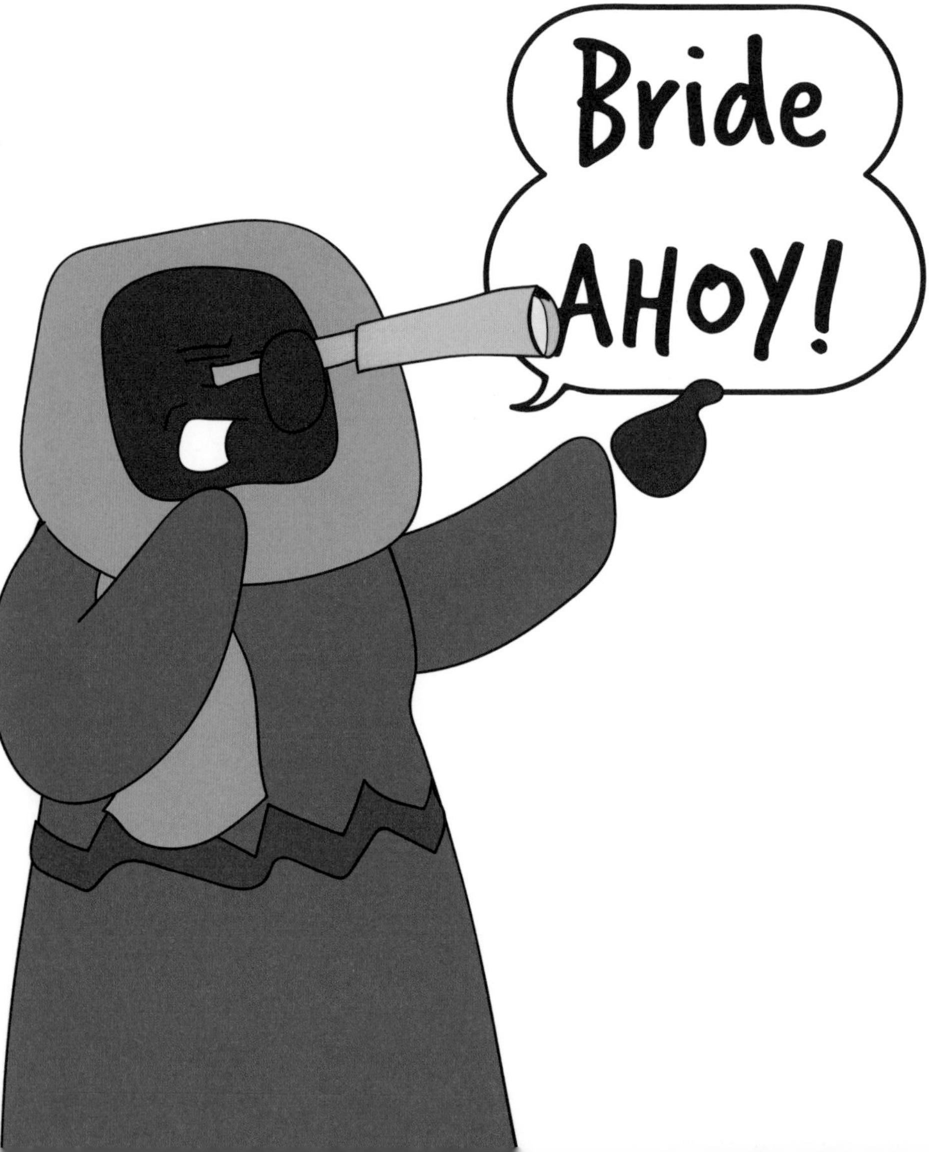
Bride AHOY!

Biodata *(noun)*: personal information about one's life, work, family, personality, goals, financial status, values, beliefs, health history, favorite Pokémon, and other preferences about things both religious and secular. Think super-detailed Tinder profile, except instead of dating, they'd get married.

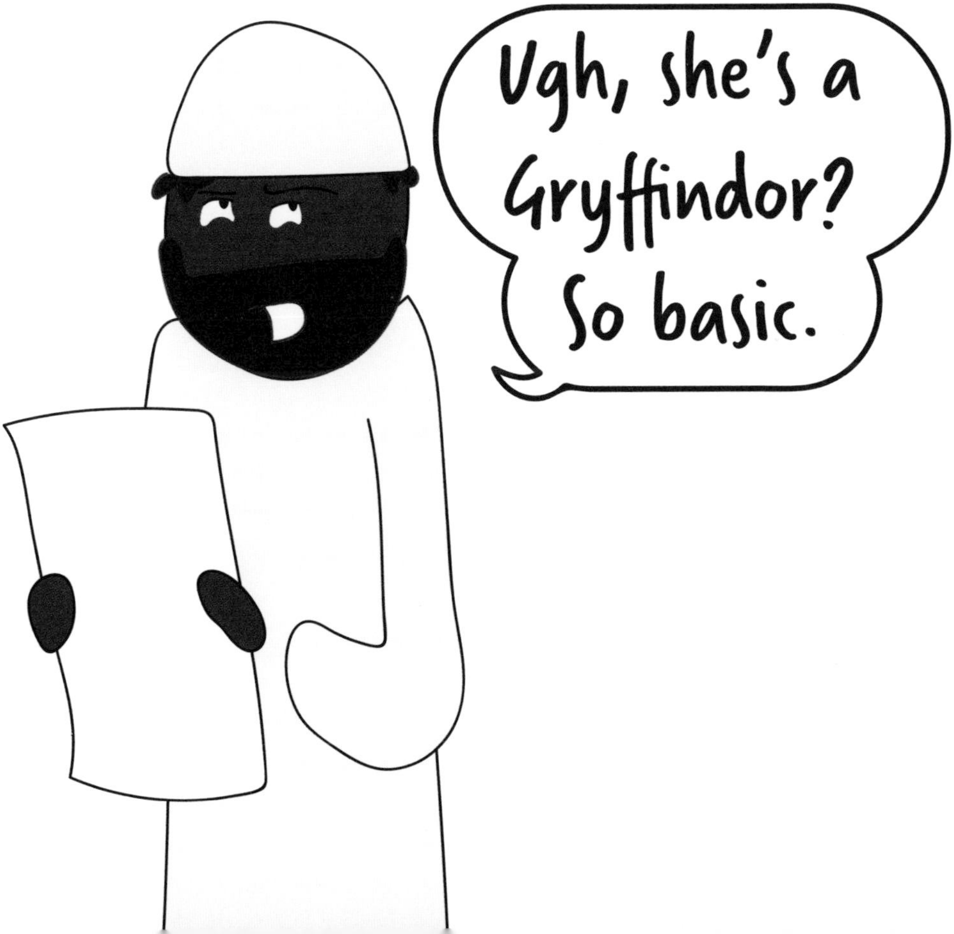
Ugh, she's a Gryffindor? So basic.

If both parties liked what they saw on paper, their parents would arrange a meet (chaperoned of course).

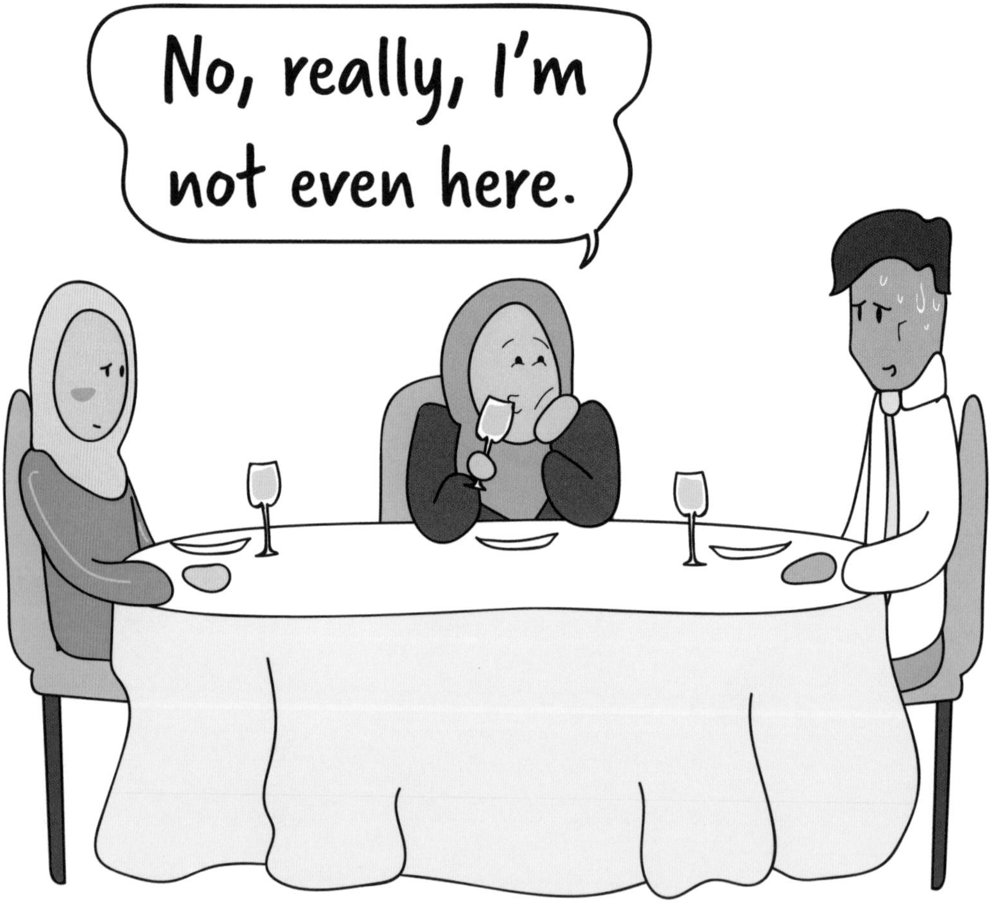
No, really, I'm not even here.

Problem was, I never made it past the first round. Moms thought I was funny, but a good personality did not a future daughter-in-law make.

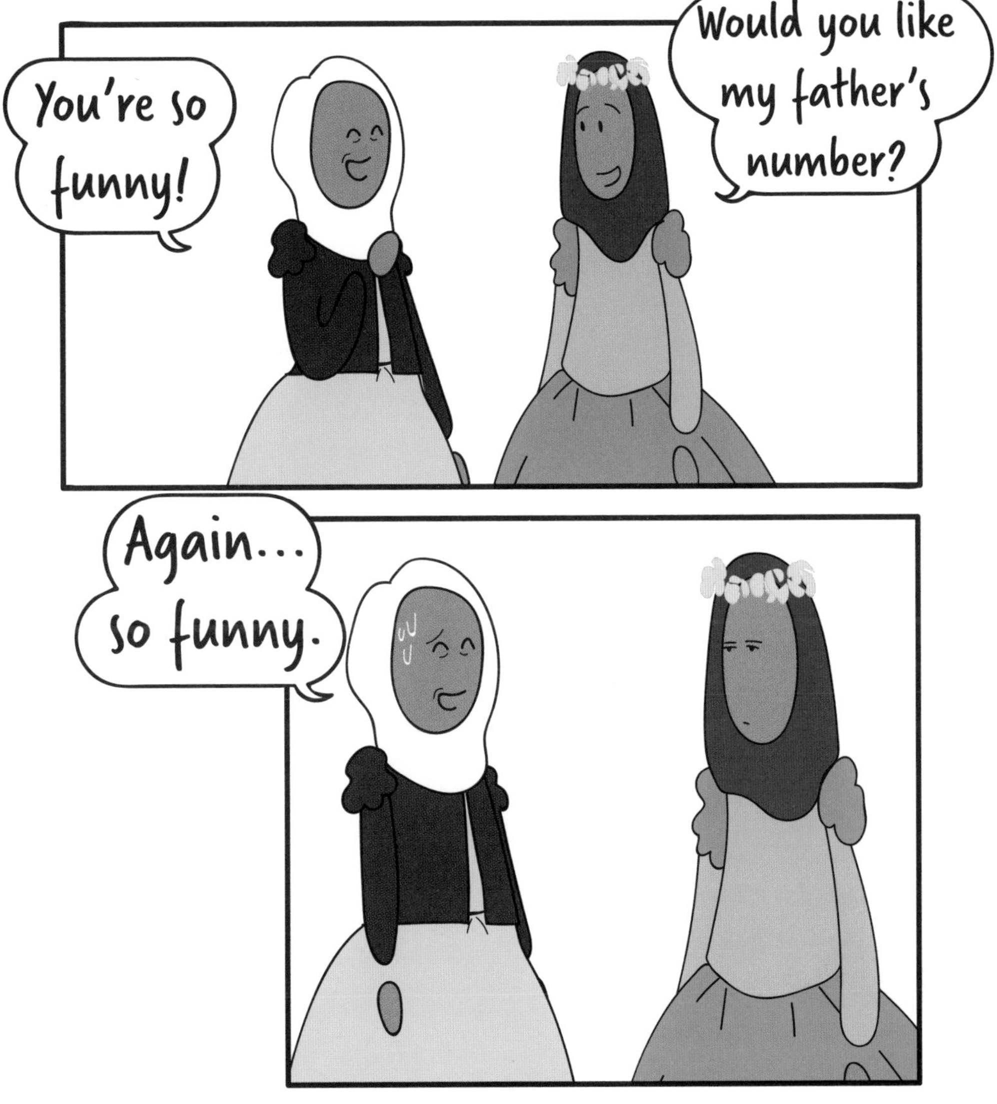
You're so funny!
Would you like my father's number?
Again... so funny.

Eventually, I got tired of waiting for someone to see me at some wedding and decide whether I was good enough to meet their son. So, I figured I'd cut out the middle-mom and meet a guy myself.

My First Proposal

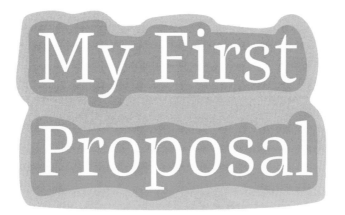

Because of the rules, I grew up avoiding guys as much as possible. What my parents didn't tell me was that there WERE rules in Islam about interacting with guys in a professional or academic setting. So, I used college to work on my social skills. I knew I couldn't avoid guys forever in the real world, and I needed to practice how to hold a simple conversation without being super weird.

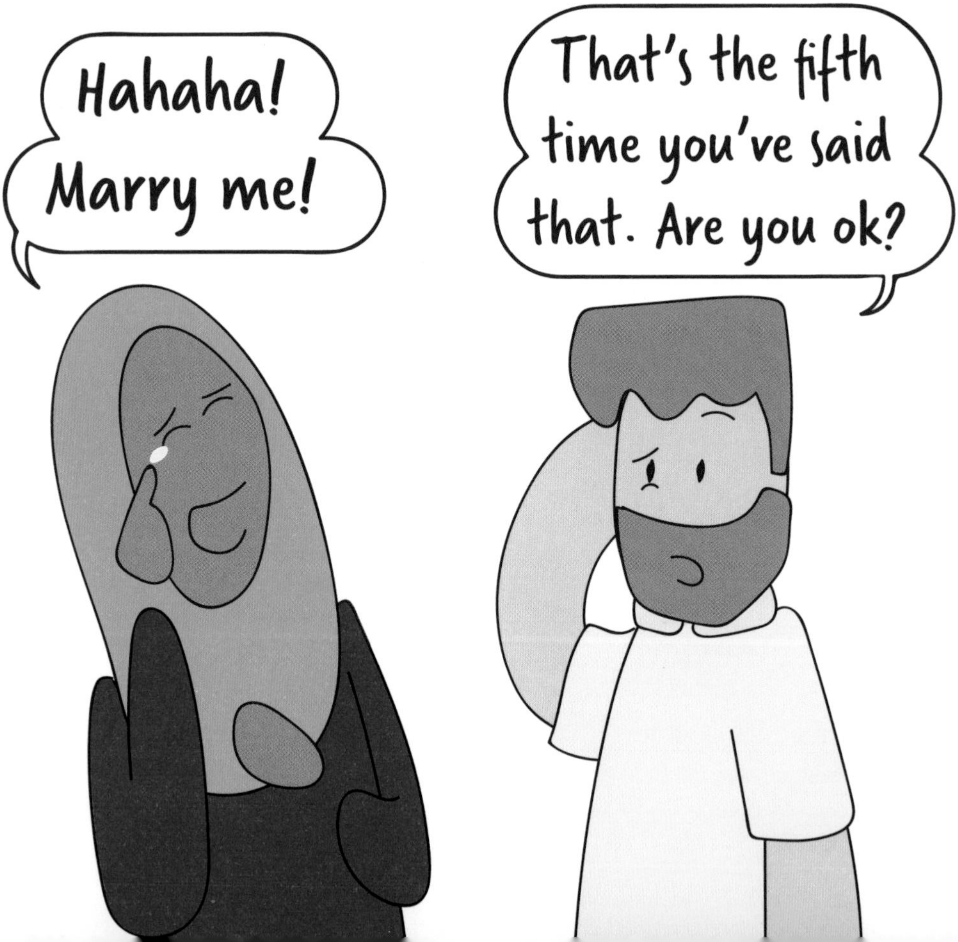
Hahaha! Marry me!
That's the fifth time you've said that. Are you ok?

Secretly, though, I was craving banter. You know the banter I'm talking about. The witty banter between the heroine and her frustratingly handsome and wholly misunderstood person of interest. Austen's banter.

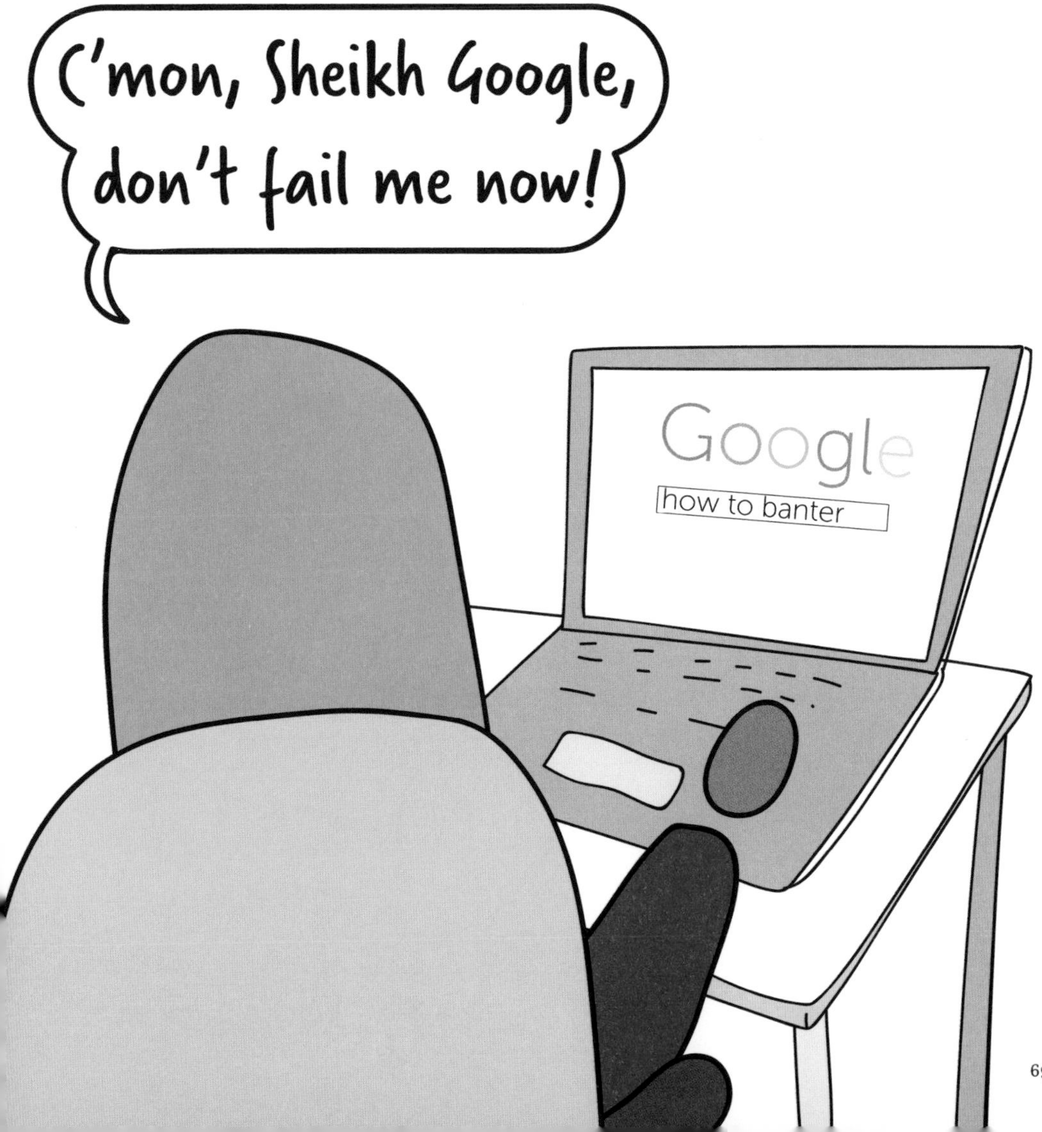
C'mon, Sheikh Google, don't fail me now!
Google
how to banter

I befriended a lot of guys and harbored many an unrequited crush. I wasn't one to beat around the bush and actually told a couple of these crushes that I would like to pursue a serious "here's my father's number" relationship. I was rejected both times. One of them told me he didn't find girls in abaya attractive.

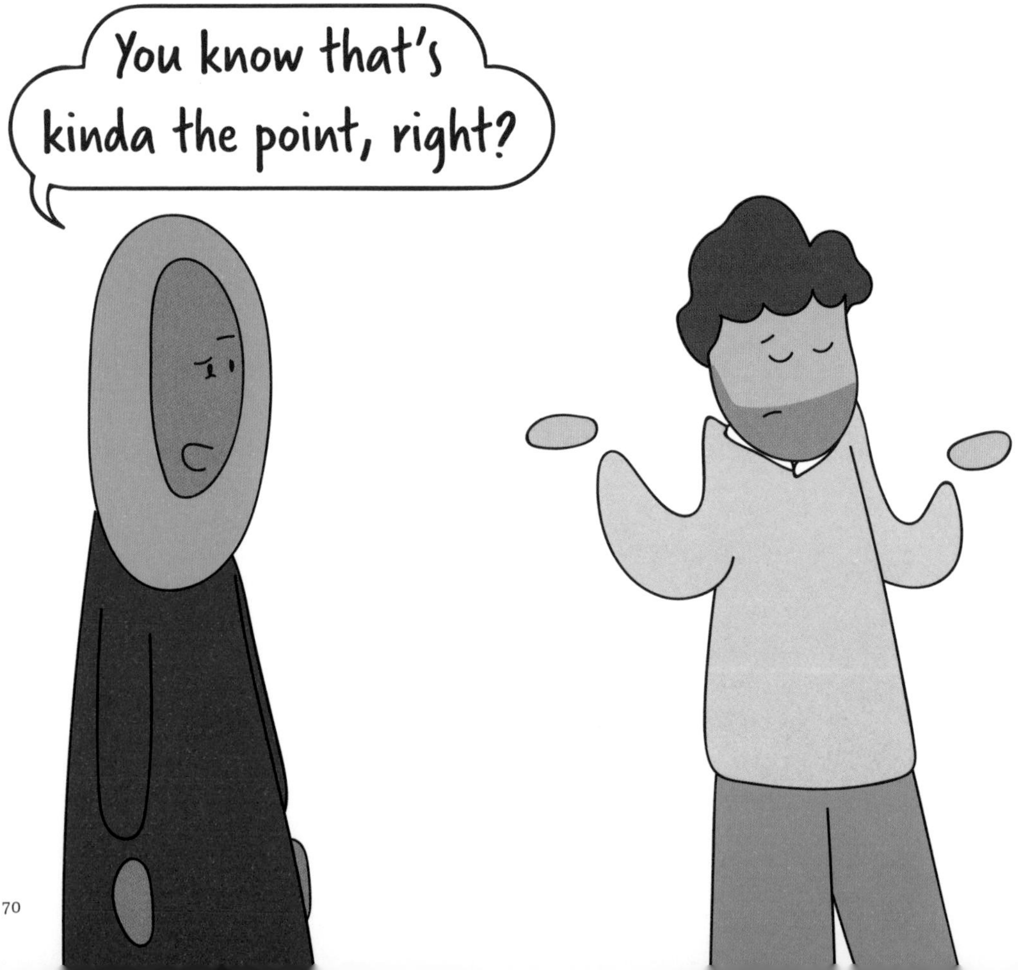
You know that's kinda the point, right?

And though I managed to improve my social skills, I left college with no marriage prospects at all. Good Lord, what was wrong with me? Why didn't these guys like me? Was it my acne? My weight? Was I too loud? Too judgy? I was 21, graduating college, and the last (and only) suitor I met was four years ago. Ticktock.

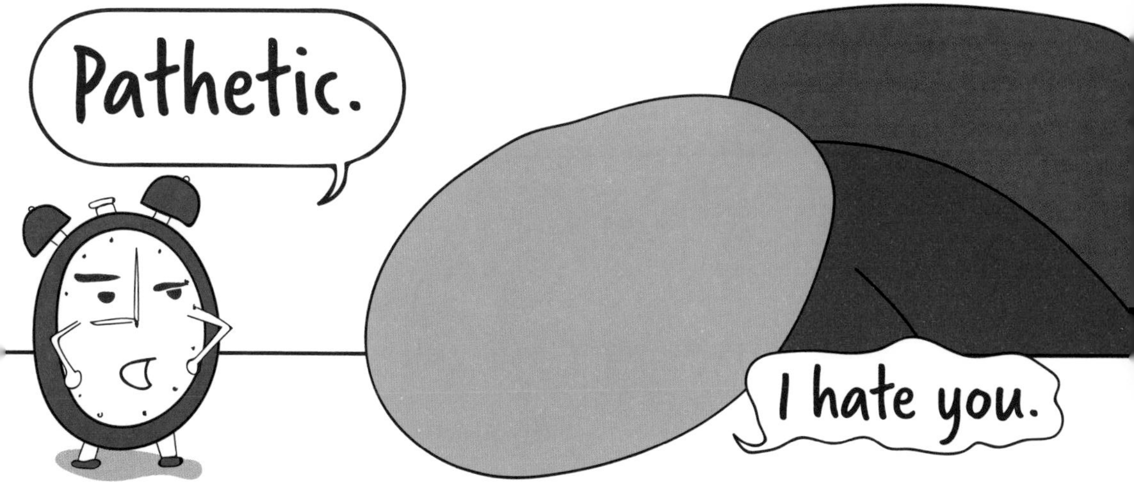

Pathetic.
I hate you.

And then . . . it happened. The summer after graduation, I met someone and received my first ever proposal.

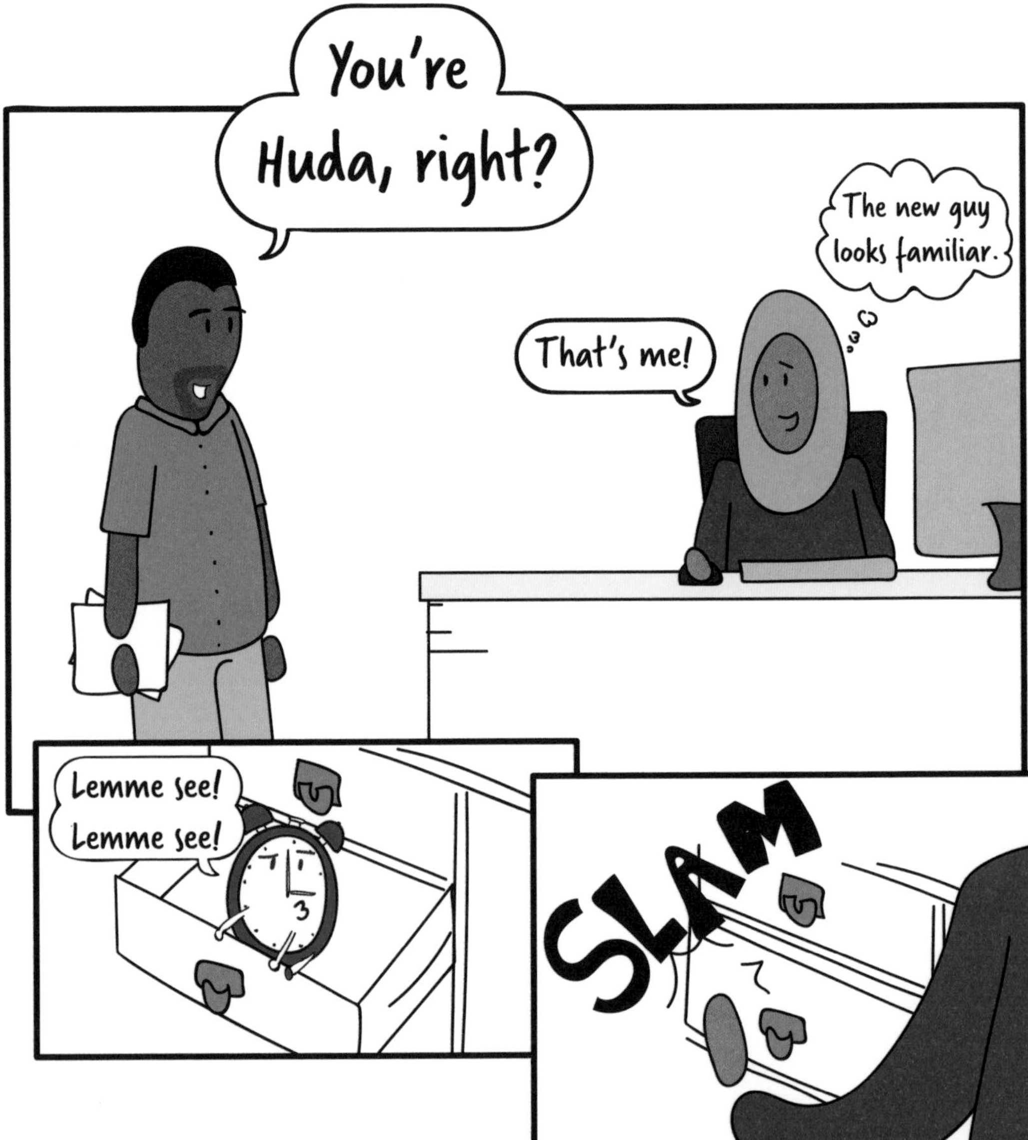
You're Huda, right?
That's me!
The new guy looks familiar.
Lemme see! Lemme see!
SLAM

I was working as a content writer for a nonprofit organization when a coworker approached me. I recognized him from college, but I'd never really paid much attention to him before.

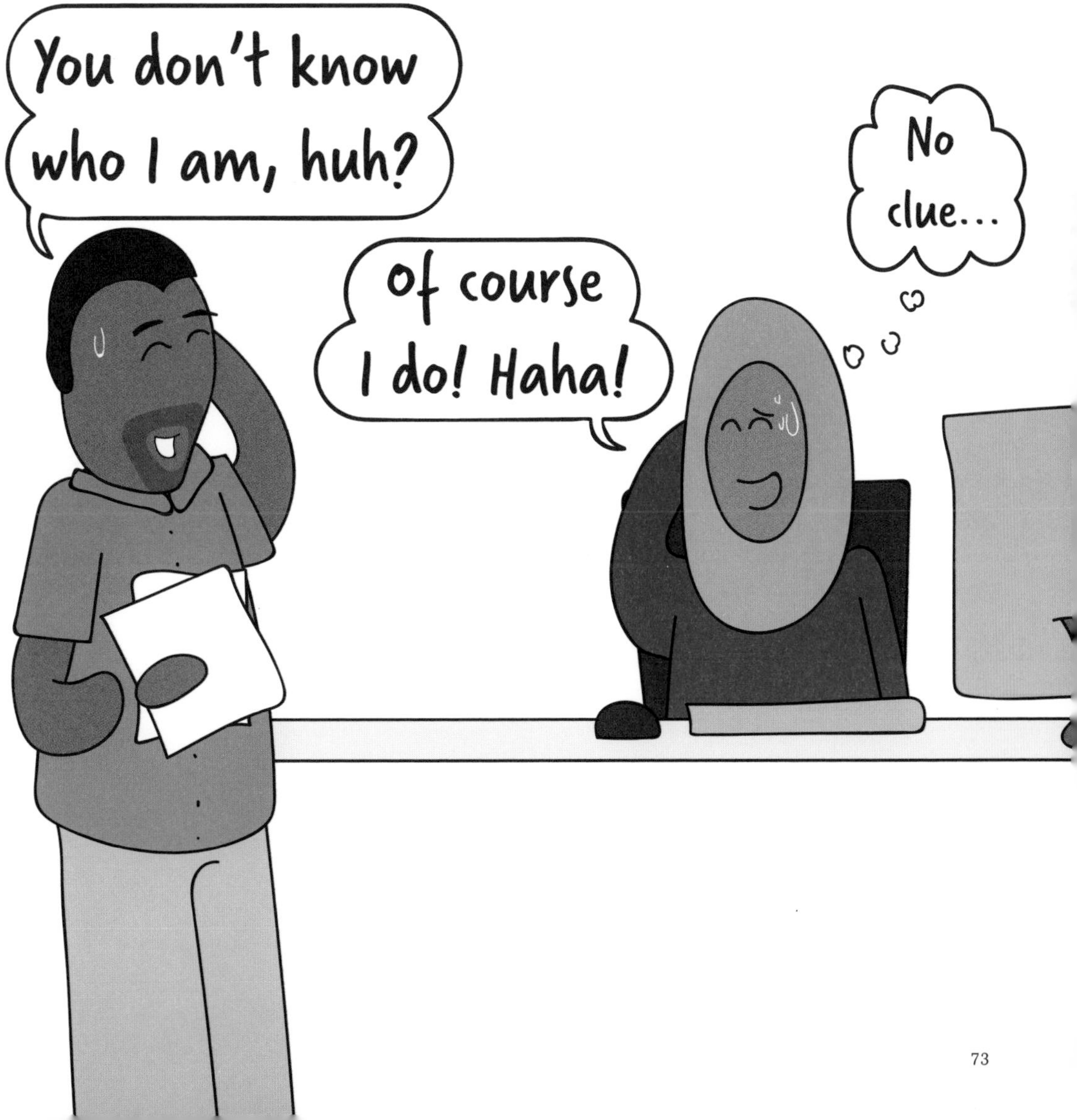
You don't know who I am, huh?
Of course I do! Haha!
No clue...

He thought I was cute and funny. Awww! He also knew the make and model of my car and said he used to watch me get out of it from the student union. Uh . . .

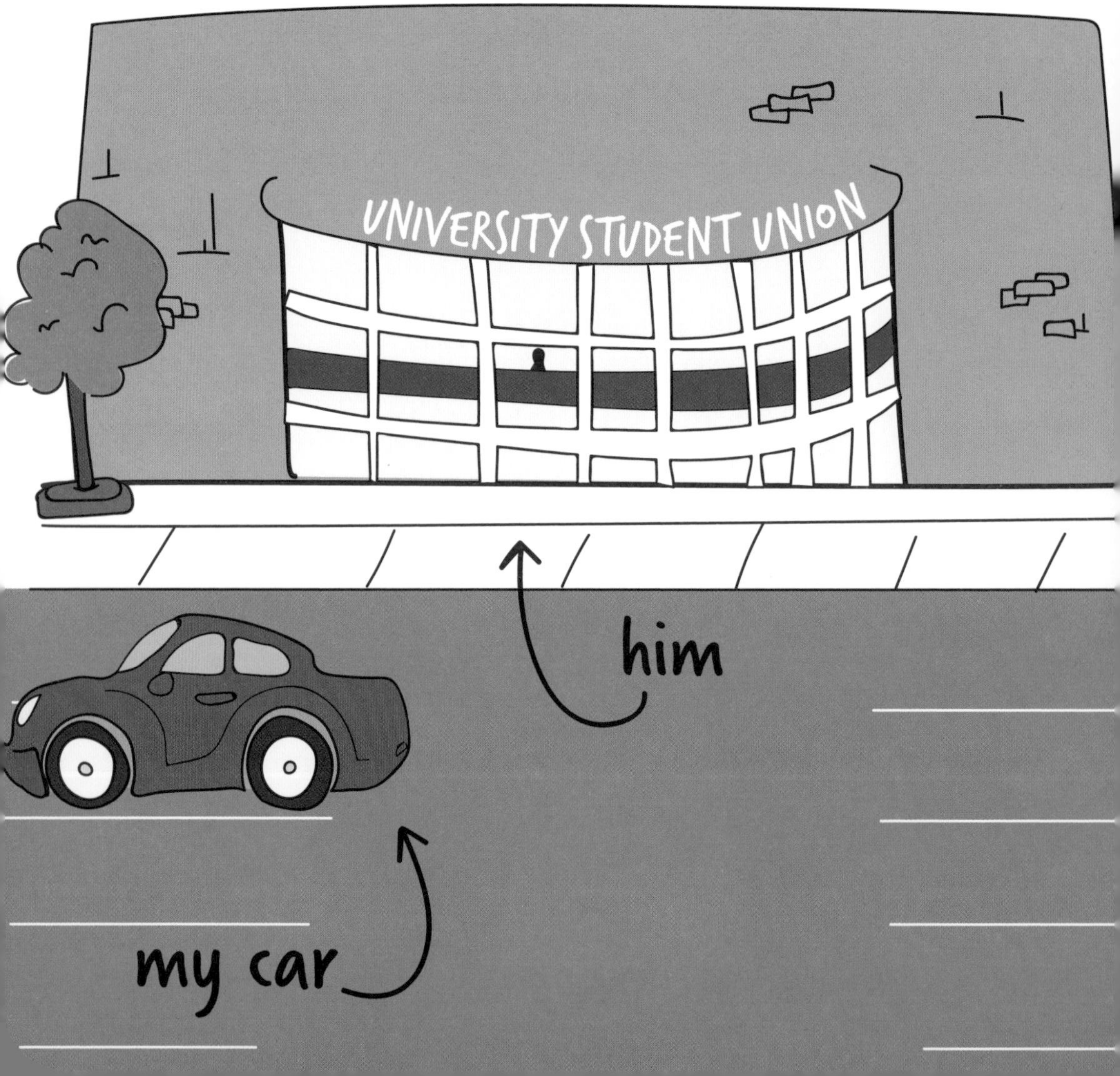
UNIVERSITY STUDENT UNION
him
my car

It was like a scene pulled straight outta one of the million rom-coms I'd watched where the guy watches his love interest from afar and silently pines for her, only to bump into her at work and finally have the courage to ask her out. So romantic! Except in real life, it just felt kinda . . . creepy?

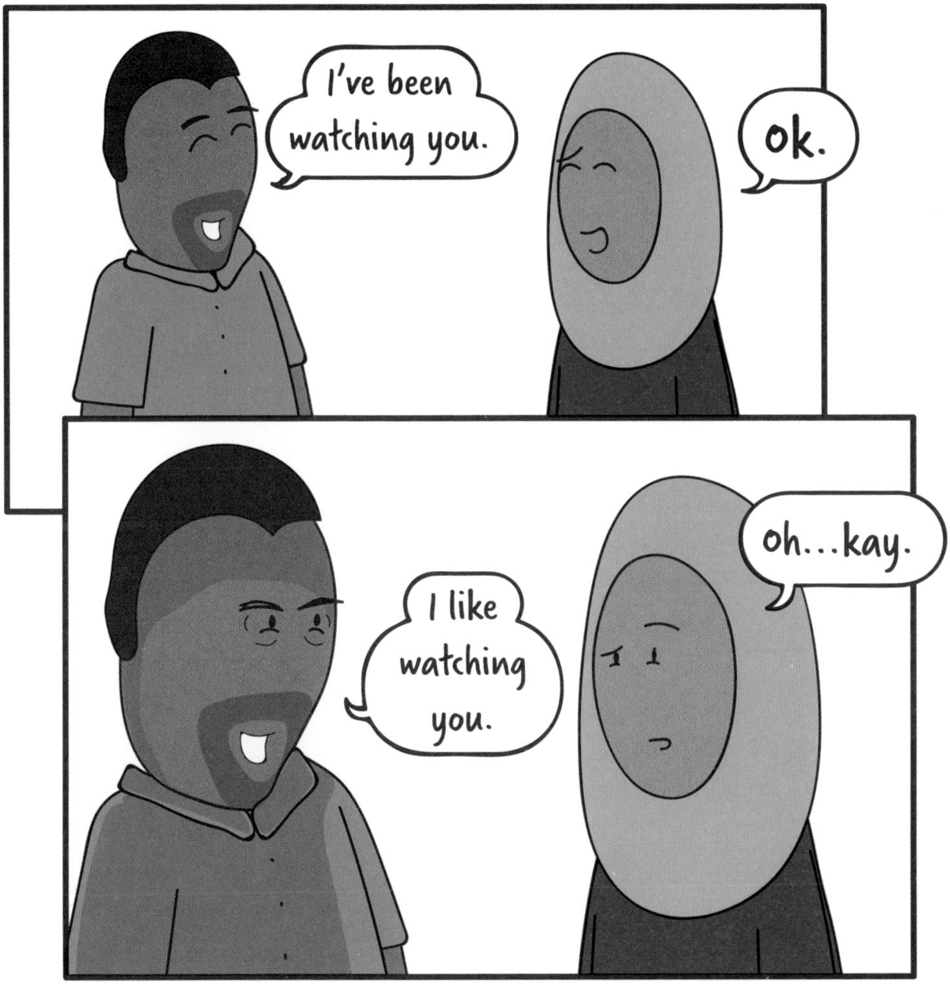
I've been watching you.
Ok.
I like watching you.
Oh...kay.

But this was the first time someone approached me for marriage who actually liked me! I could forgive a little creepiness, couldn't I?

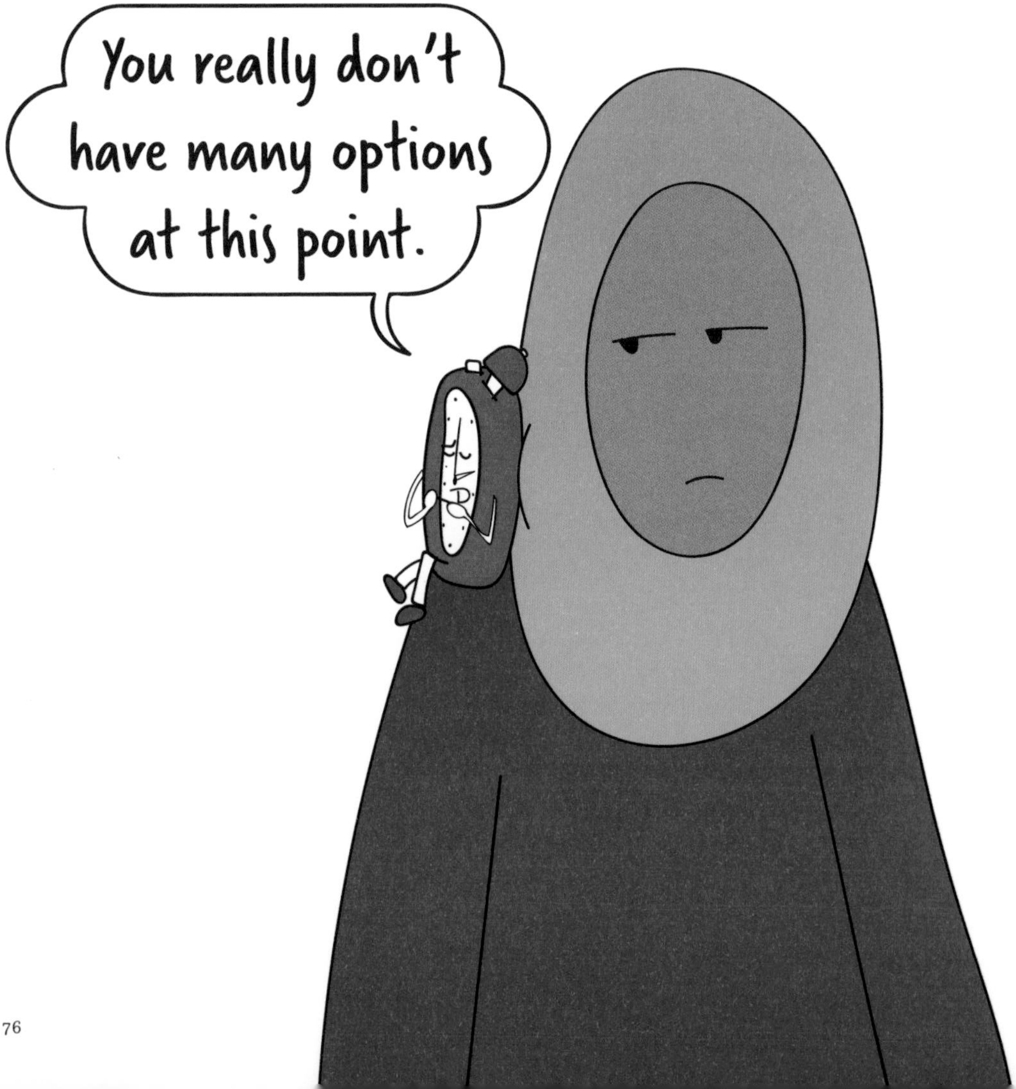
You really don't have many options at this point.

My mom liked him.

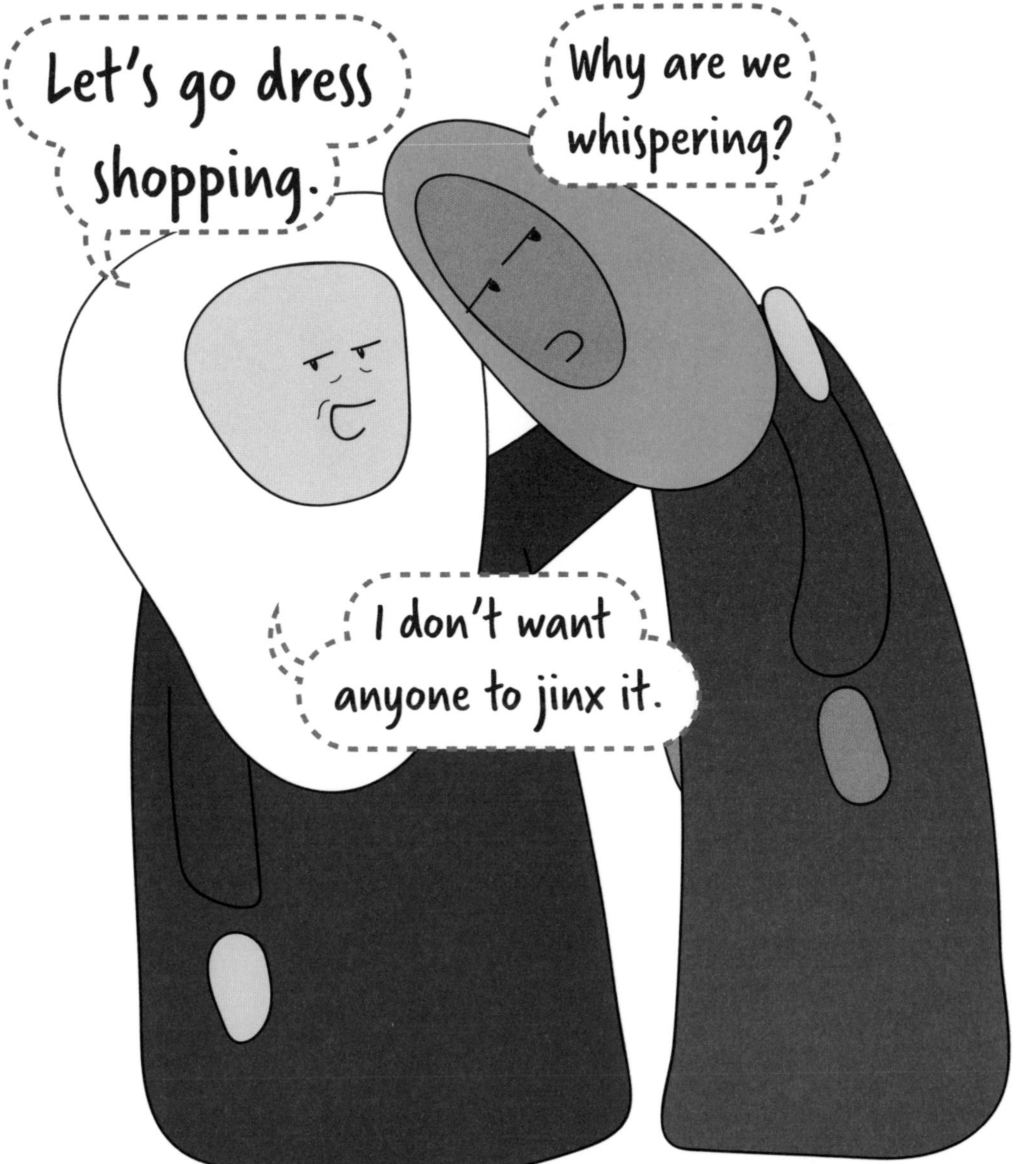
Let's go dress shopping.
Why are we whispering?
I don't want anyone to jinx it.

My dad . . . not so much.

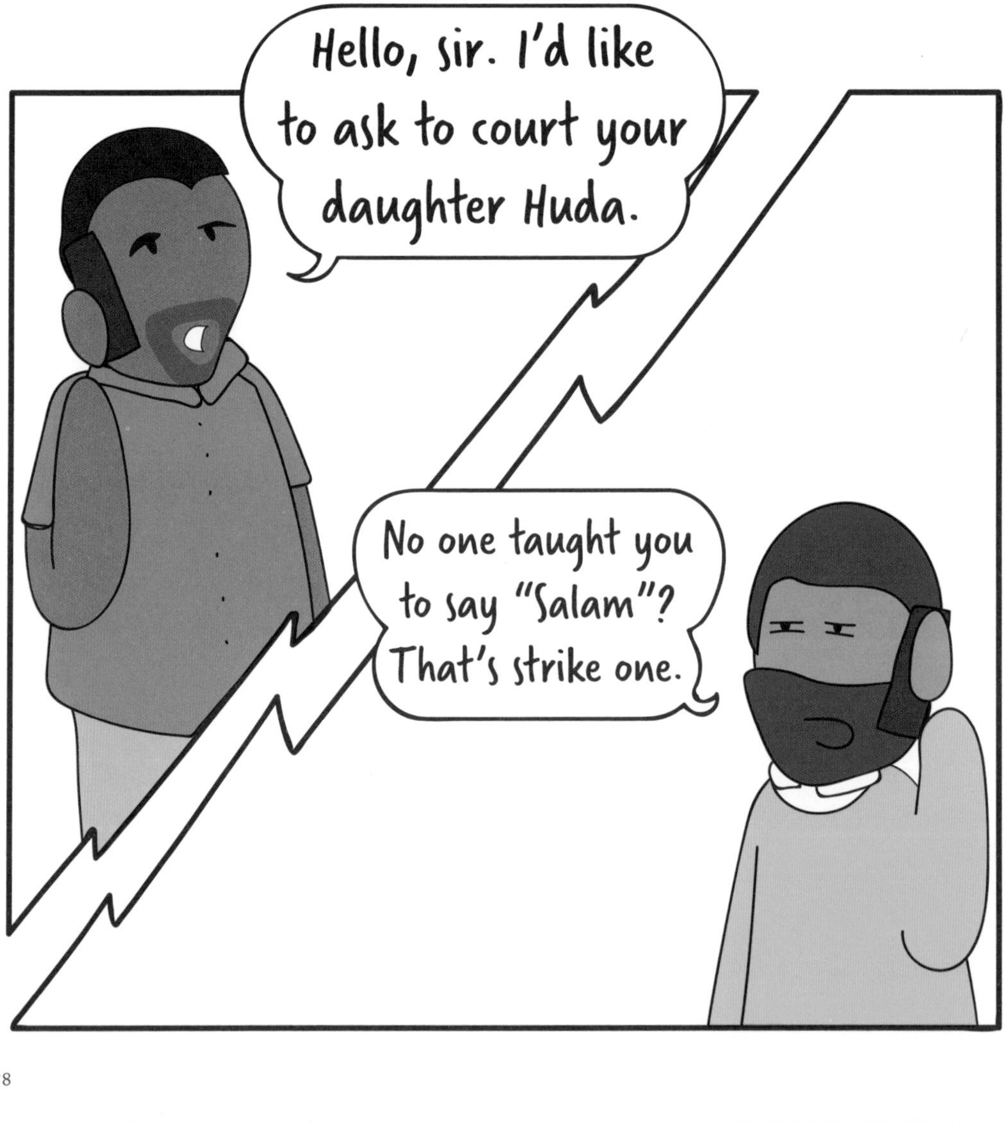
Hello, sir. I'd like to ask to court your daughter Huda.
No one taught you to say "Salam"? That's strike one.

I used to think my dad was too hard on some of the guys who came to see my sisters. As I grew older, though, I appreciated him for what he really was: a master interrogator and the first line of defense. Before a guy was allowed to court me, he had to go through an intense and thorough cross-examination. My dad did not play around. And he most definitely was not impressed with this guy.

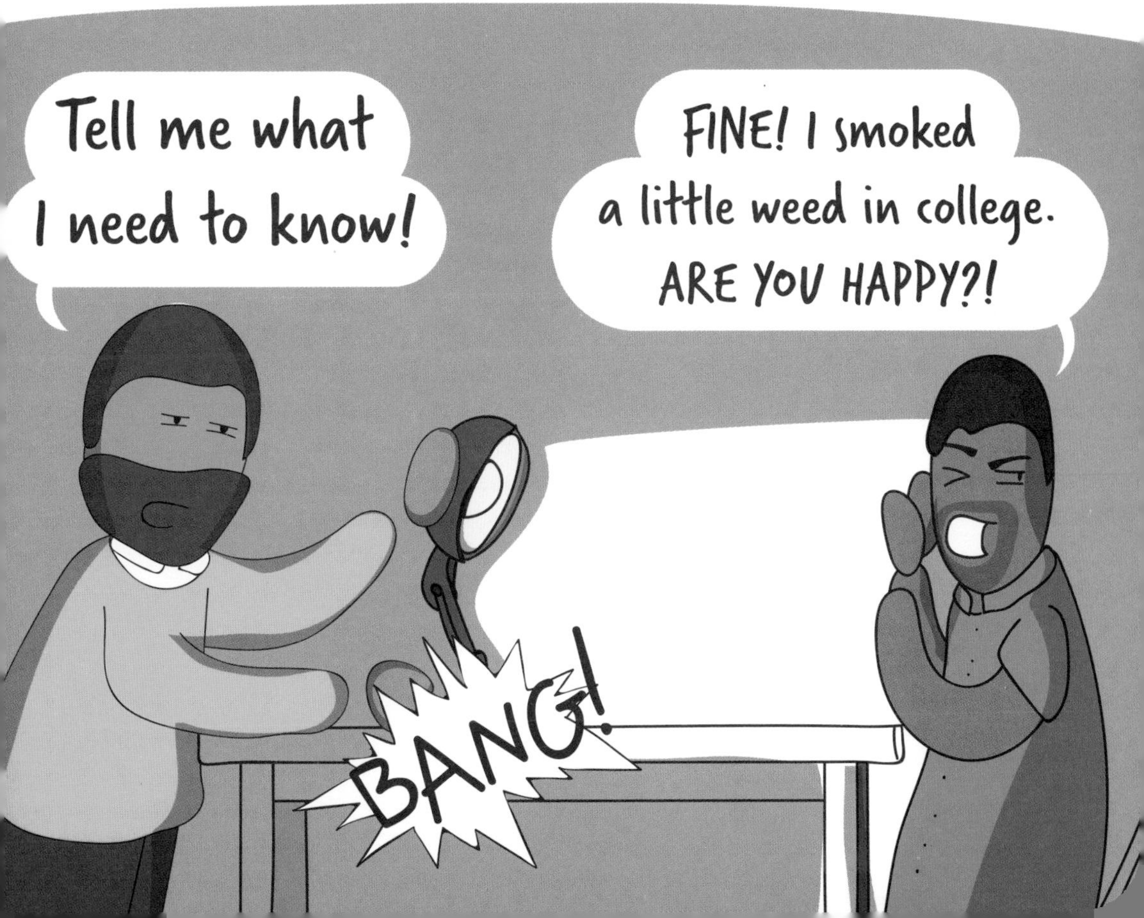
Tell me what I need to know!
FINE! I smoked a little weed in college. ARE YOU HAPPY?!
BANG!

My dad not liking this dude-bro wasn't the only thing he had going against him. There were a lot of red flags (he was controlling, lied a lot, insulted my family just to get a rise outta me), but . . . could I really afford to pass on this guy? Would I ever get another chance at marriage? What if no one ever asked for me again?

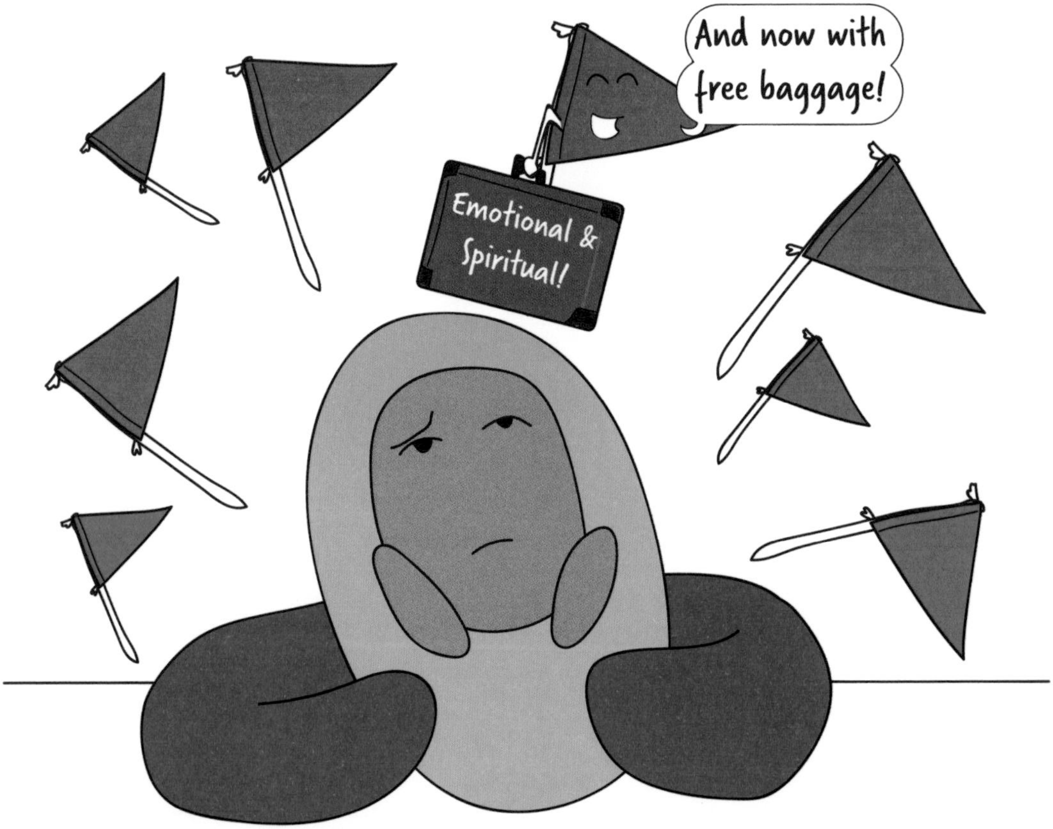
And now with free baggage!
Emotional & Spiritual!

In the end, I made one of the hardest decisions I'd ever had to make. I listened to my gut, decided I deserved better, and I turned him down.

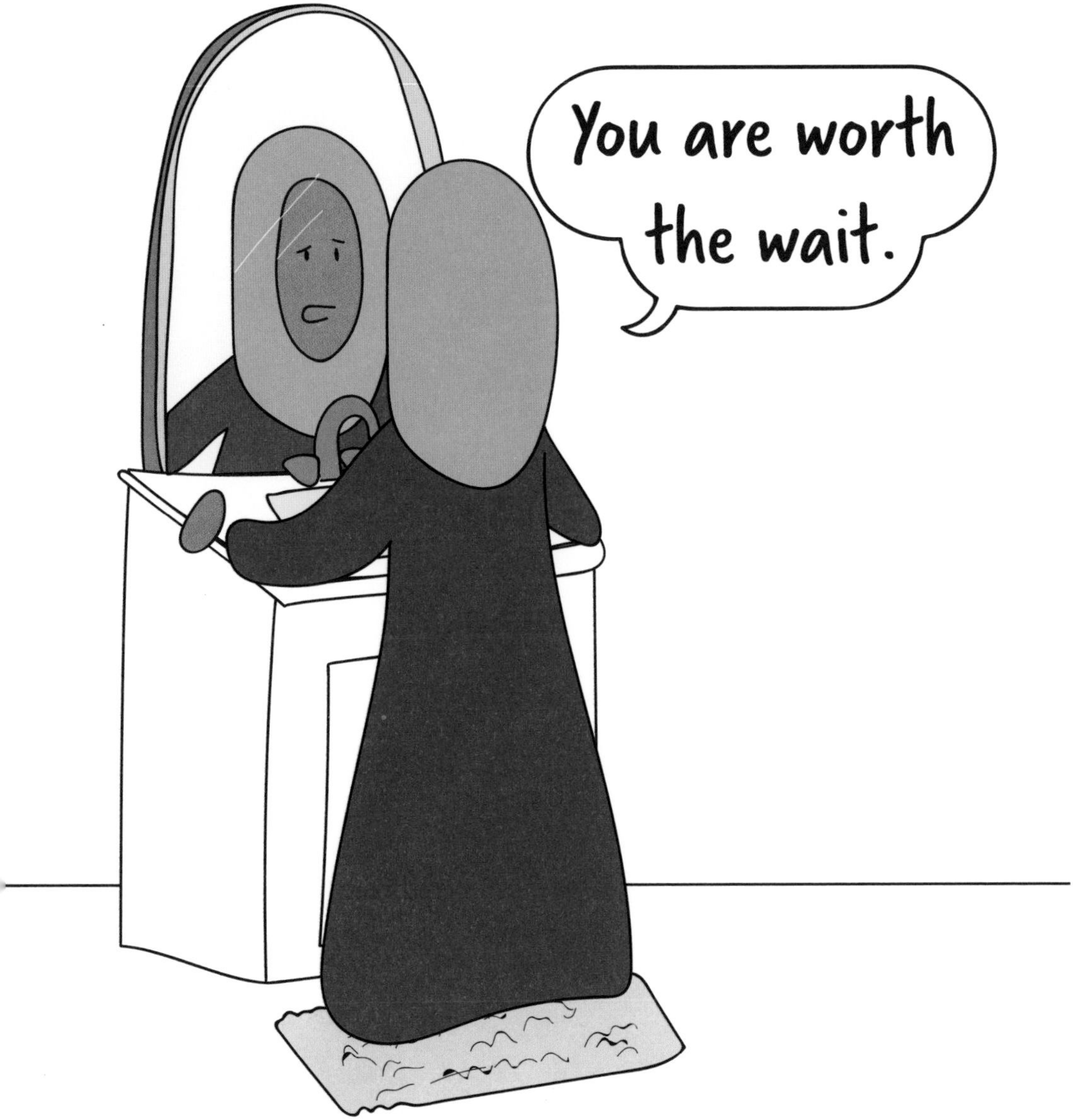
You are worth the wait.

Unfortunately, he turned into a real psycho when I said no, but thankfully that meant NO REGRETS, BABY.

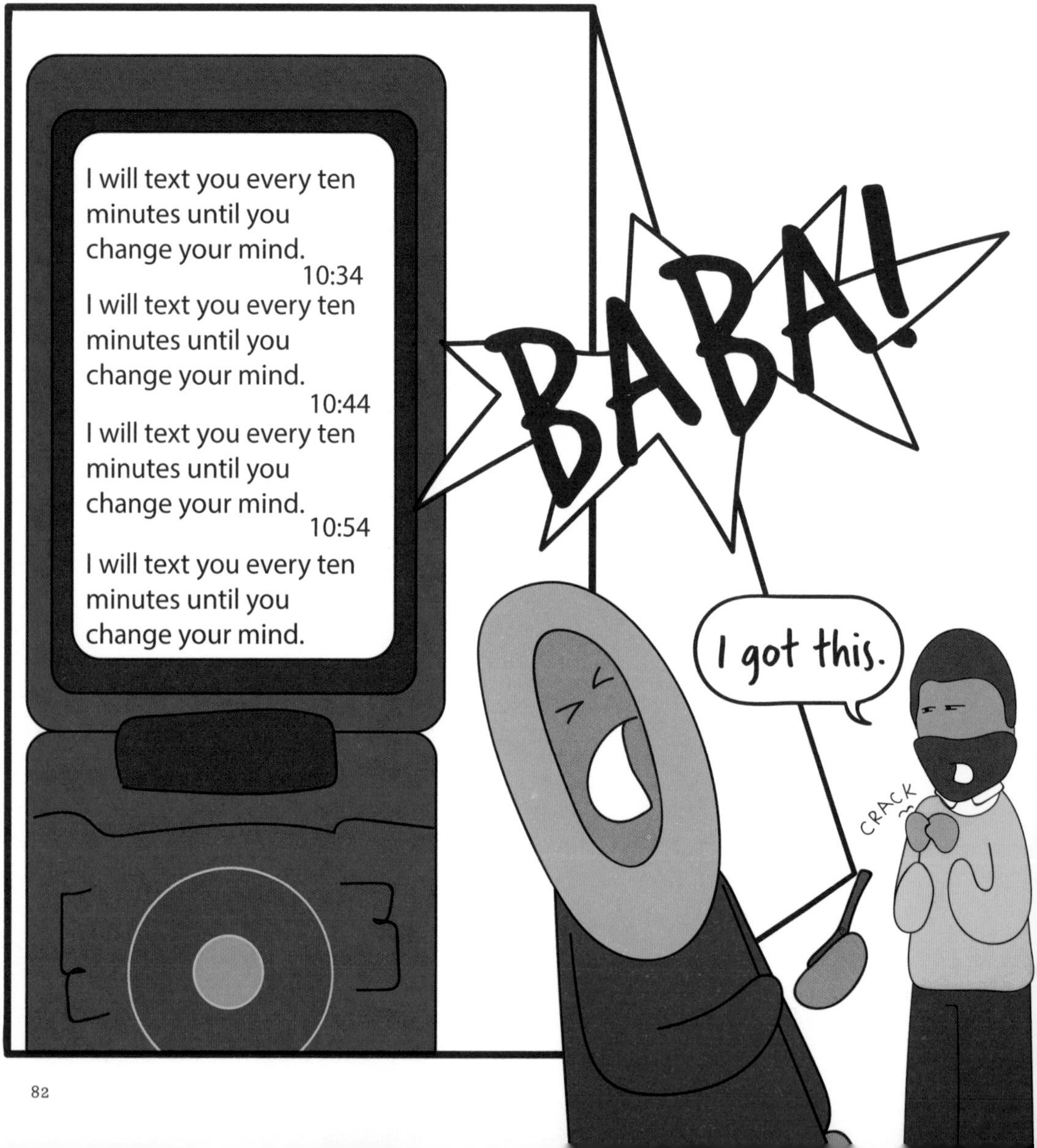
I will text you every ten minutes until you change your mind.
10:34
I will text you every ten minutes until you change your mind.
10:44
I will text you every ten minutes until you change your mind.
10:54
I will text you every ten minutes until you change your mind.
BABA!
I got this.
CRACK

Is this what it feels like to have self-worth??

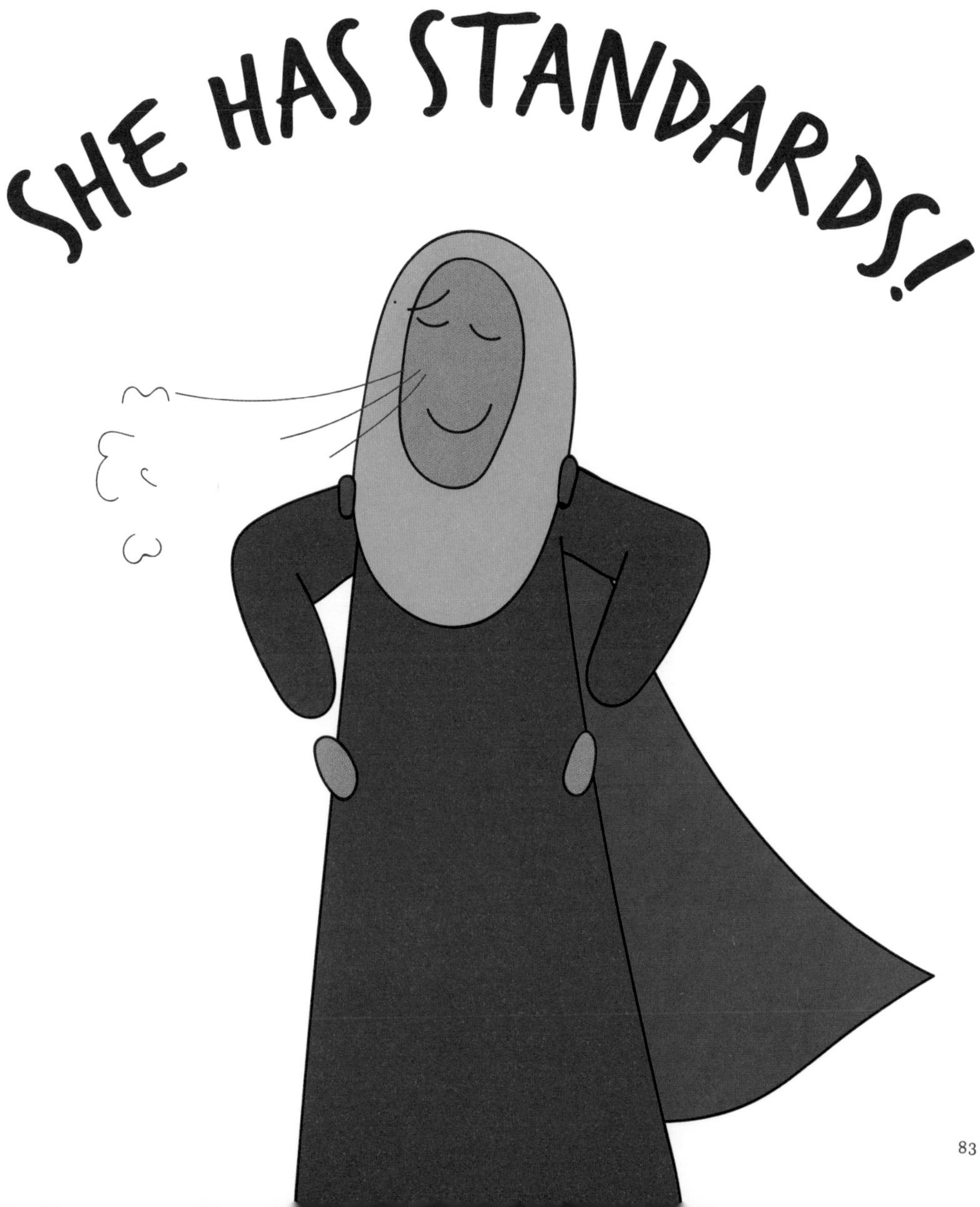
SHE HAS STANDARDS!

That whole experience forced me to take a hard look at myself. I didn't know when it happened, but at some point, I started believing that marriage meant I would be with someone who saw how much I'd invested in making myself the most desirable woman *for him* . . . and marrying me meant he would want to invest in me, too. My worth became tied to his approval of me in the form of a proposal. So saying no to my first (and possibly only) proposal was, in a way, a huge step in my journey to understanding the importance of self-love. Maybe marriage didn't have to be the end-all be-all of my life.

It was a very freeing thought.

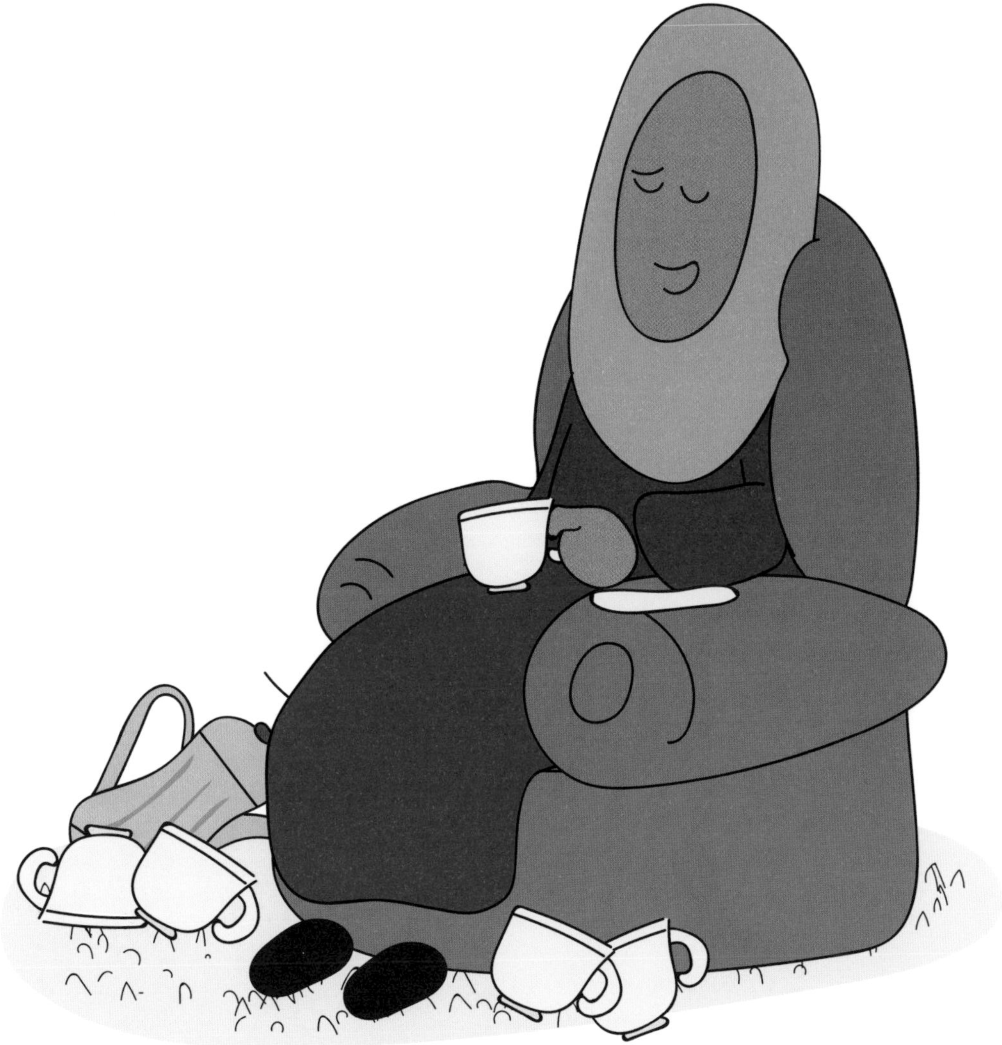

Qadr

(destiny)

So here I was at 21, super ripe future cat lady, turning down the only *real* prospect I'd ever, or would ever, get. *I thought.*

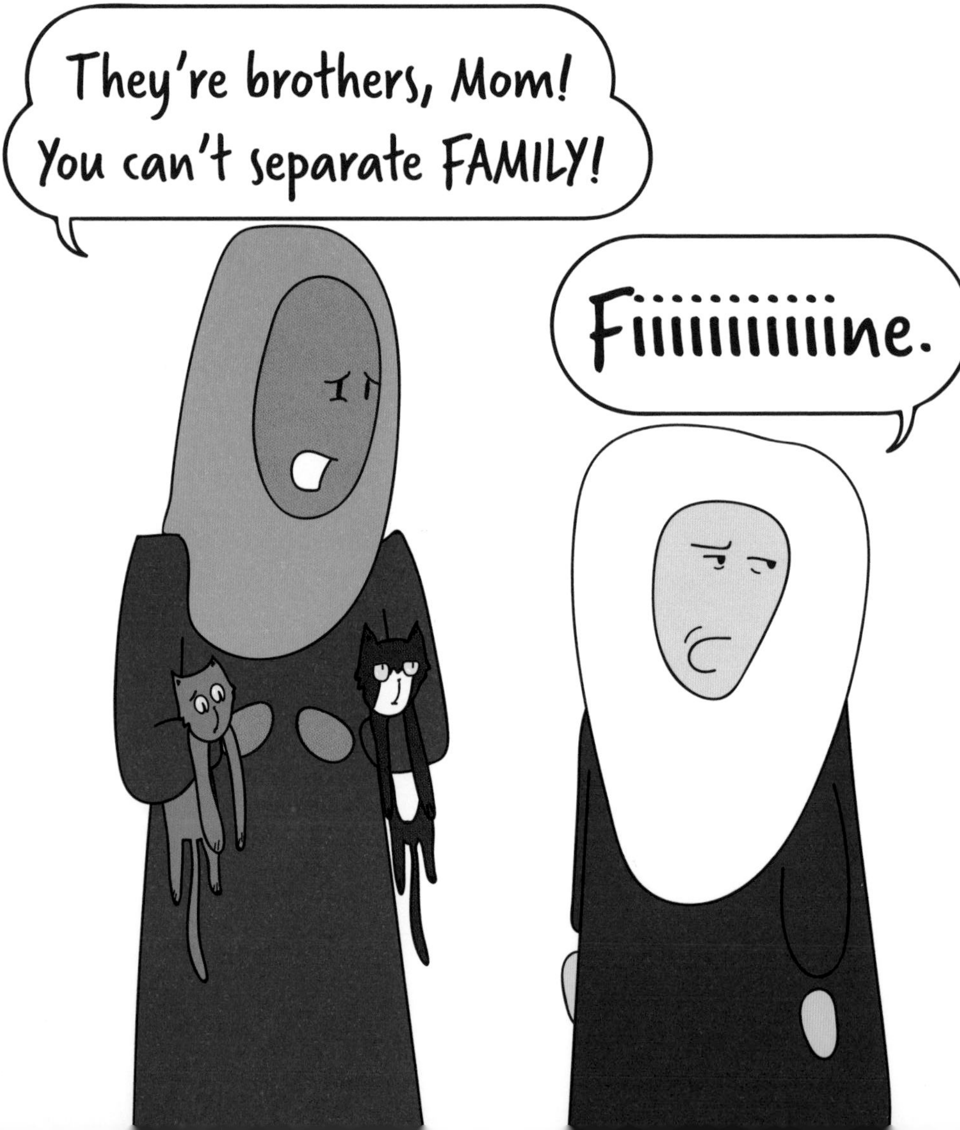
They're brothers, Mom! You can't separate FAMILY!
Fiiiiiiiiiiine.

I could've just said, "Screw it!" to the whole system and dated guys on my own. So why didn't I?

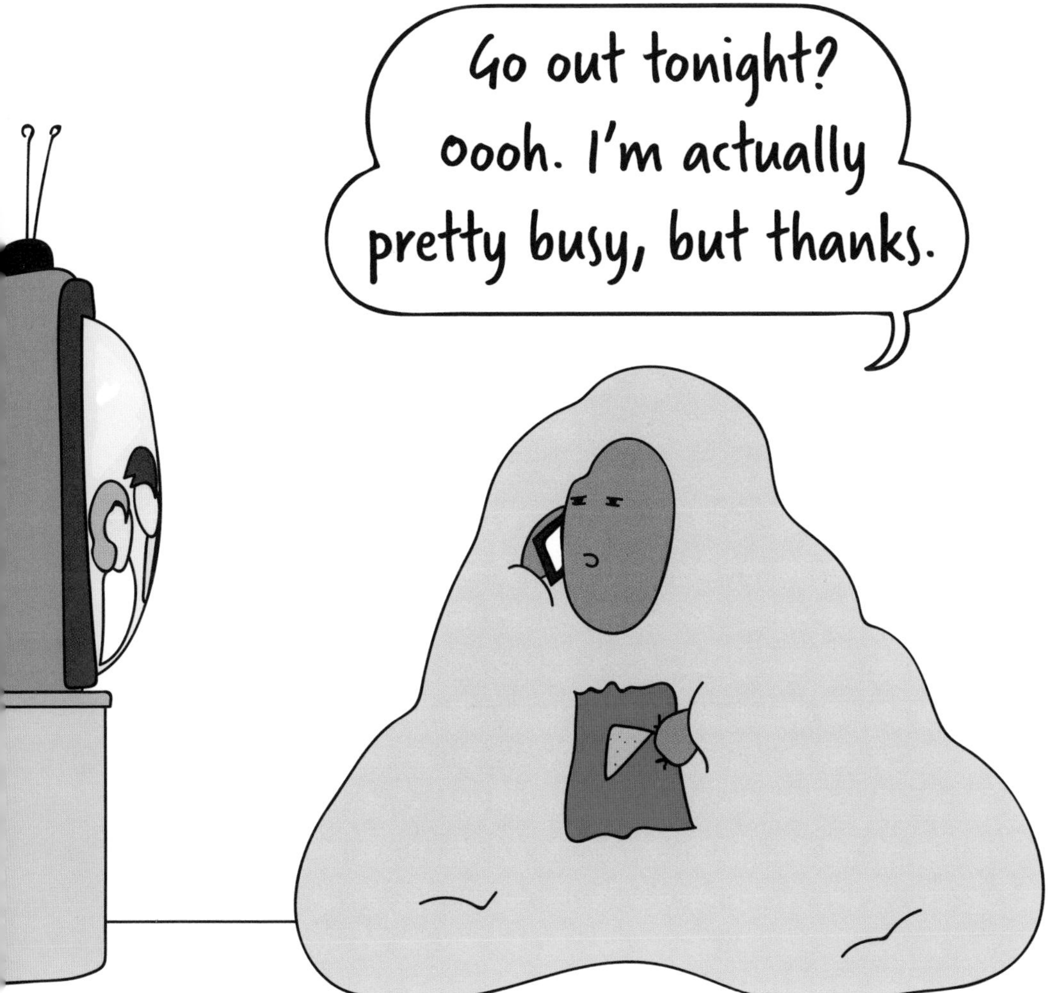
Go out tonight? Oooh. I'm actually pretty busy, but thanks.

For one, it would've meant going behind my parents' backs, and I definitely didn't want to start a relationship based on lies. Their approval meant a lot to me. And also, they were both, like, really good at weeding out the losers.

Is Your Suitor a Loser?
Not sure if your stud is a dud?

We can help.
Call 1-800-GTHO

More importantly, I put my trust in God.

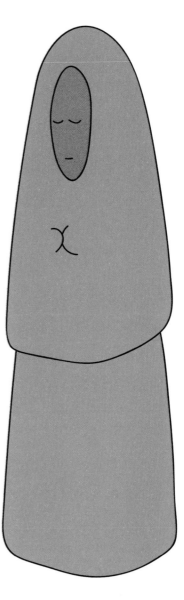

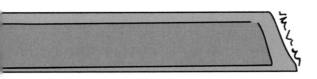

So I focused on myself. See . . . I realized that when I wanted a guy to like me, I had a tendency to mold and shape myself into the person I thought he'd like (while my own likes took a back seat). I mean, did you miss the part where I was about ready to marry a grade-A stalker because I badly wanted to feel like I was worthy? When I turned him down, a fire started burning inside me. I found I actually had a lot to say about what I wanted in a partner. And more than that, I stopped asking what was wrong with me.

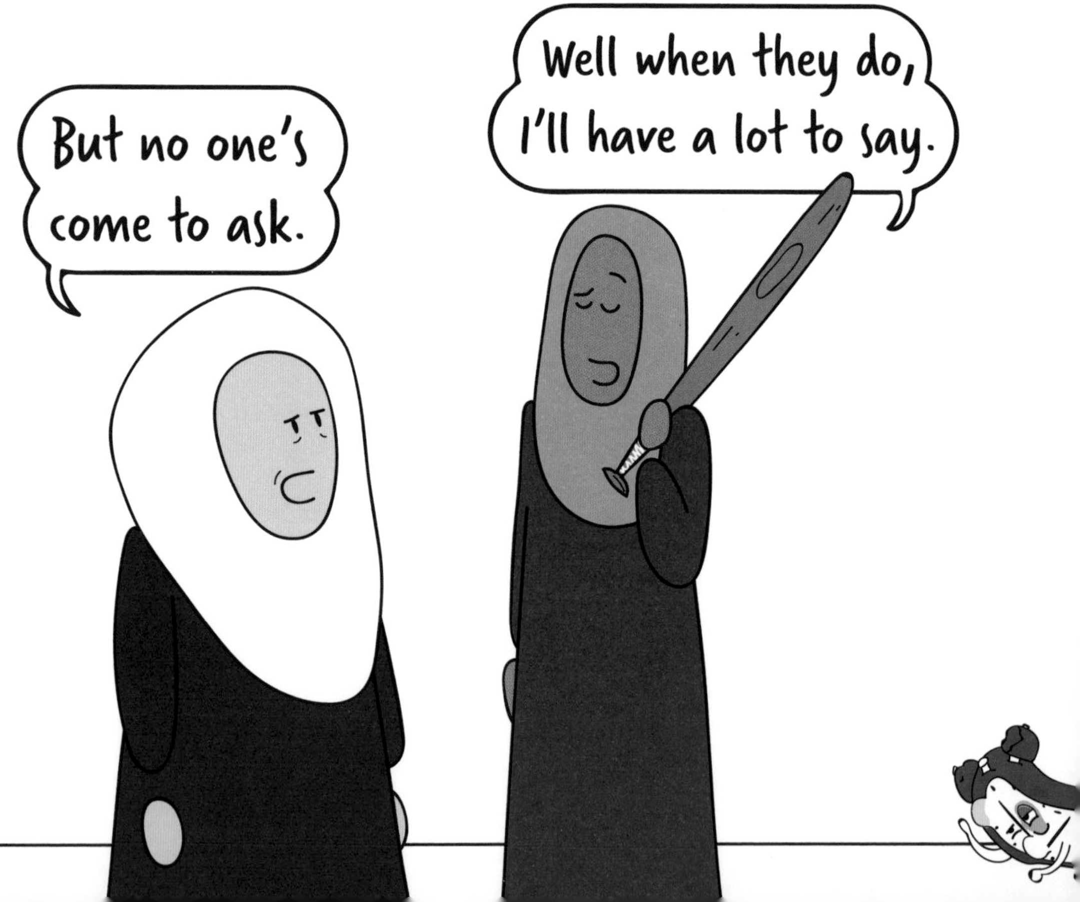
But no one's come to ask.
Well when they do, I'll have a lot to say.

In the process of learning to love myself, I took religious studies classes about love, family, and religion. And time, as it does, ticked on.

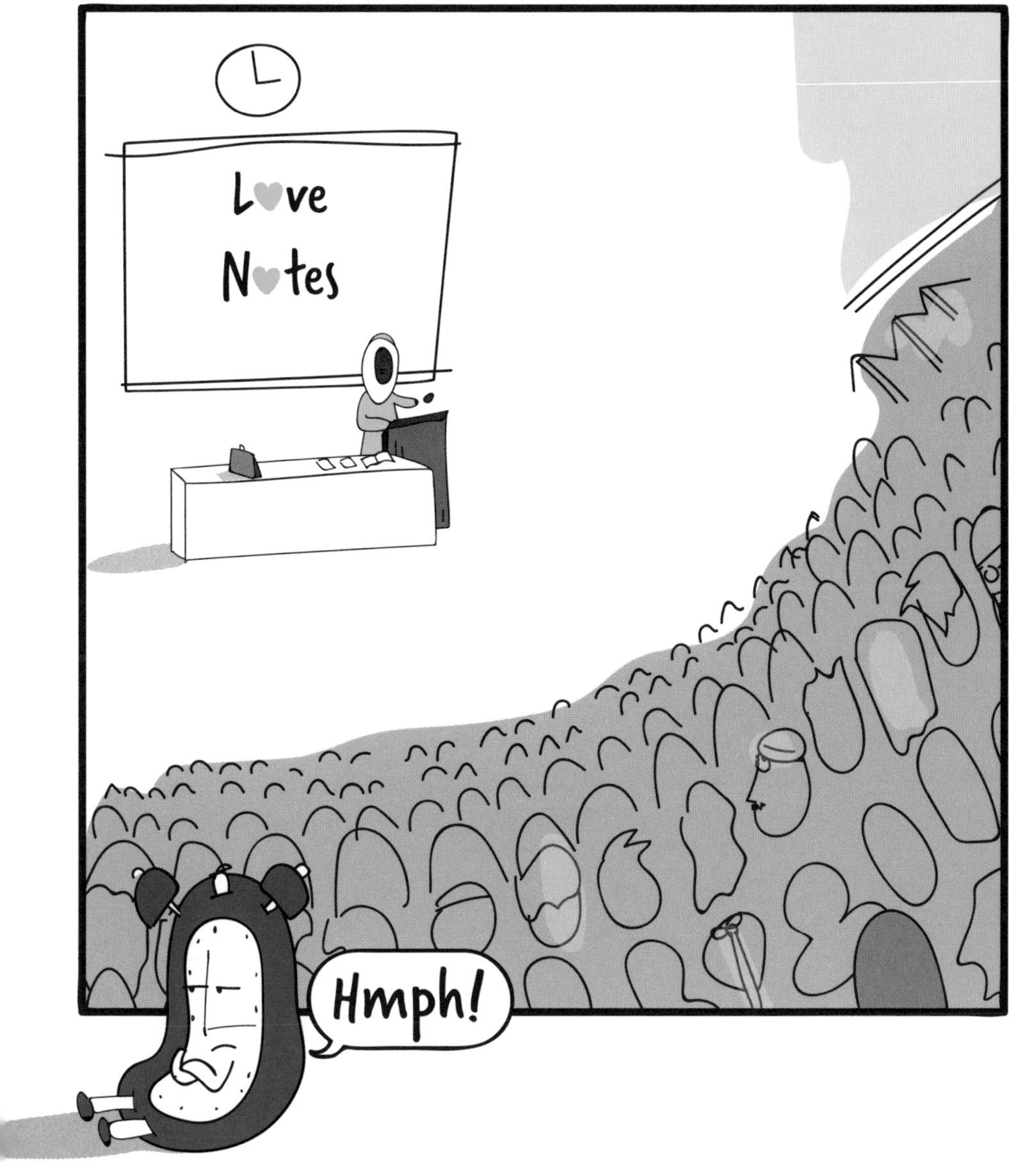
Love
Notes
Hmph!

Friends got married.

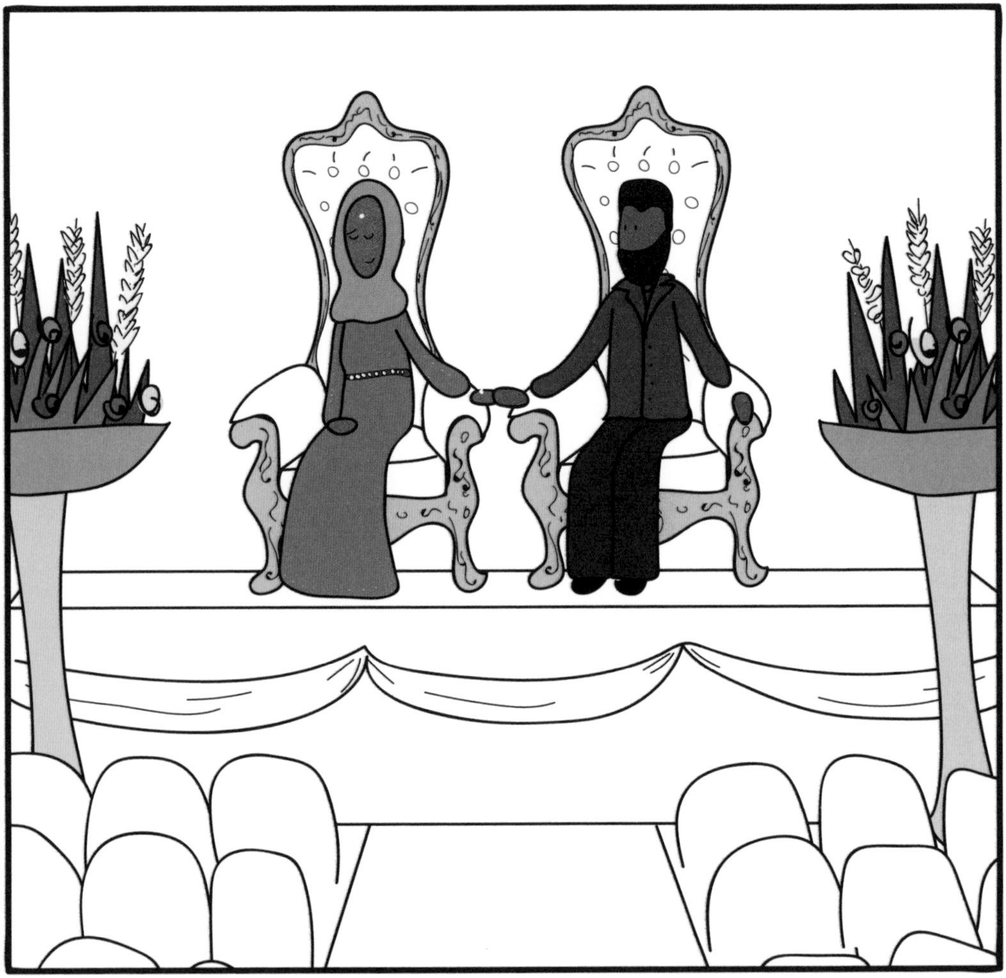

Friends got divorced.

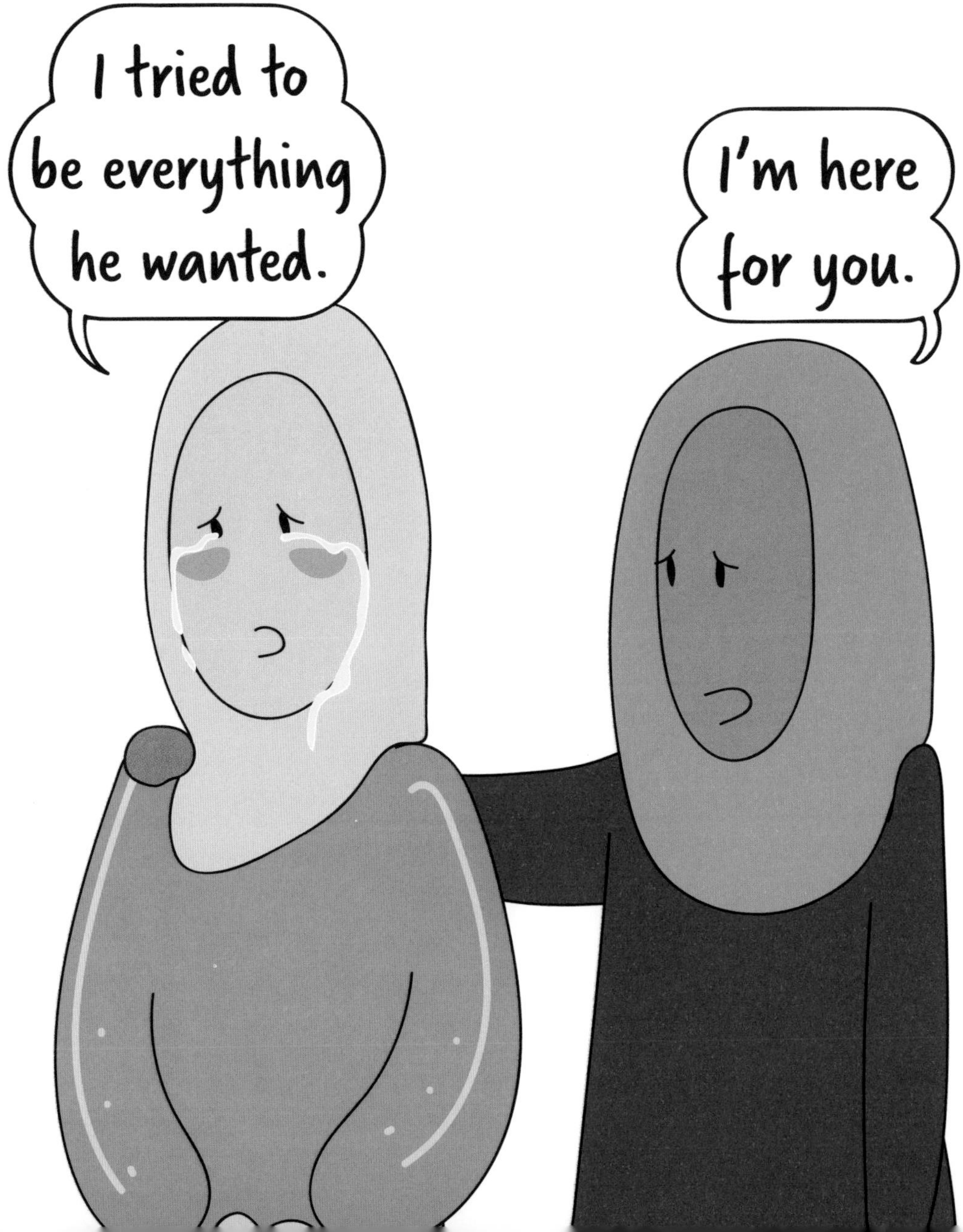
I tried to be everything he wanted.
I'm here for you.

My sisters got married.

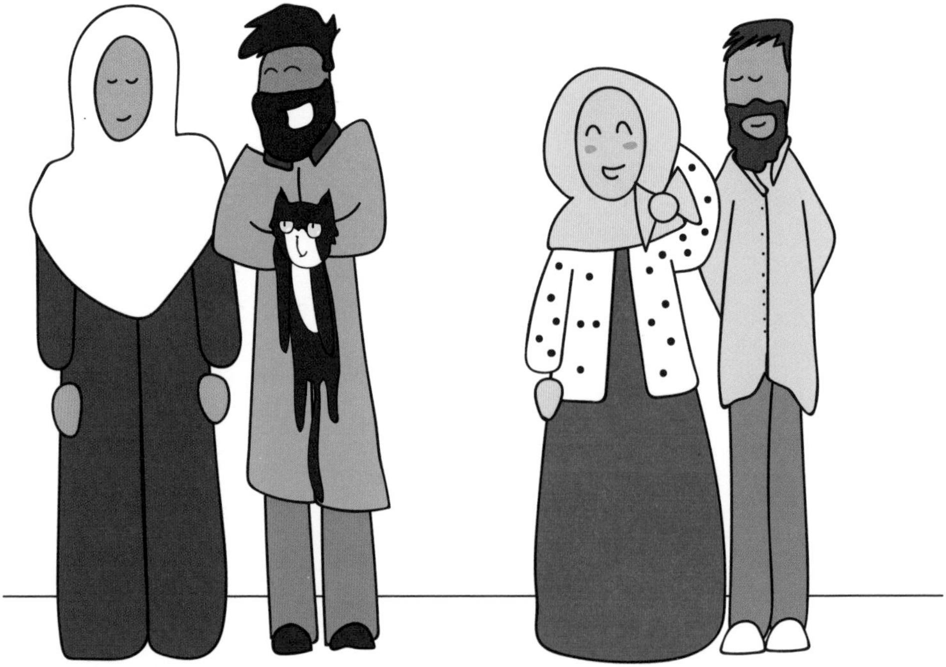

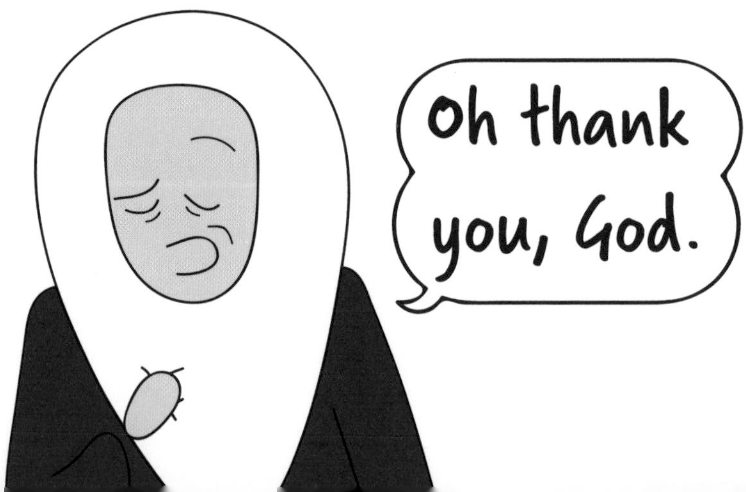
Oh thank you, God.

My parents got divorced.

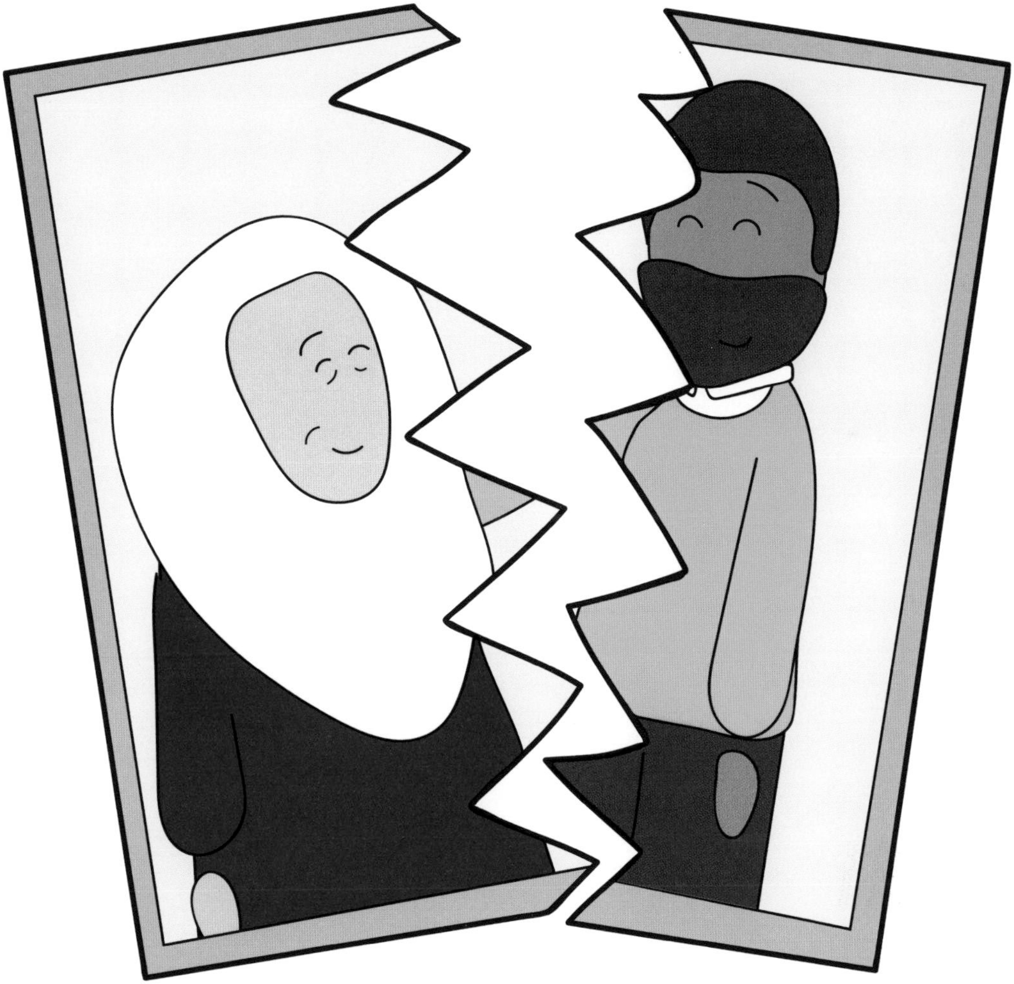

Four years passed, and even though I grew to love myself more and more every day, I couldn't deny I was lonely.

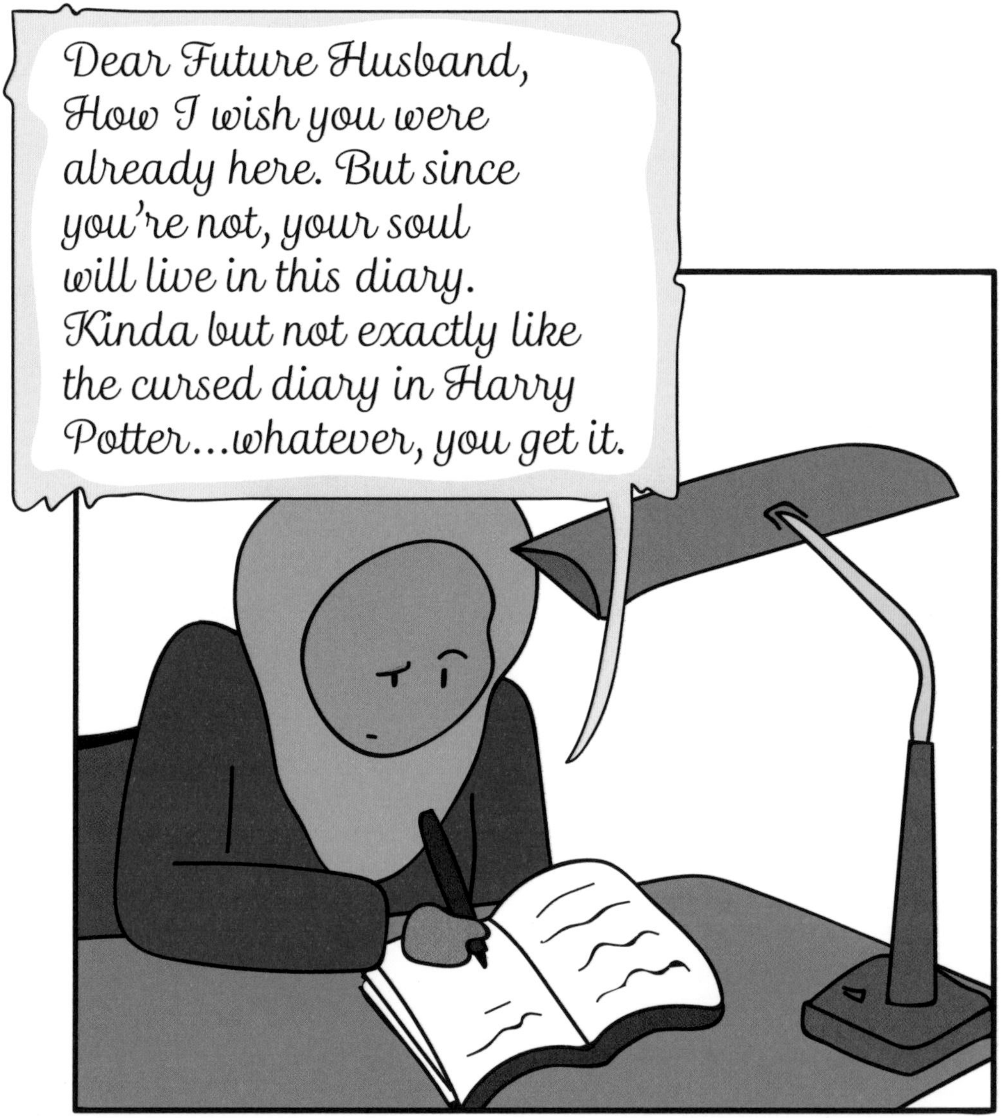
Dear Future Husband,
How I wish you were already here. But since you're not, your soul will live in this diary. Kinda but not exactly like the cursed diary in Harry Potter...whatever, you get it.

I dunno, maybe that's why I signed up for a weeklong conference on Islamic studies. What better way to cure my loneliness than to throw myself into books?

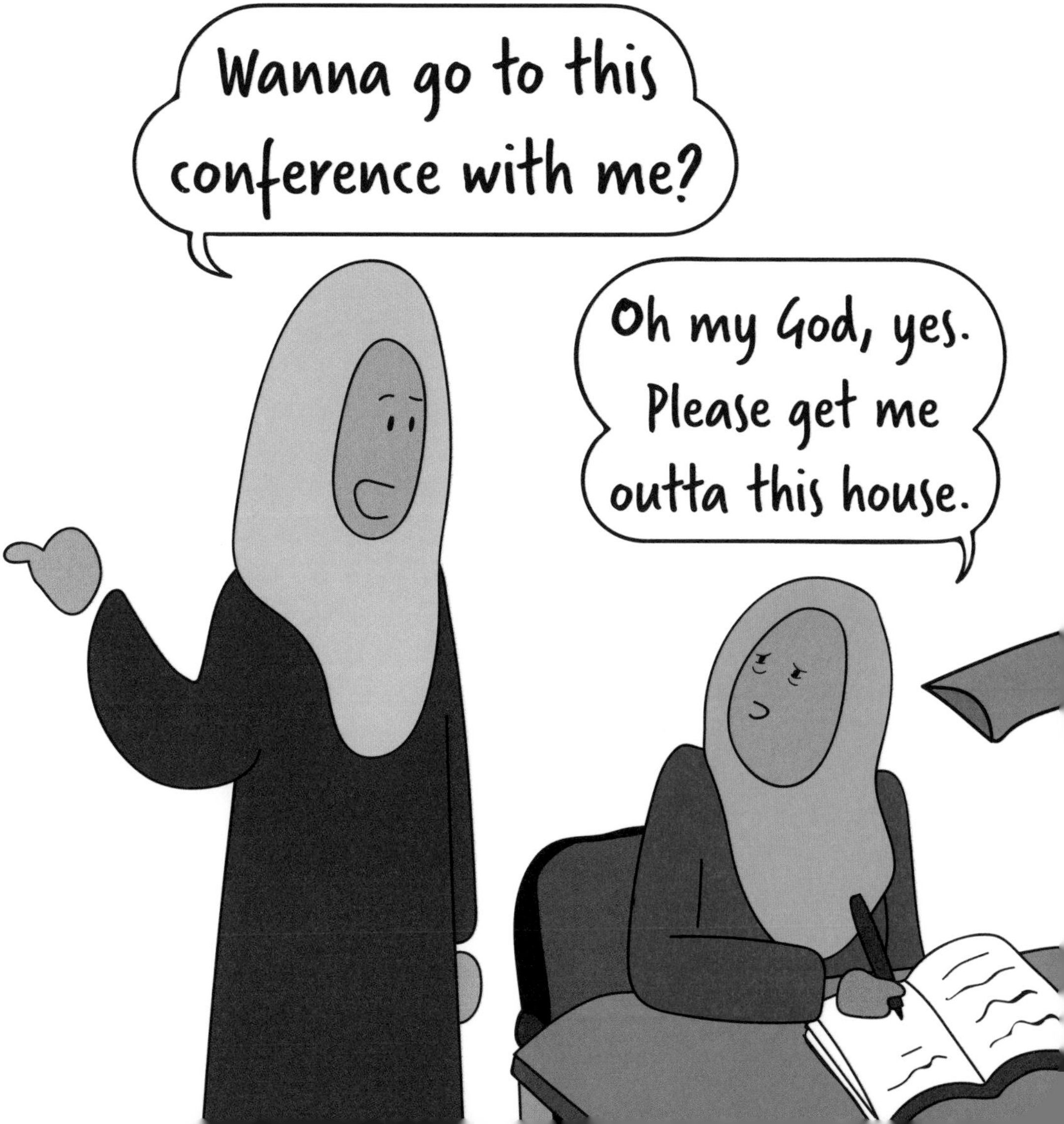
Wanna go to this conference with me?
Oh my God, yes. Please get me outta this house.

The conference had classes about understanding the Quran, studying the life of the Prophet (peace be upon him), and learning Islamic history.

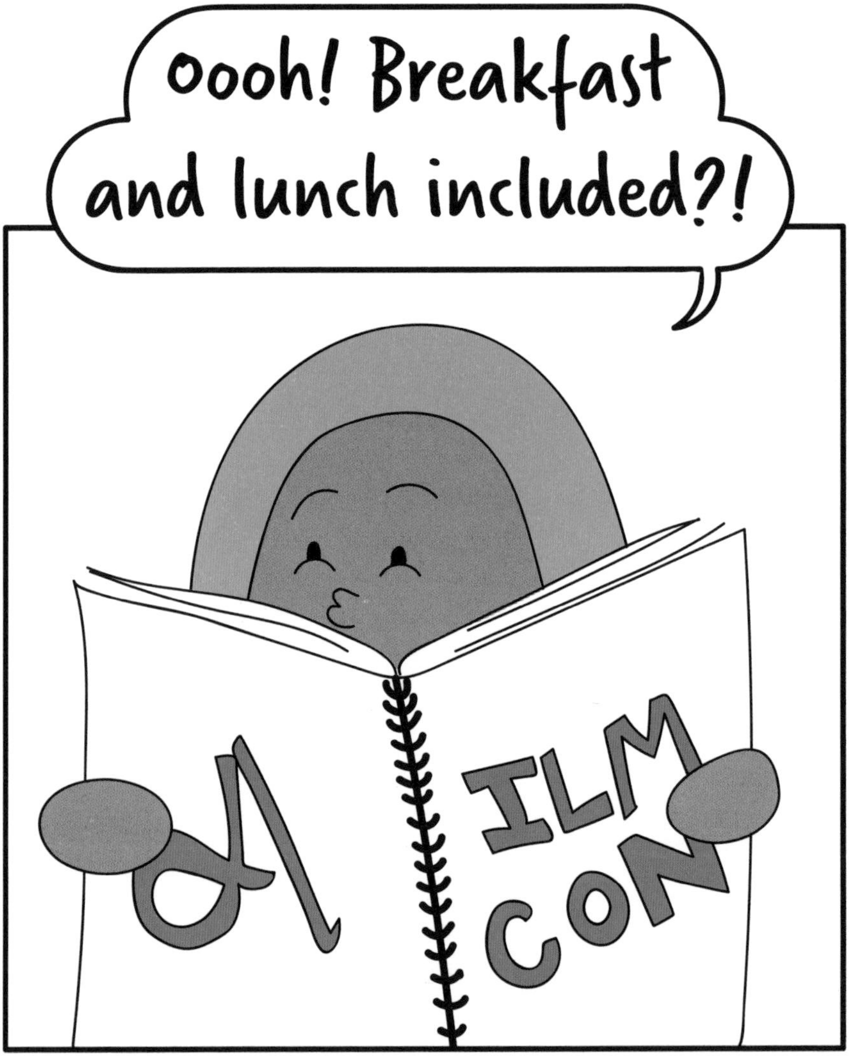
Oooh! Breakfast and lunch included?!
ILM CON

My point is, it wasn't exactly a pickup scene, and I sure as shay wasn't there to meet anyone.

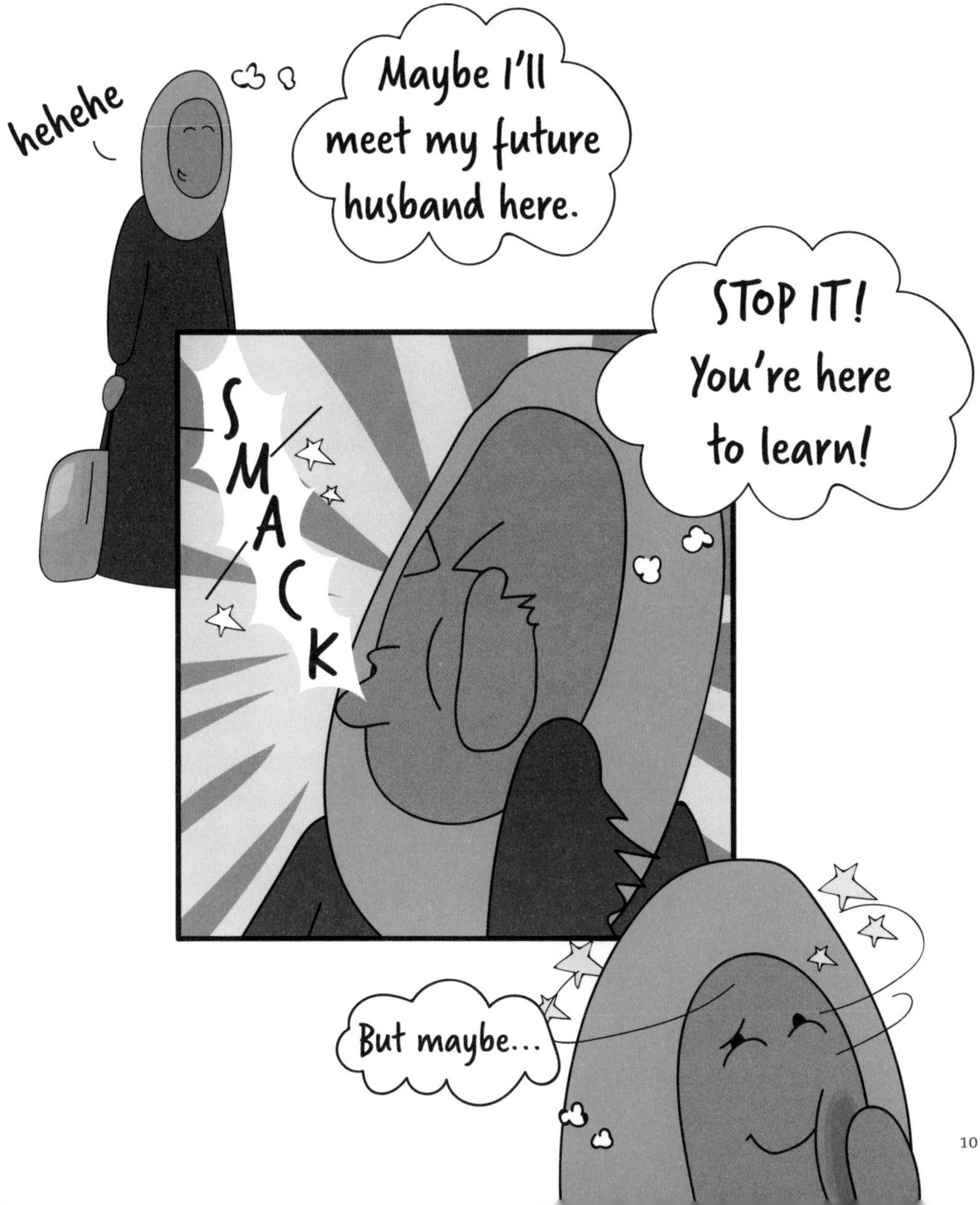
hehehe
Maybe I'll meet my future husband here.
SMACK
STOP IT! You're here to learn!
But maybe...

When I got on the plane to go to the conference, my priorities were intact, you see.

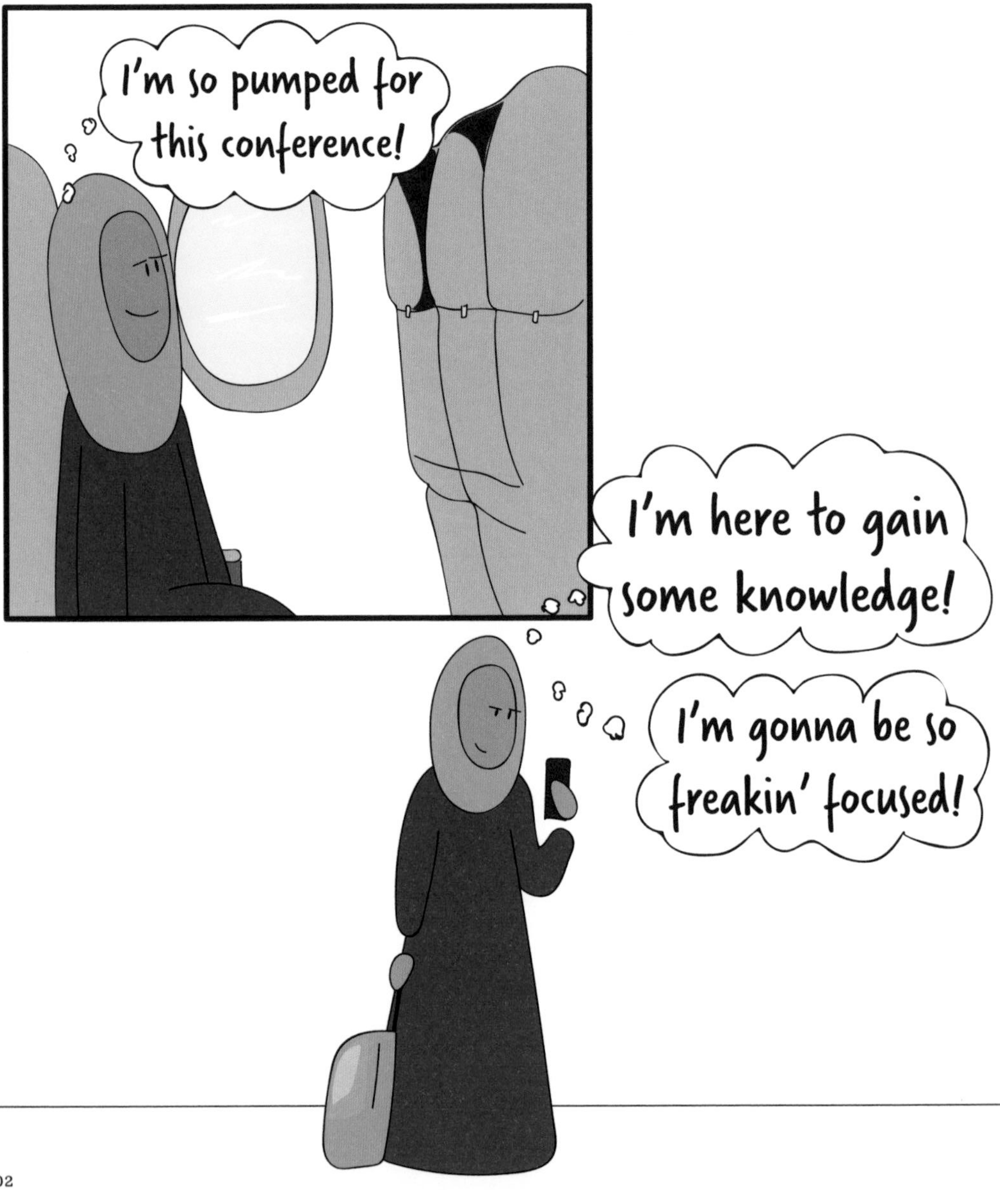
I'm so pumped for this conference!
I'm here to gain some knowledge!
I'm gonna be so freakin' focused!

But day one, there he had to go and be.

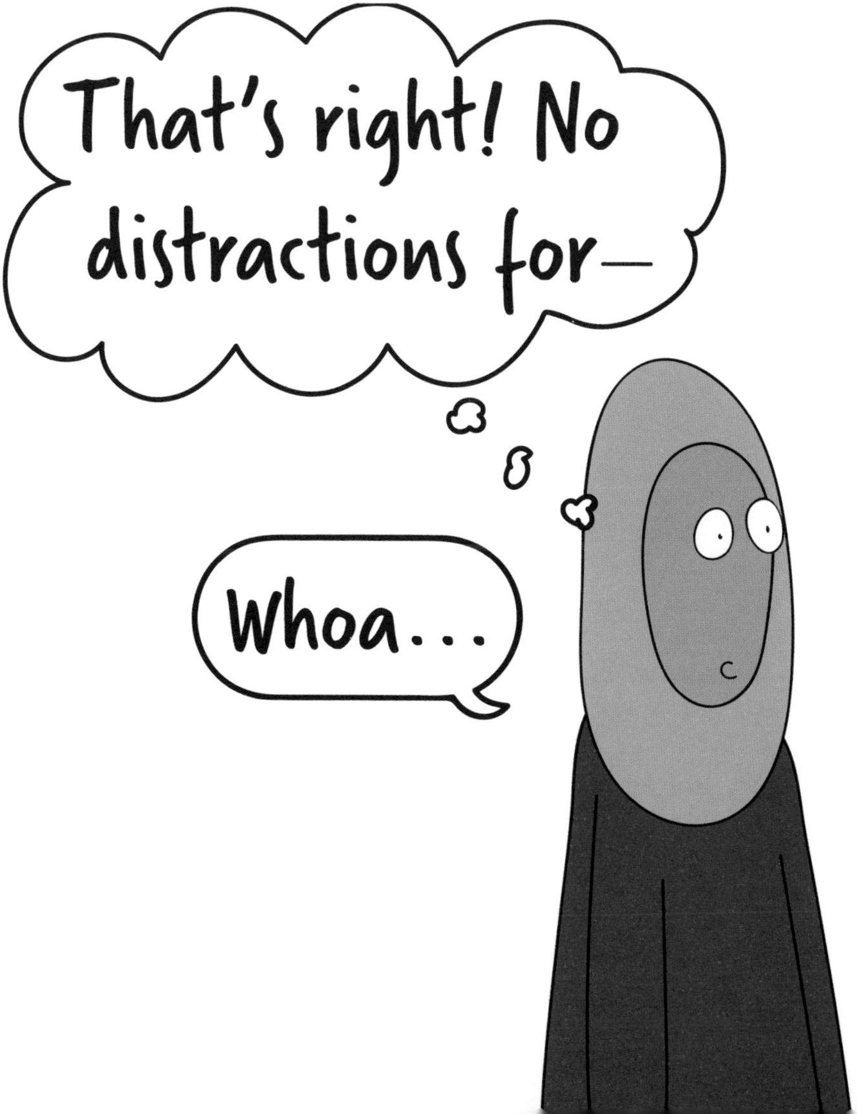
That's right! No distractions for—
Whoa...

It was qadr.

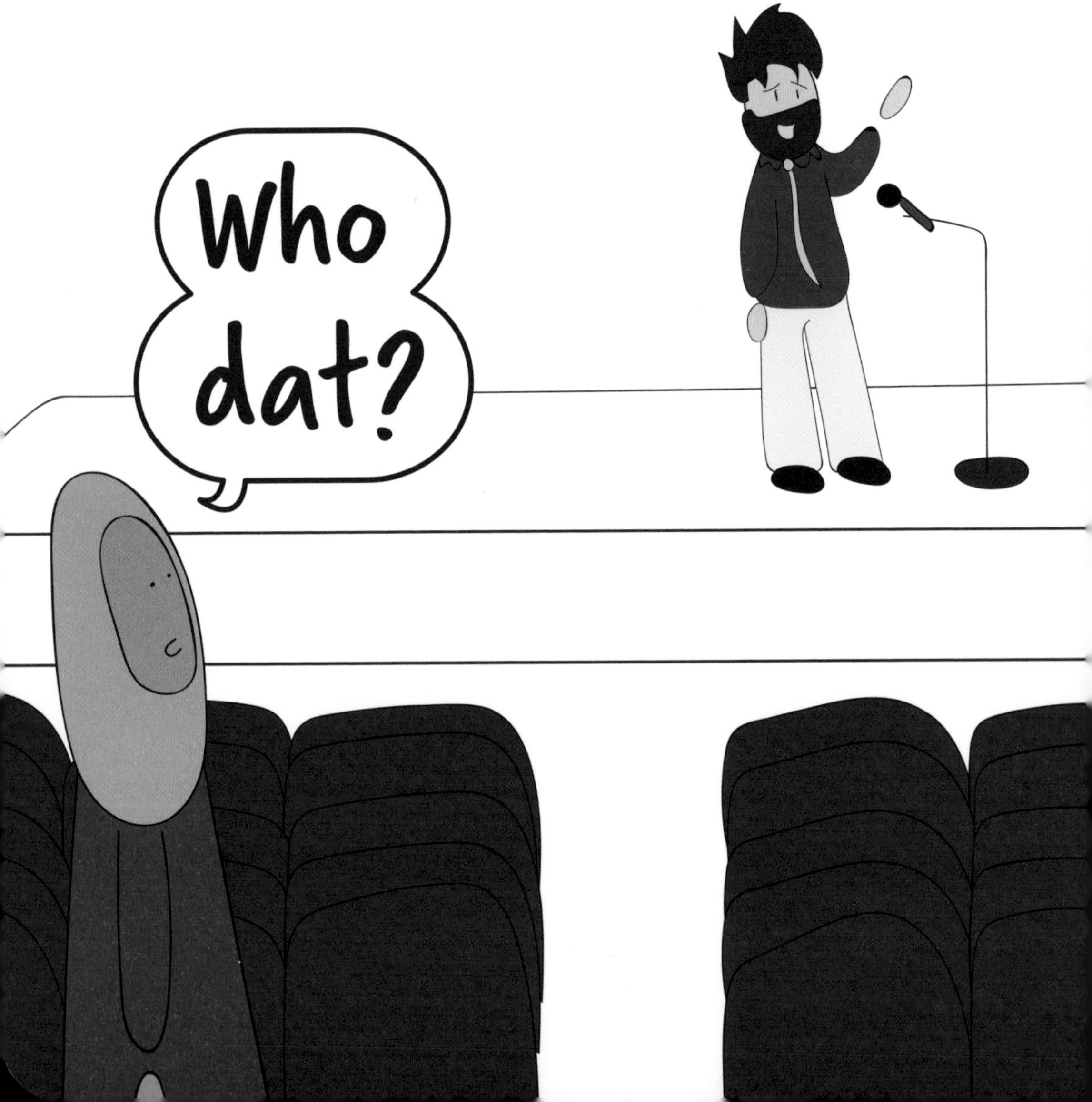
Who dat?

Arranged

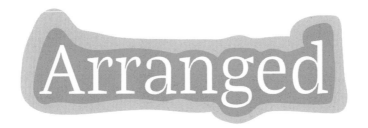

I was not about to let *some guy* become the center of what was supposed to be my week of religious self-improvement.

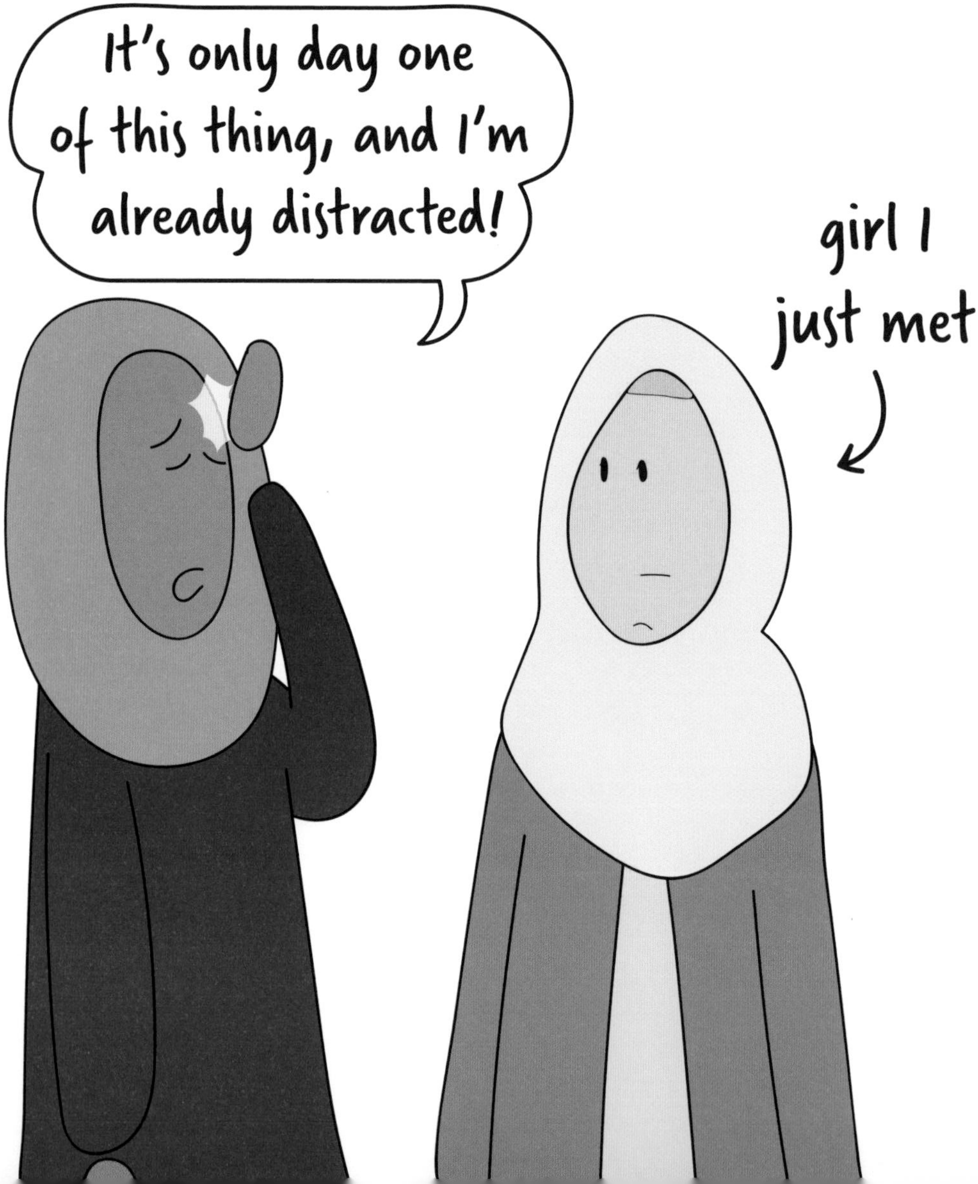
It's only day one of this thing, and I'm already distracted!
girl I just met

No! I can do this. I'm gonna snap outta this and focus on studying!

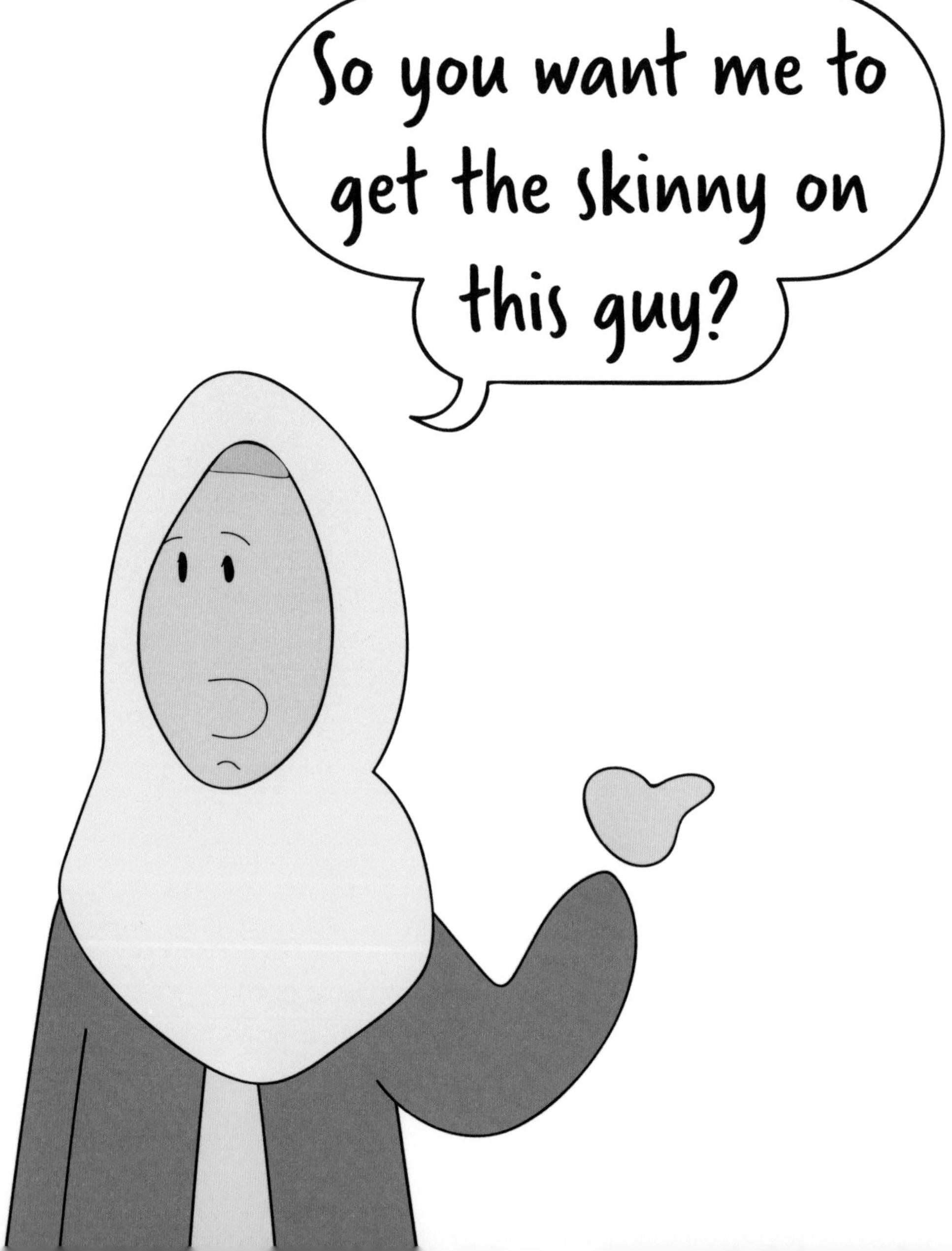
So you want me to get the skinny on this guy?

She would actually go on to become one of my closest friends.

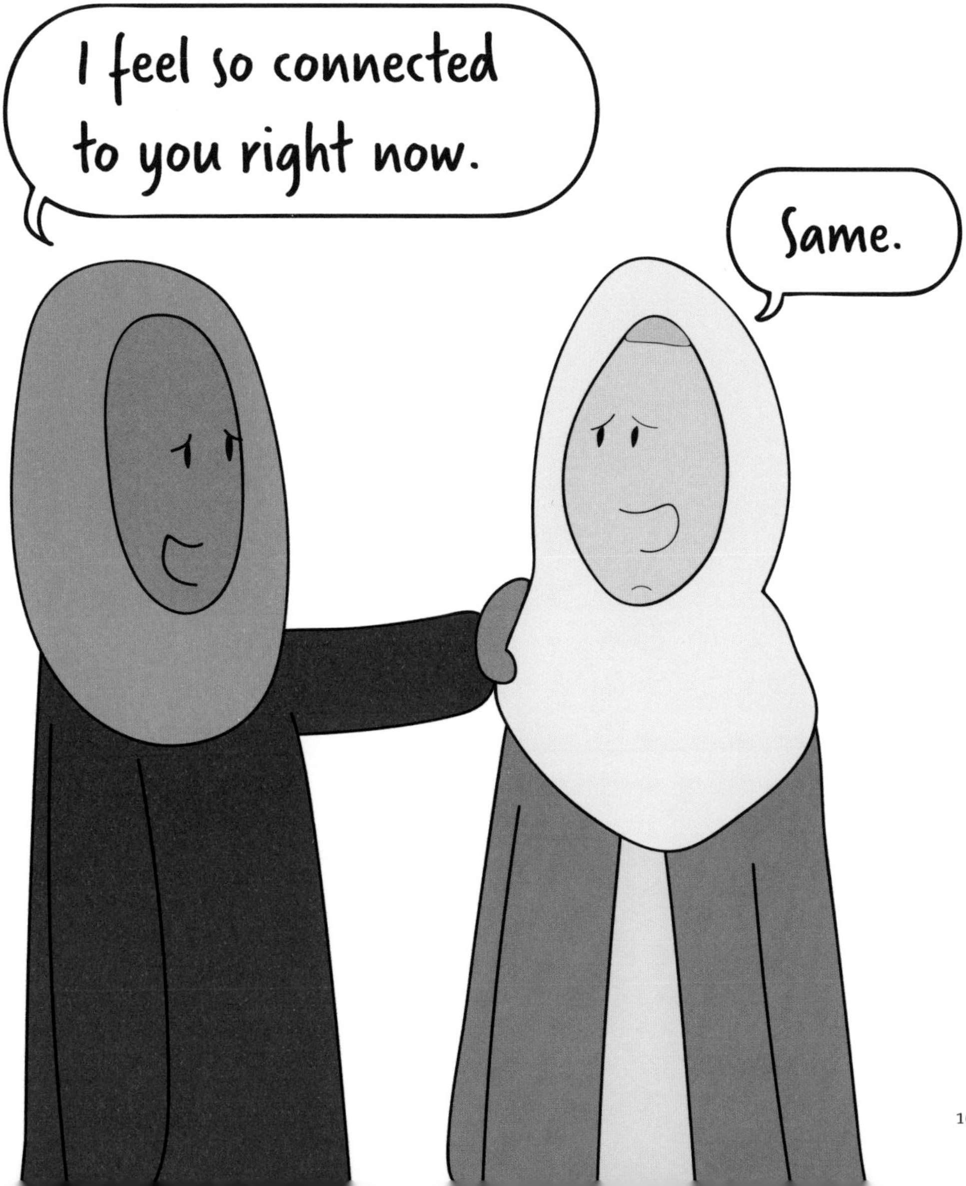
I feel so connected to you right now.
Same.

And so began the longest week ever recorded.

Day 1

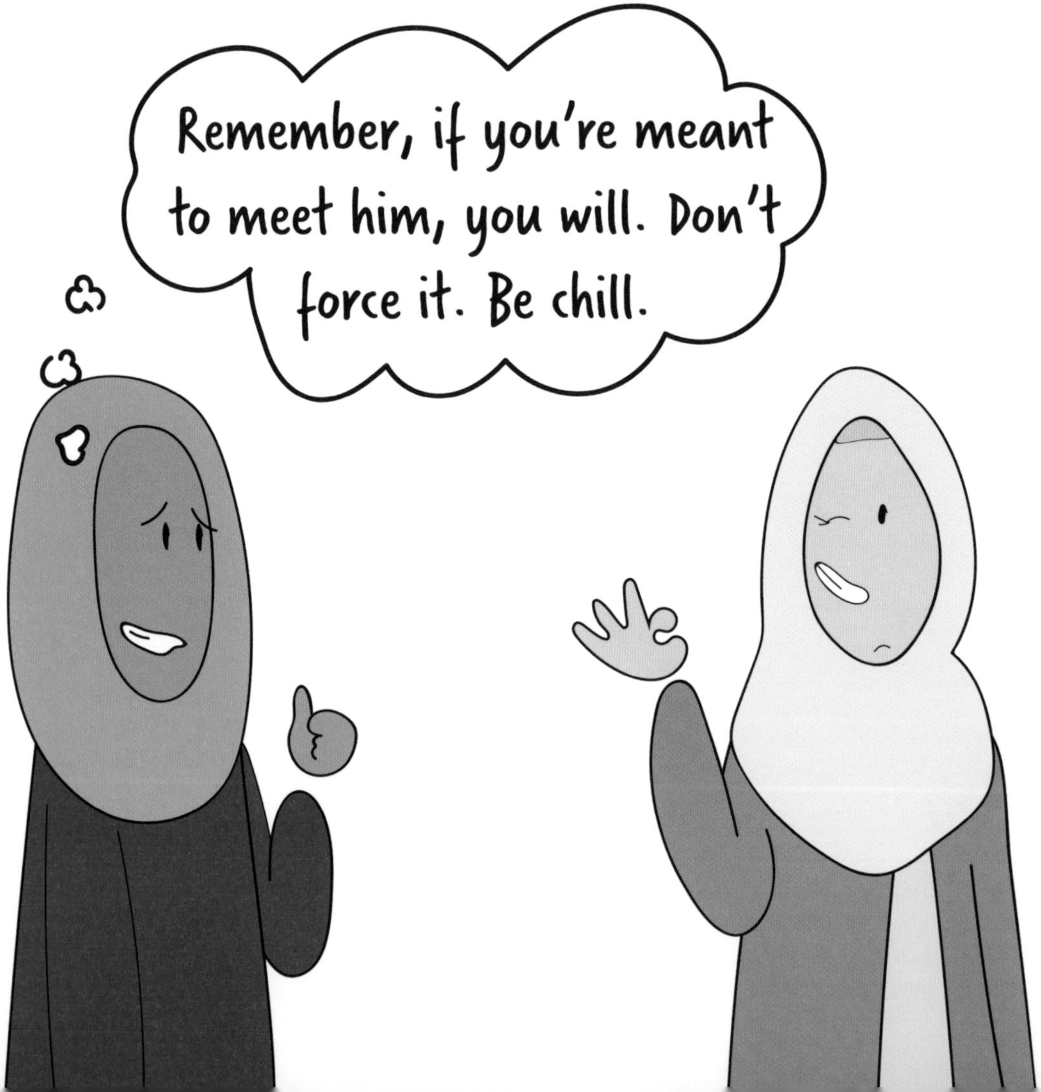
Remember, if you're meant to meet him, you will. Don't force it. Be chill.

Day 3

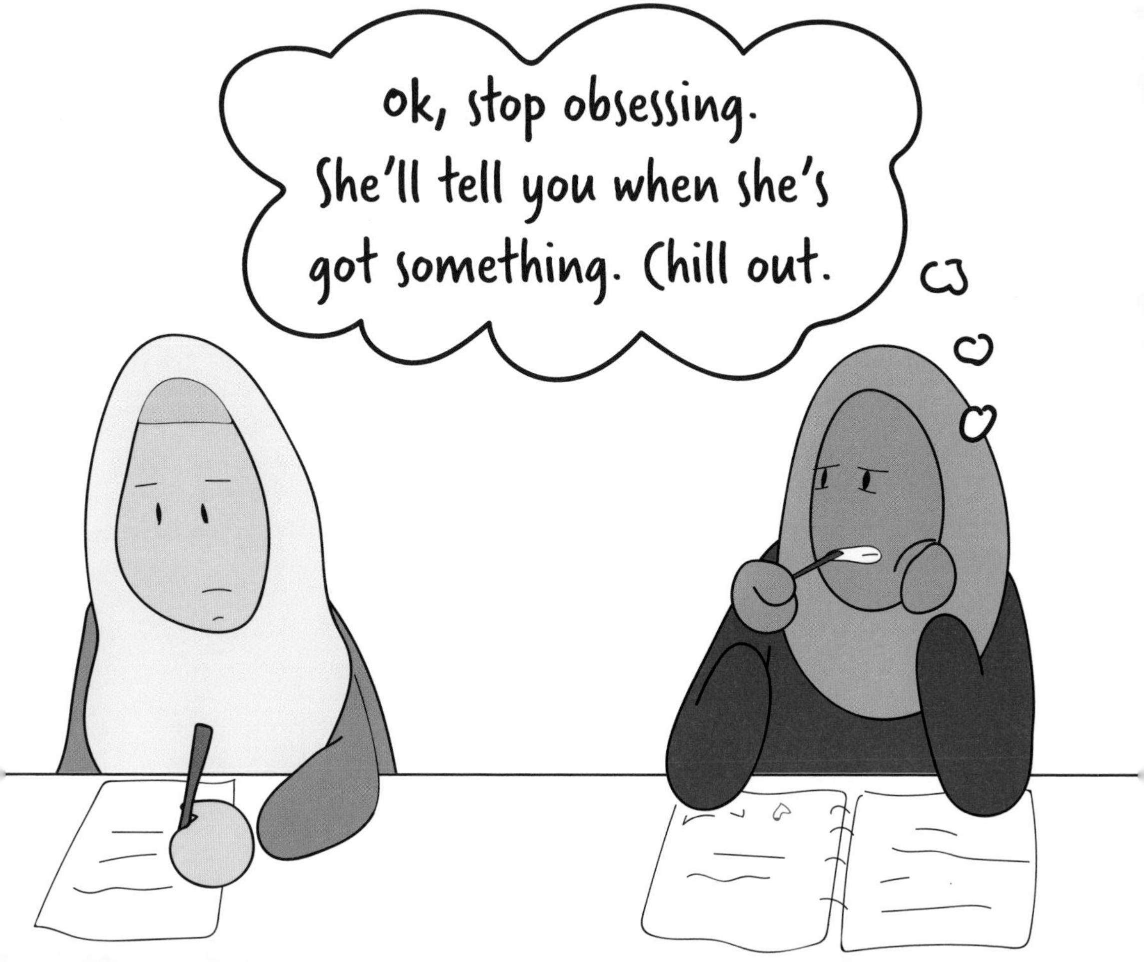
Ok, stop obsessing. She'll tell you when she's got something. Chill out.

Day 5

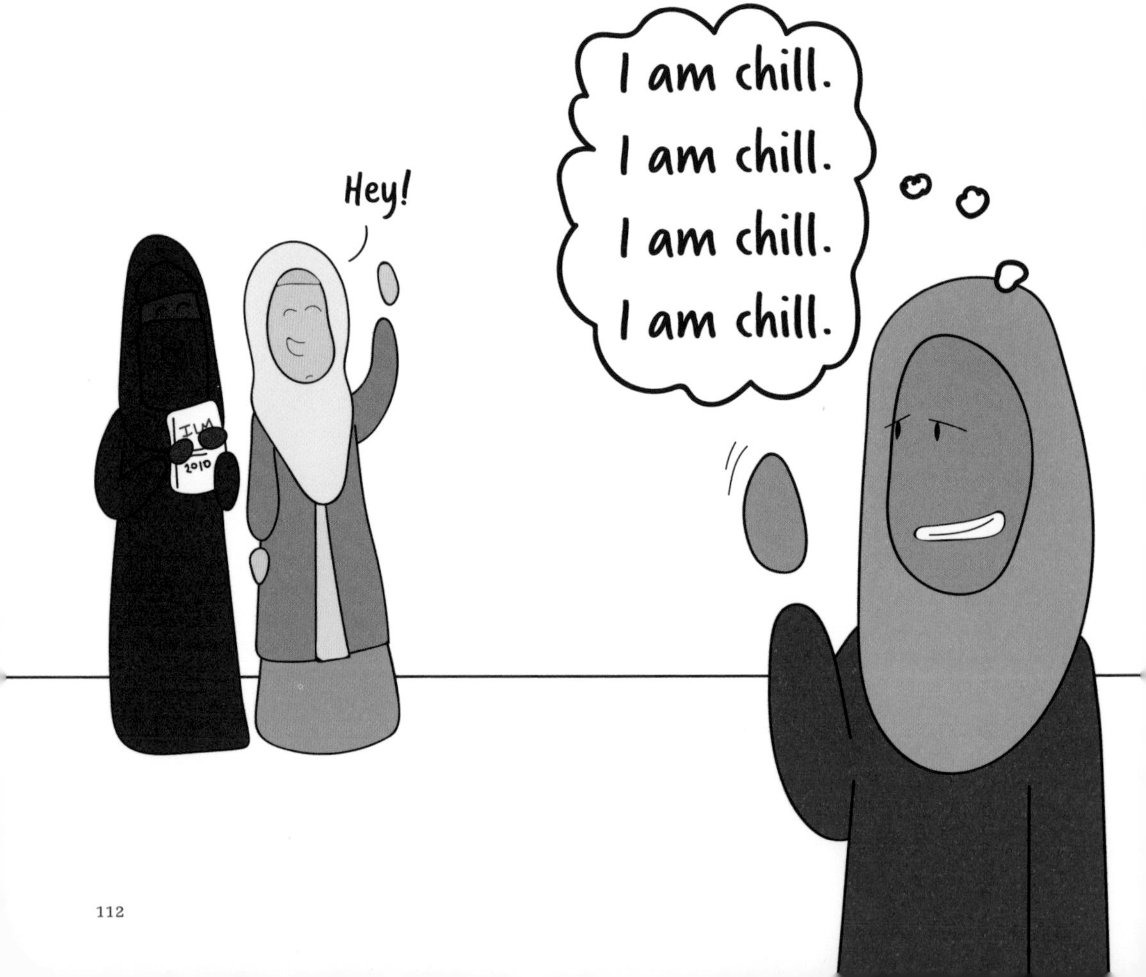
Hey!
I am chill.
I am chill.
I am chill.
I am chill.

I was not chill.

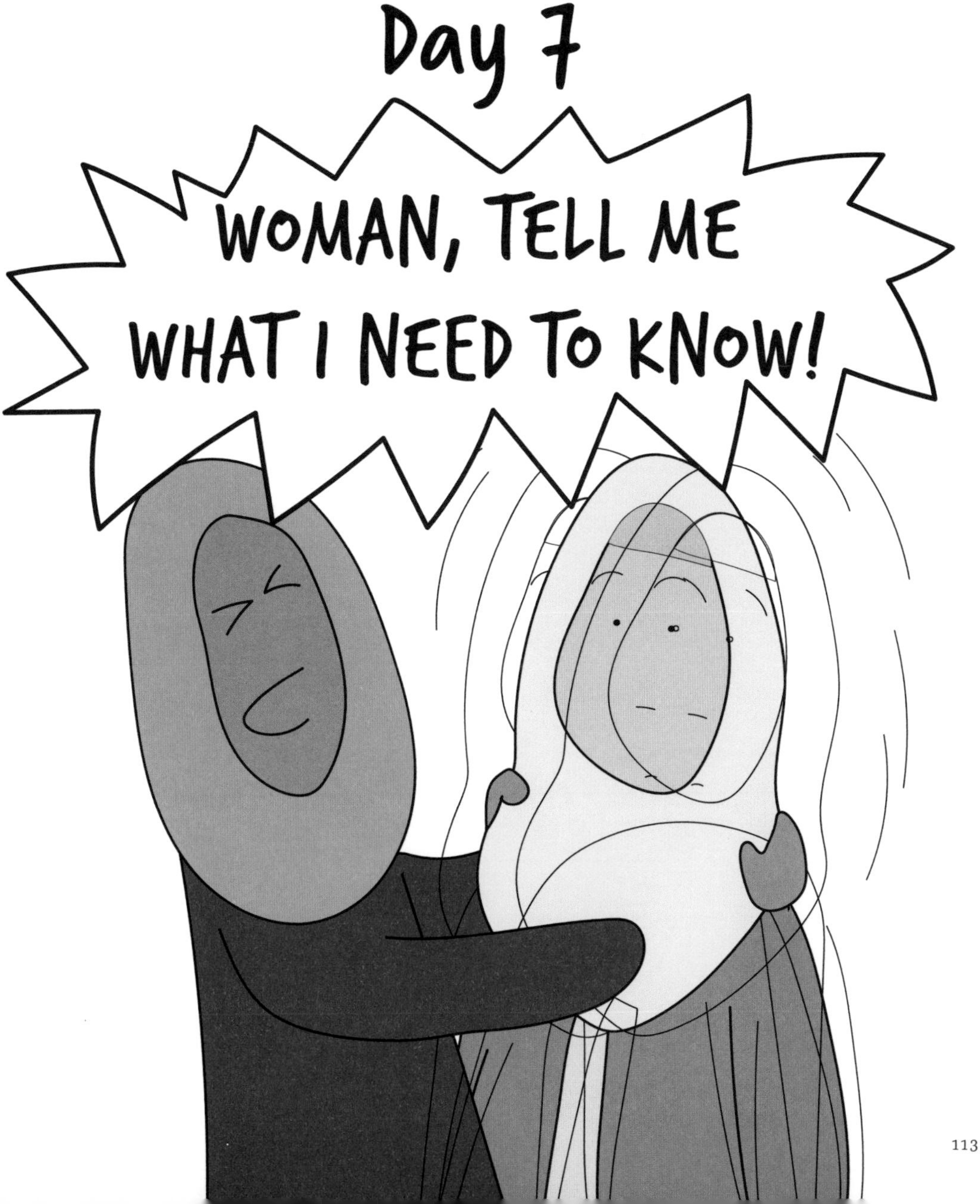
Day 7
WOMAN, TELL ME WHAT I NEED TO KNOW!

When we finally got a chance to talk, I learned that all she managed to get was that his name was Gehad.

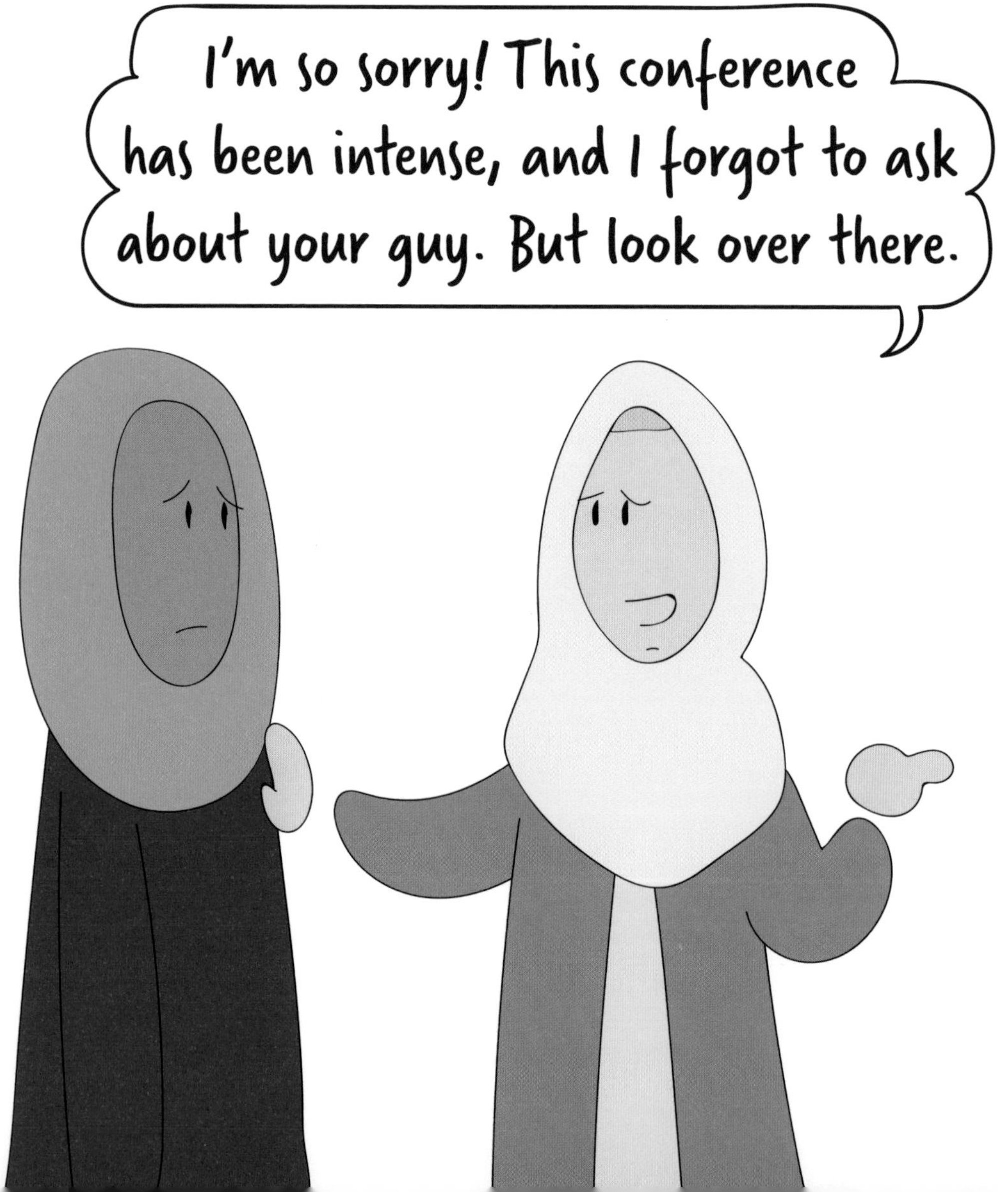
I'm so sorry! This conference has been intense, and I forgot to ask about your guy. But look over there.

That's Sheikh Z. They call him "Dr. Love" because he's great at setting people up! Go talk to him!

It wasn't unusual to ask a sheikh for help finding a spouse, but, still, I was nervous. I gave myself a little pep talk, and I was good to go.

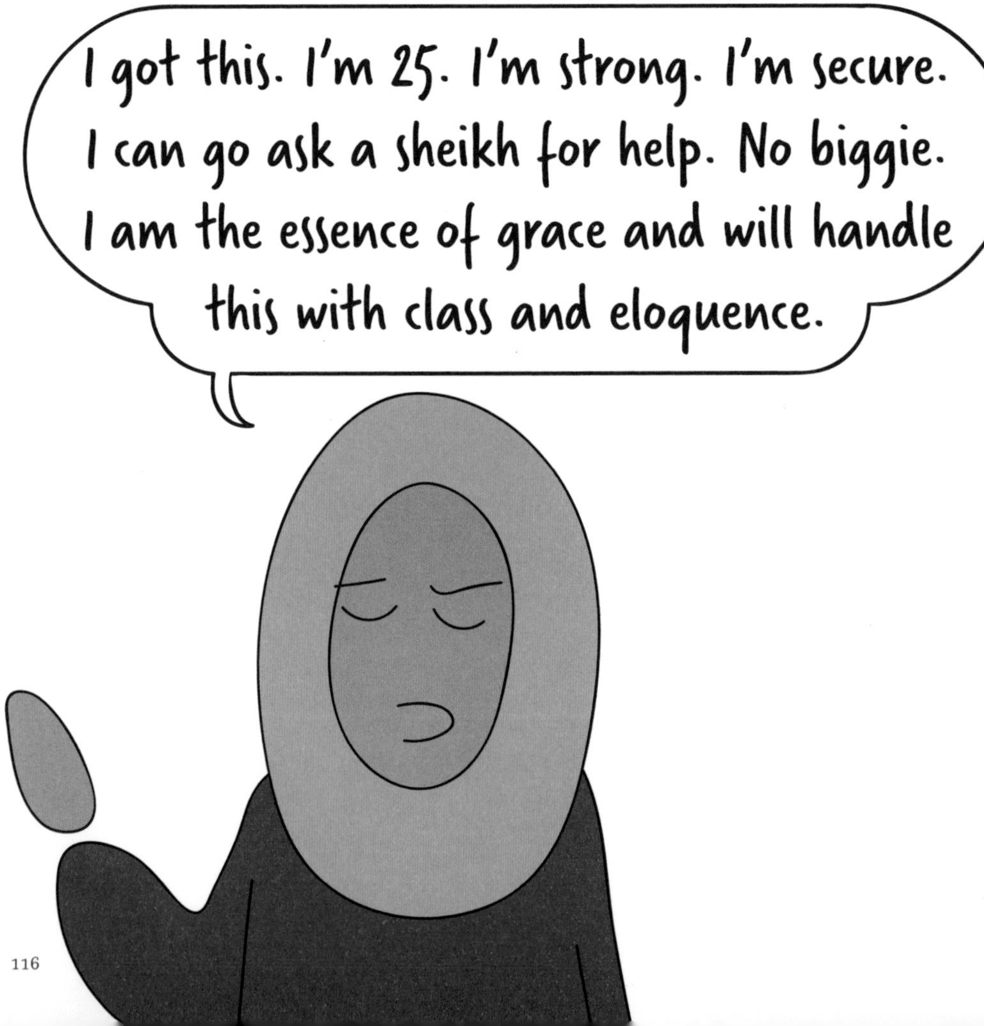
I got this. I'm 25. I'm strong. I'm secure. I can go ask a sheikh for help. No biggie. I am the essence of grace and will handle this with class and eloquence.

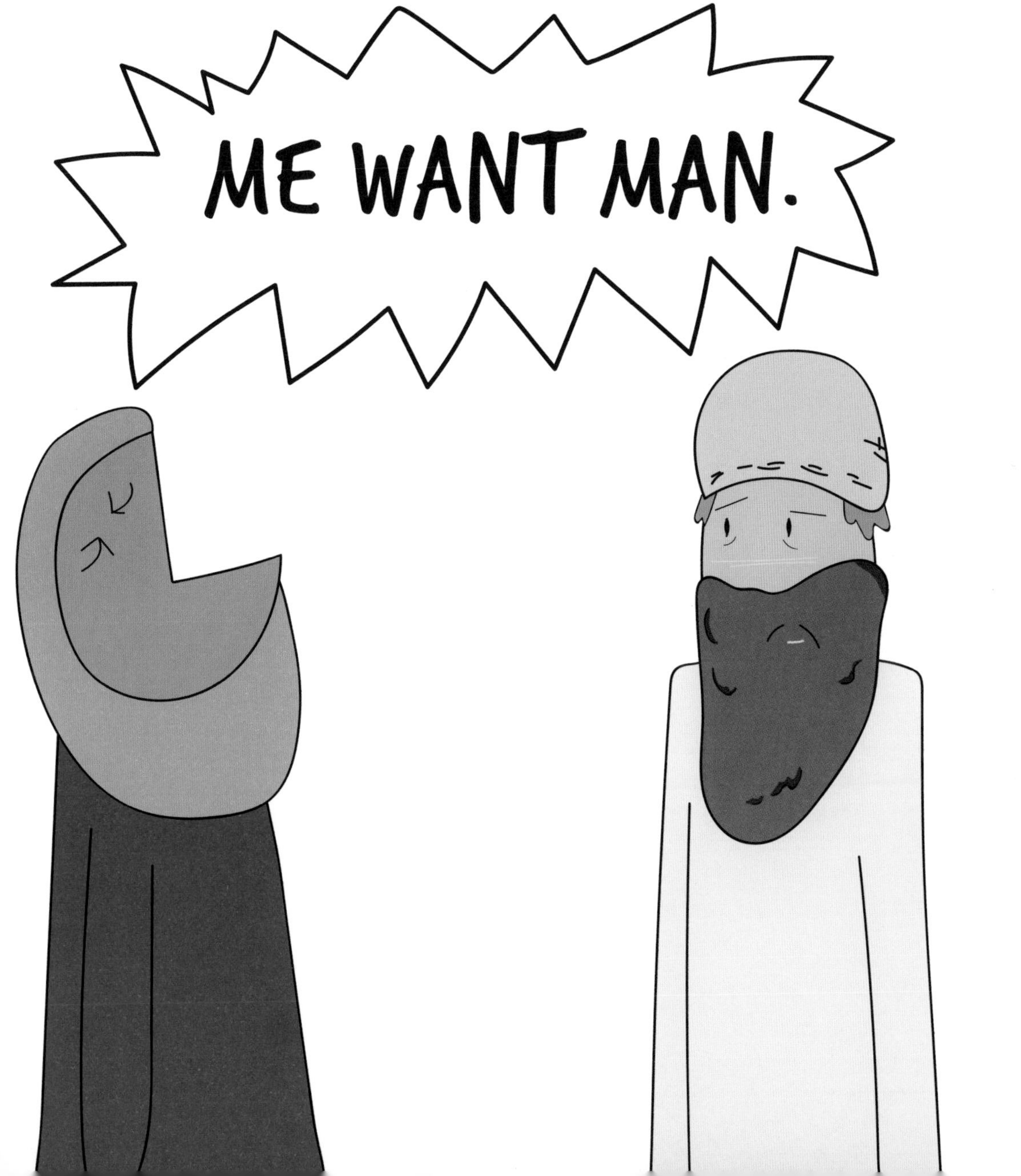
ME WANT MAN.

I didn't mention Gehad. Looking back now, I think I was protecting myself from possible rejection. If I never mentioned him, he could never reject me. Smart. So instead, Sheikh Z and I talked about relationships and what I was looking for in an ideal partner. I still remember it as one of the most important conversations of my life.

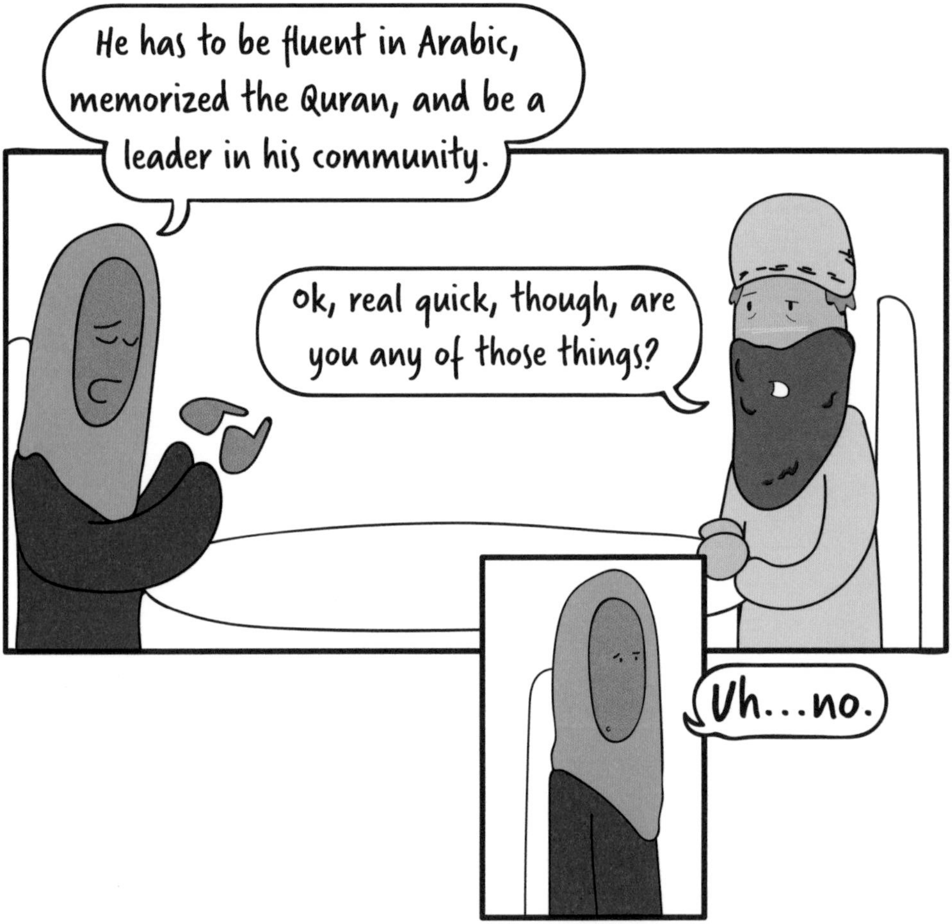
He has to be fluent in Arabic, memorized the Quran, and be a leader in his community.
Ok, real quick, though, are you any of those things?
Uh...no.

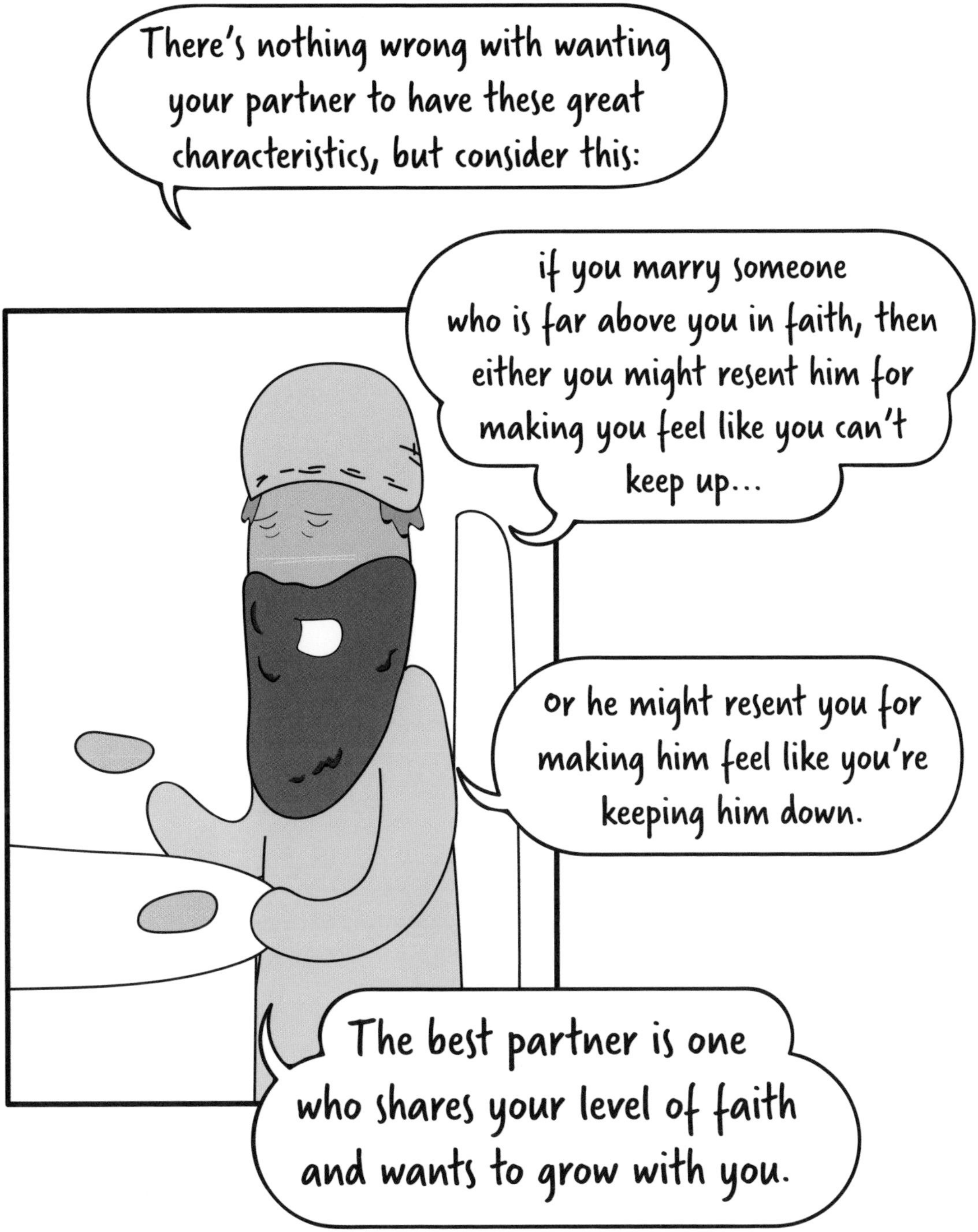
There's nothing wrong with wanting your partner to have these great characteristics, but consider this:
if you marry someone who is far above you in faith, then either you might resent him for making you feel like you can't keep up...
or he might resent you for making him feel like you're keeping him down.
The best partner is one who shares your level of faith and wants to grow with you.

It felt like I'd just been slapped with the realest relationship advice I'd ever gotten. I'd never admitted it until then, but the idea of marrying someone who was at a much higher spiritual level than me was terrifying, and for the exact reasons he listed. I didn't want to be a burden, and I certainly didn't want to feel like a failure. A weight I never even knew I carried had been lifted.

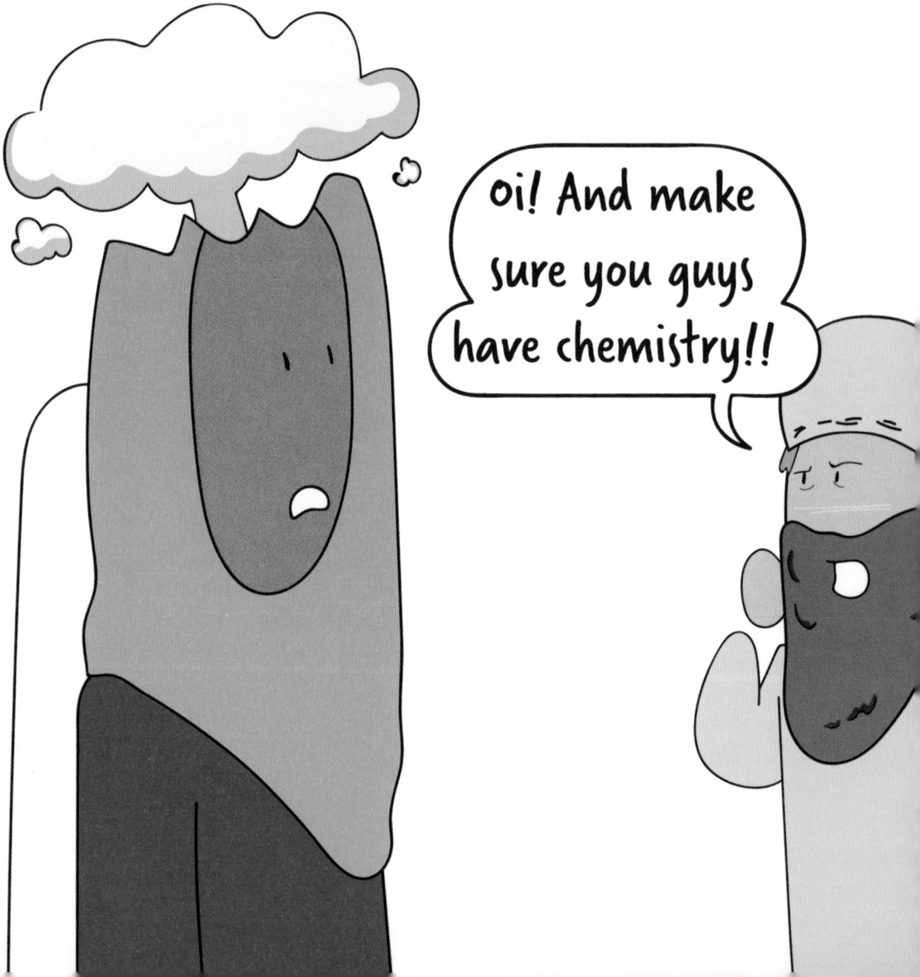
Oi! And make sure you guys have chemistry!!

I didn't expect much to happen after my conversation with the sheikh. Almost every other woman at the conference had lined up behind me to request he keep her in mind if there were guys looking. I knew I wouldn't hear back from him anytime soon.

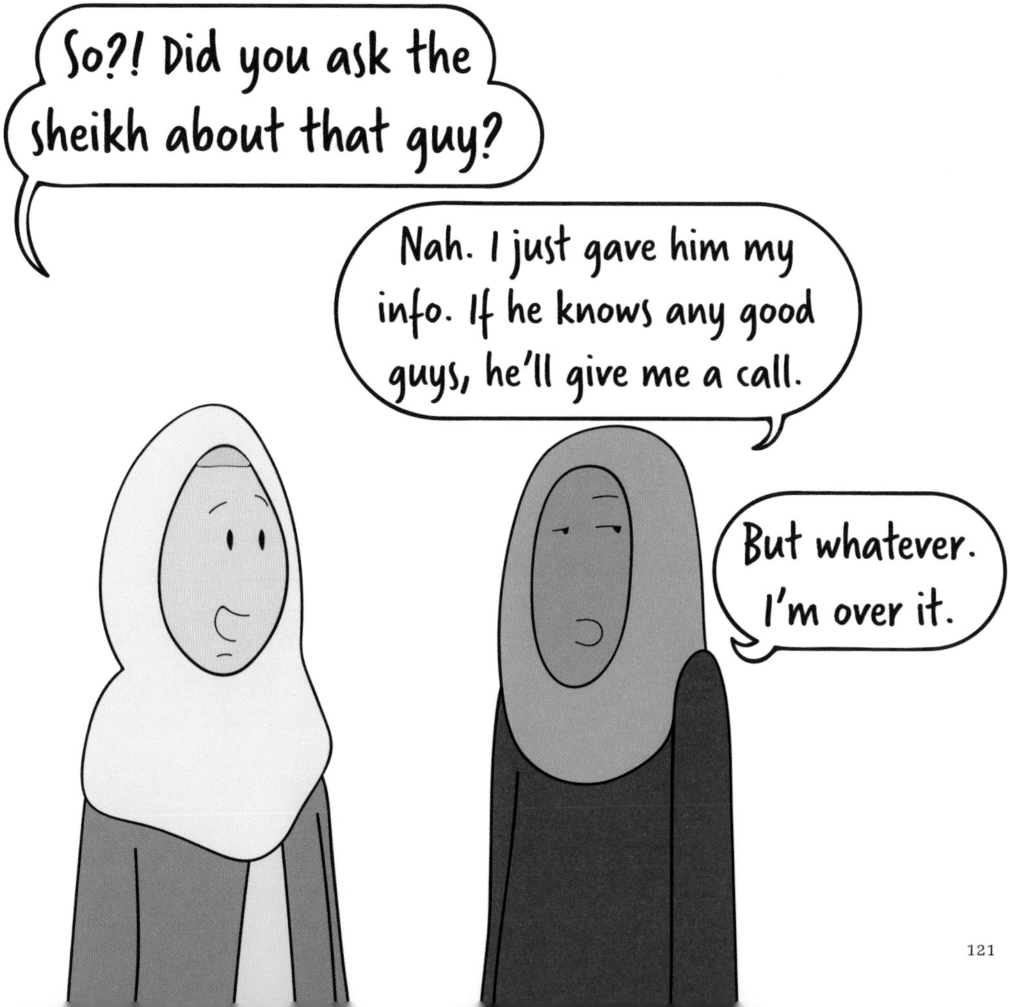
So?! Did you ask the sheikh about that guy?
Nah. I just gave him my info. If he knows any good guys, he'll give me a call.
But whatever. I'm over it.

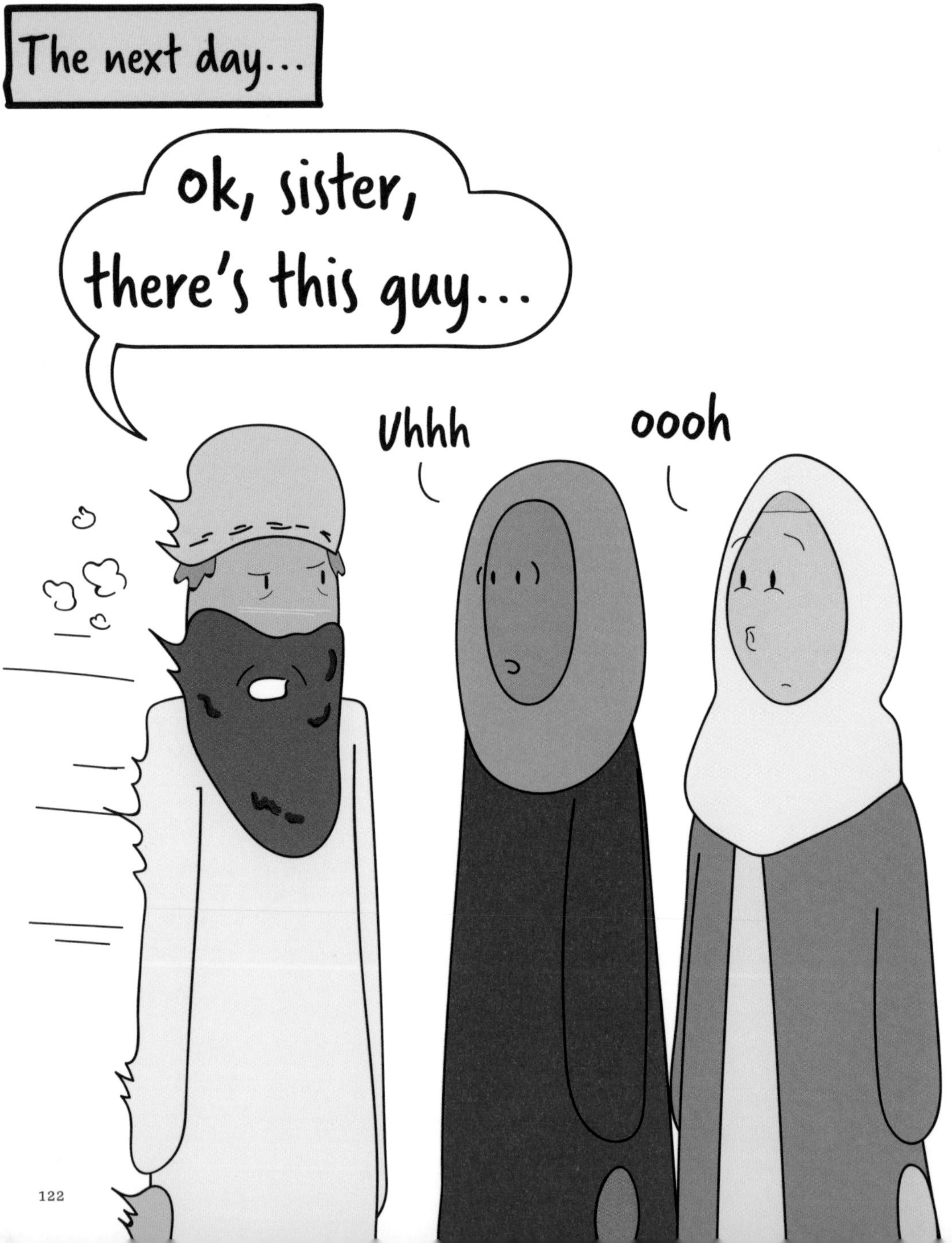
The next day...
ok, sister, there's this guy...
Uhhh
oooh

And wouldn't ya know it . . .

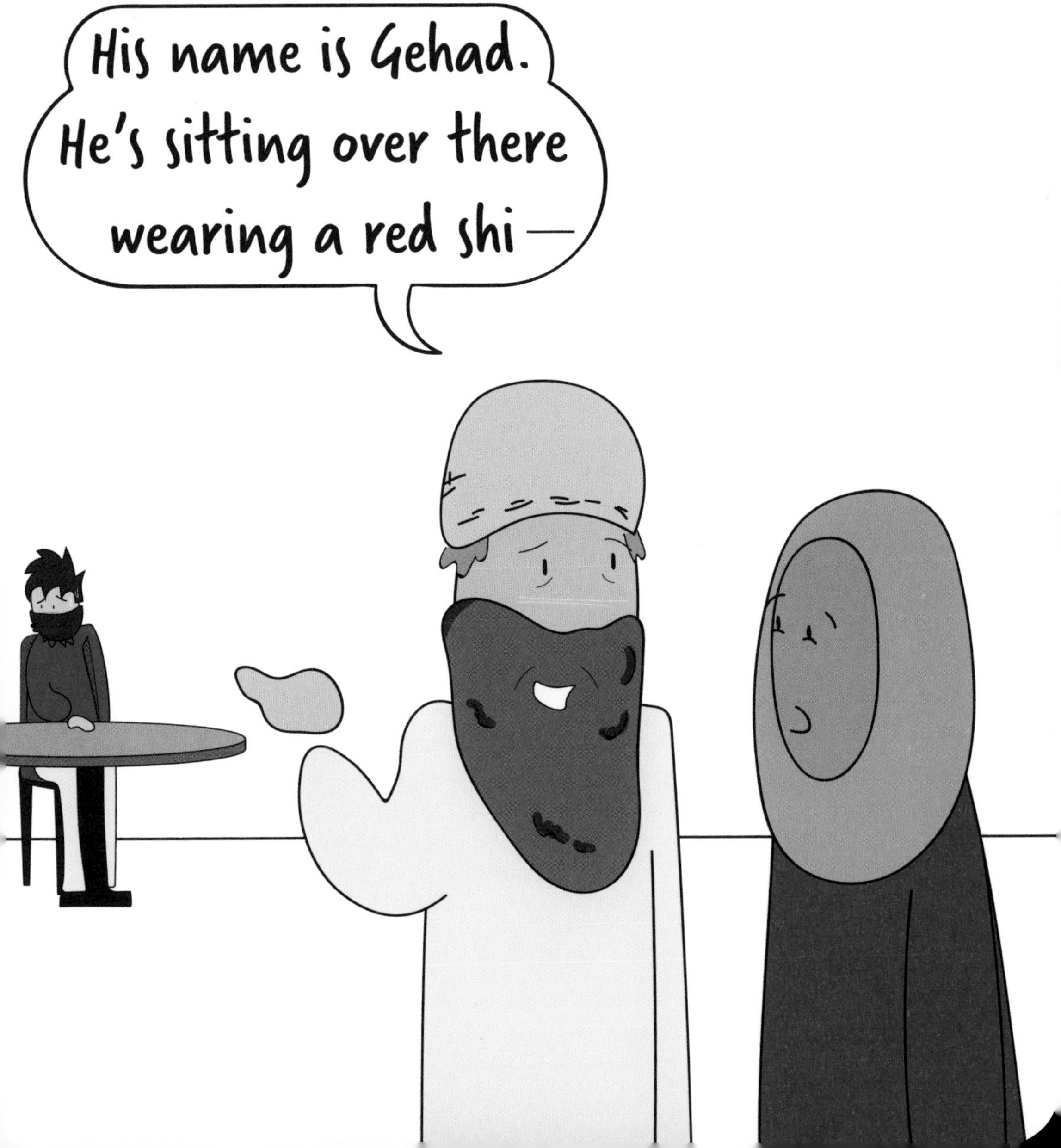

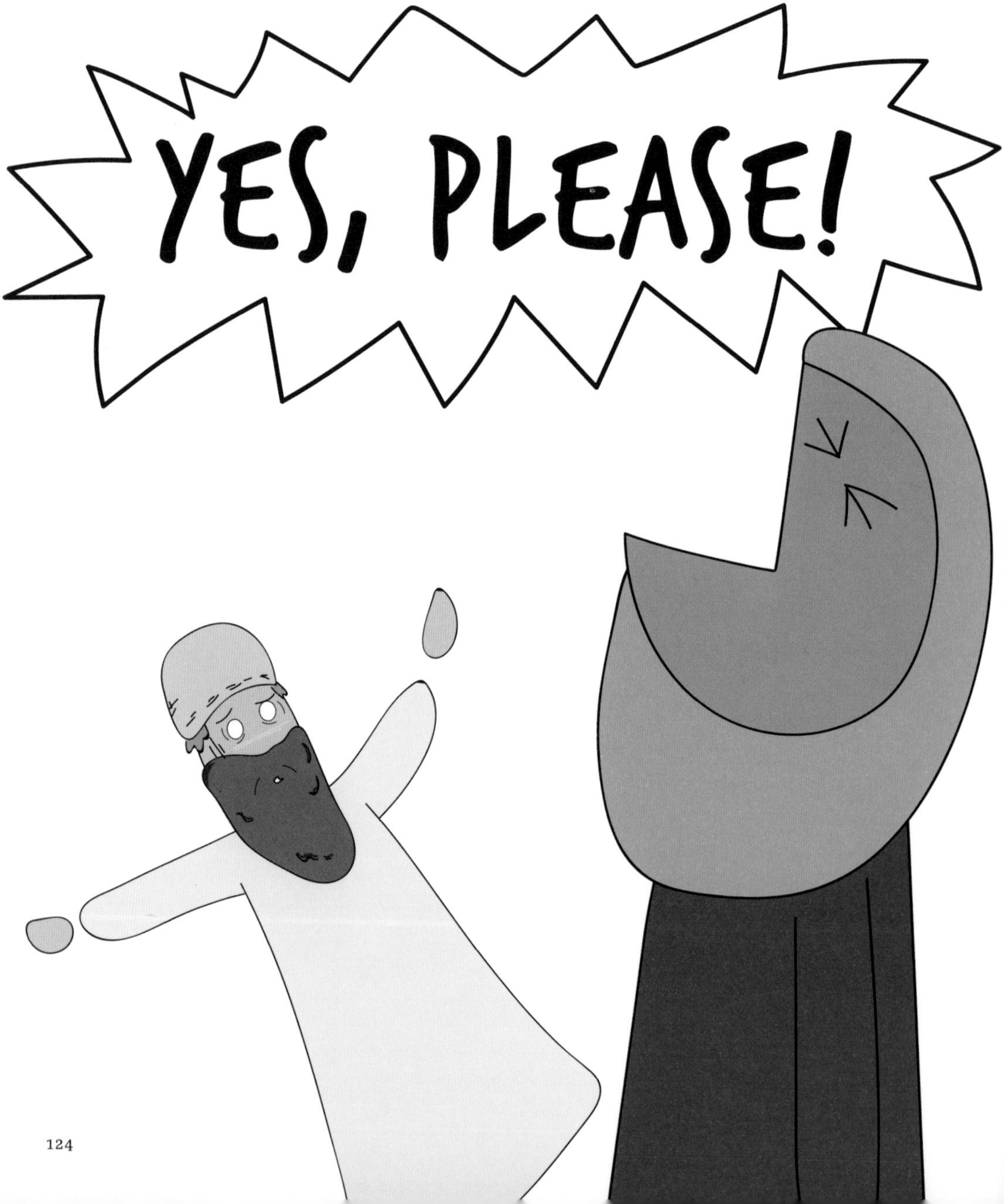
YES, PLEASE!

The First Meeting

Biodata was sent, and he was as perfect on paper as he looked in person.

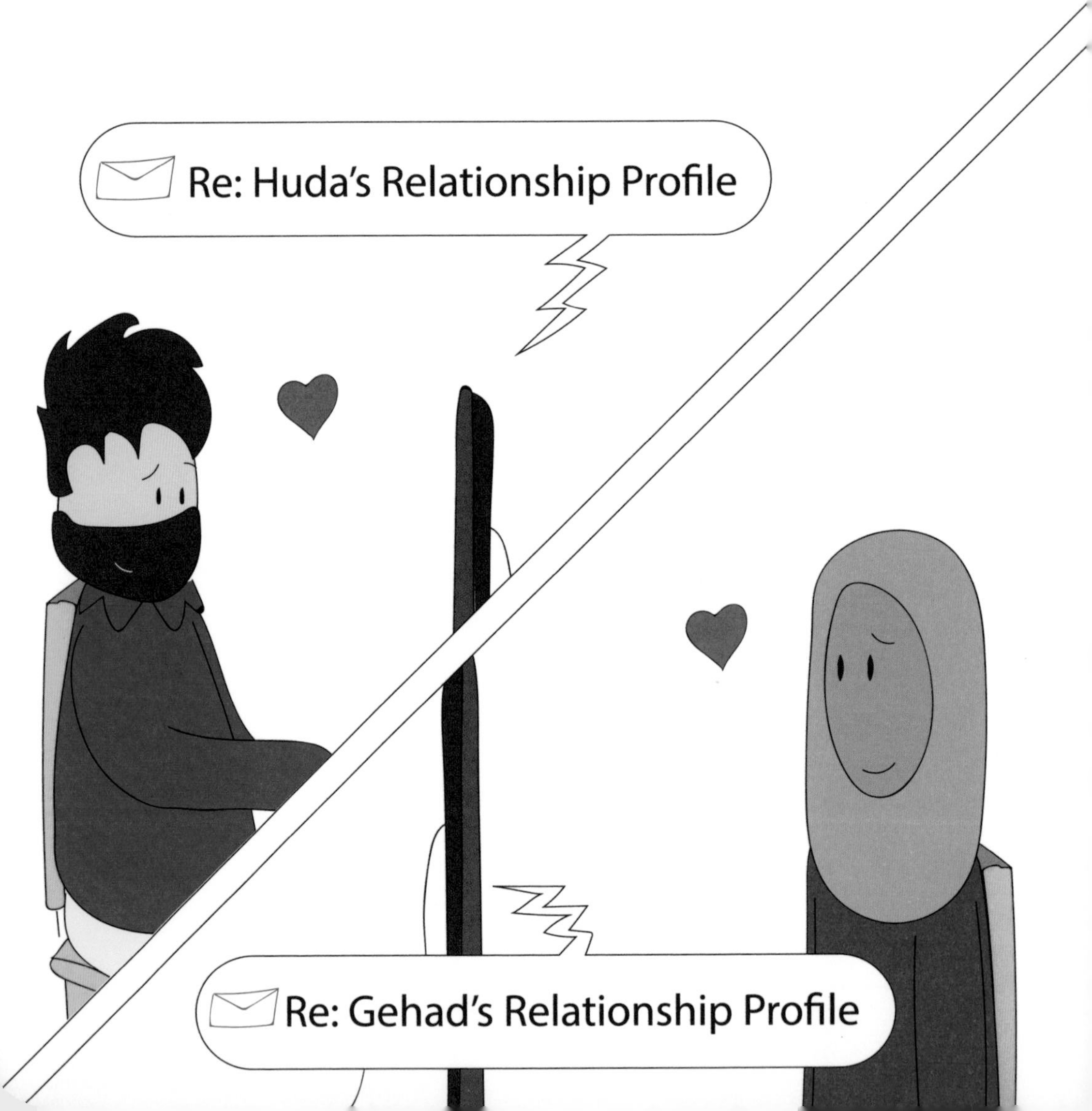
Re: Huda's Relationship Profile
Re: Gehad's Relationship Profile

He called my dad–who was as tough on him as I'd come to expect (and want).

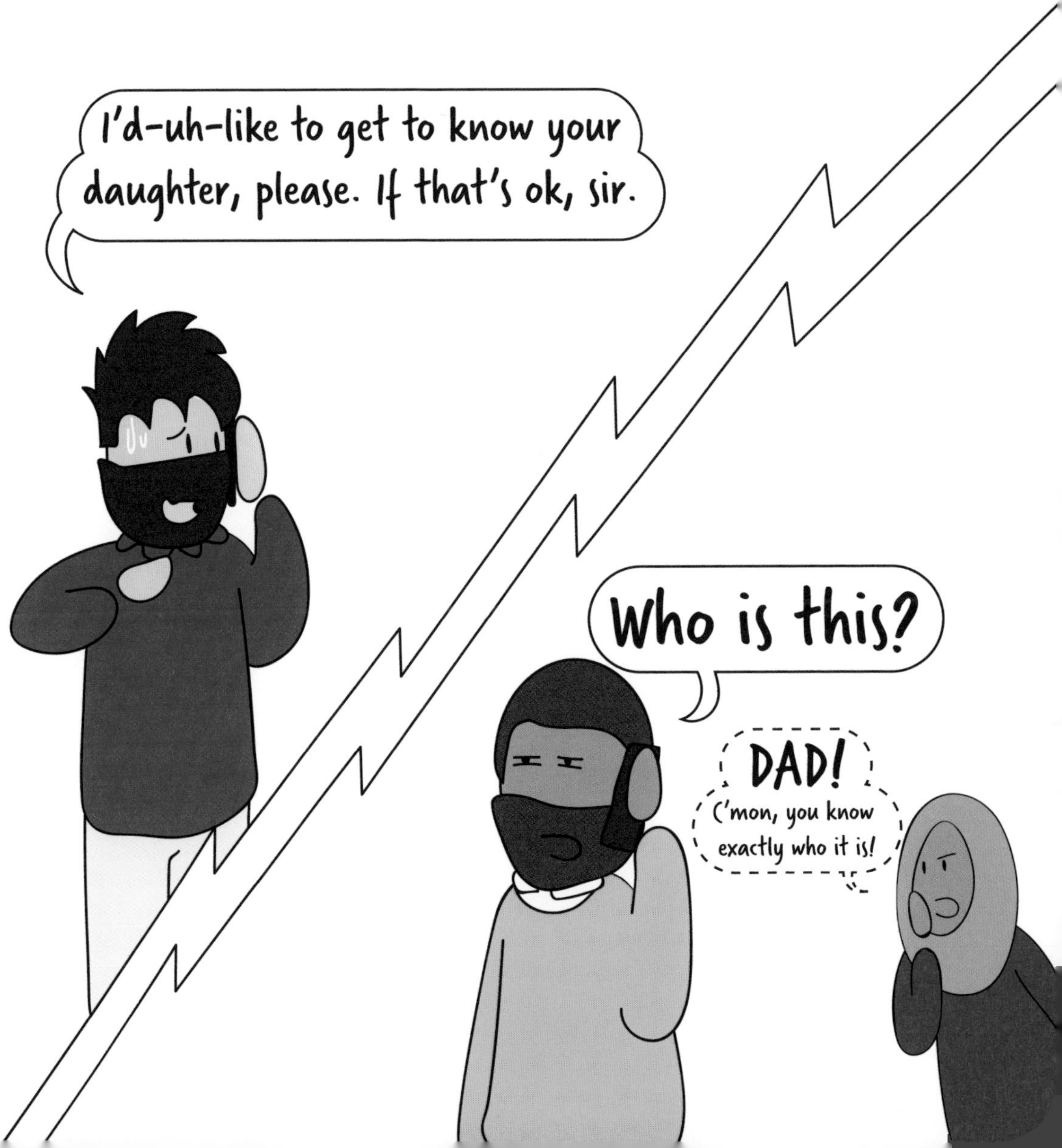
I'd-uh-like to get to know your daughter, please. If that's ok, sir.
Who is this?
DAD!
C'mon, you know exactly who it is!

And finally . . .

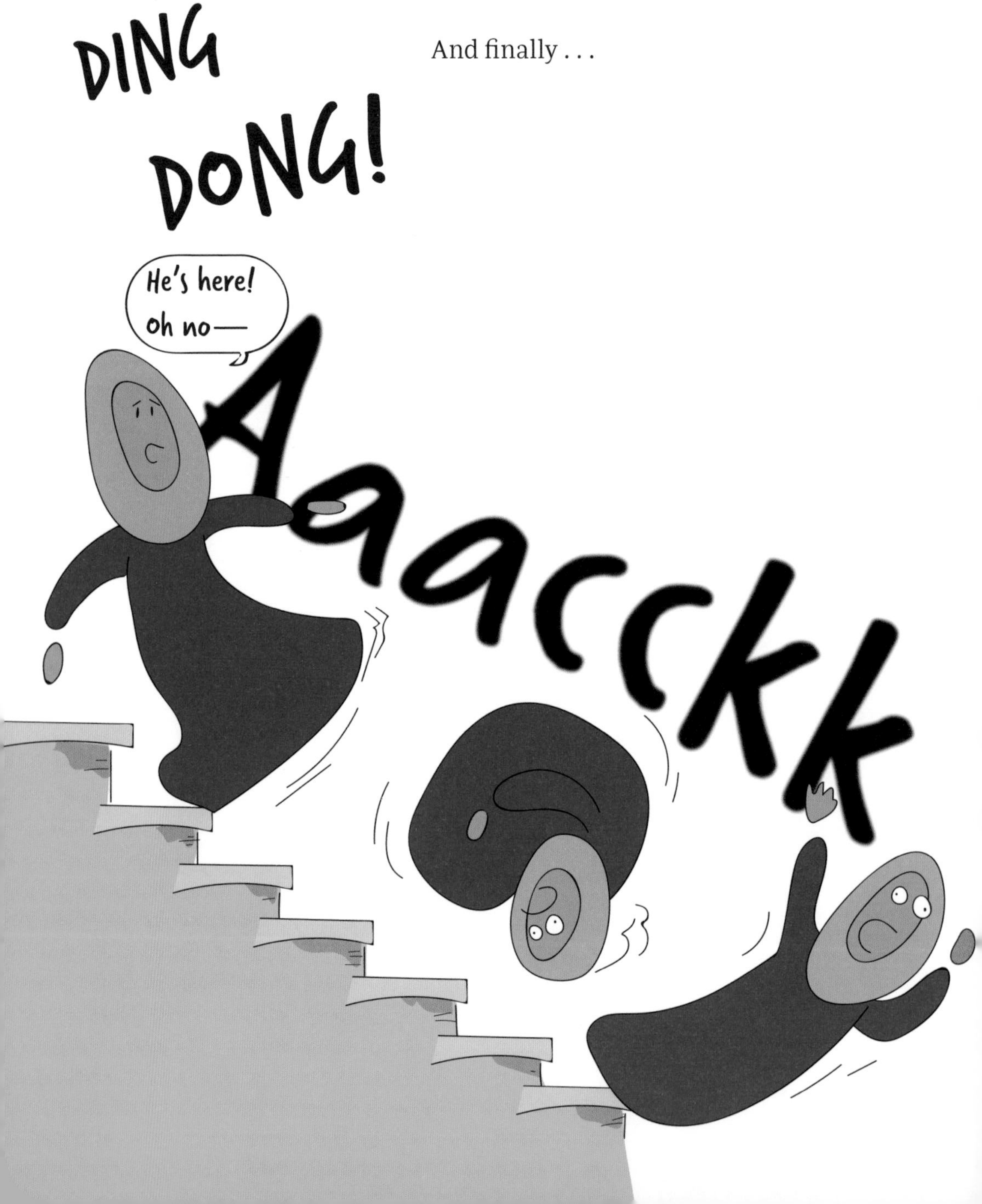
DING DONG!
He's here! oh no—
Aaacckk

I went on my first ever date.

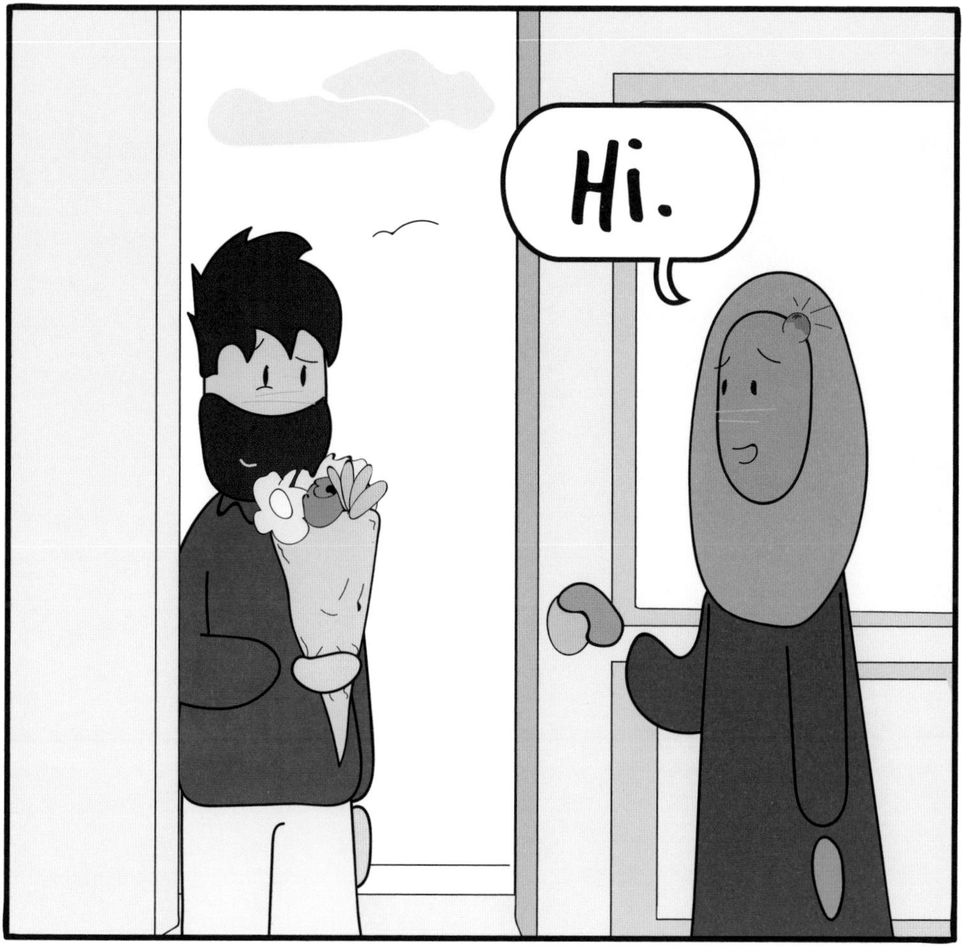
Hi.

It was at home and chaperoned. But still.

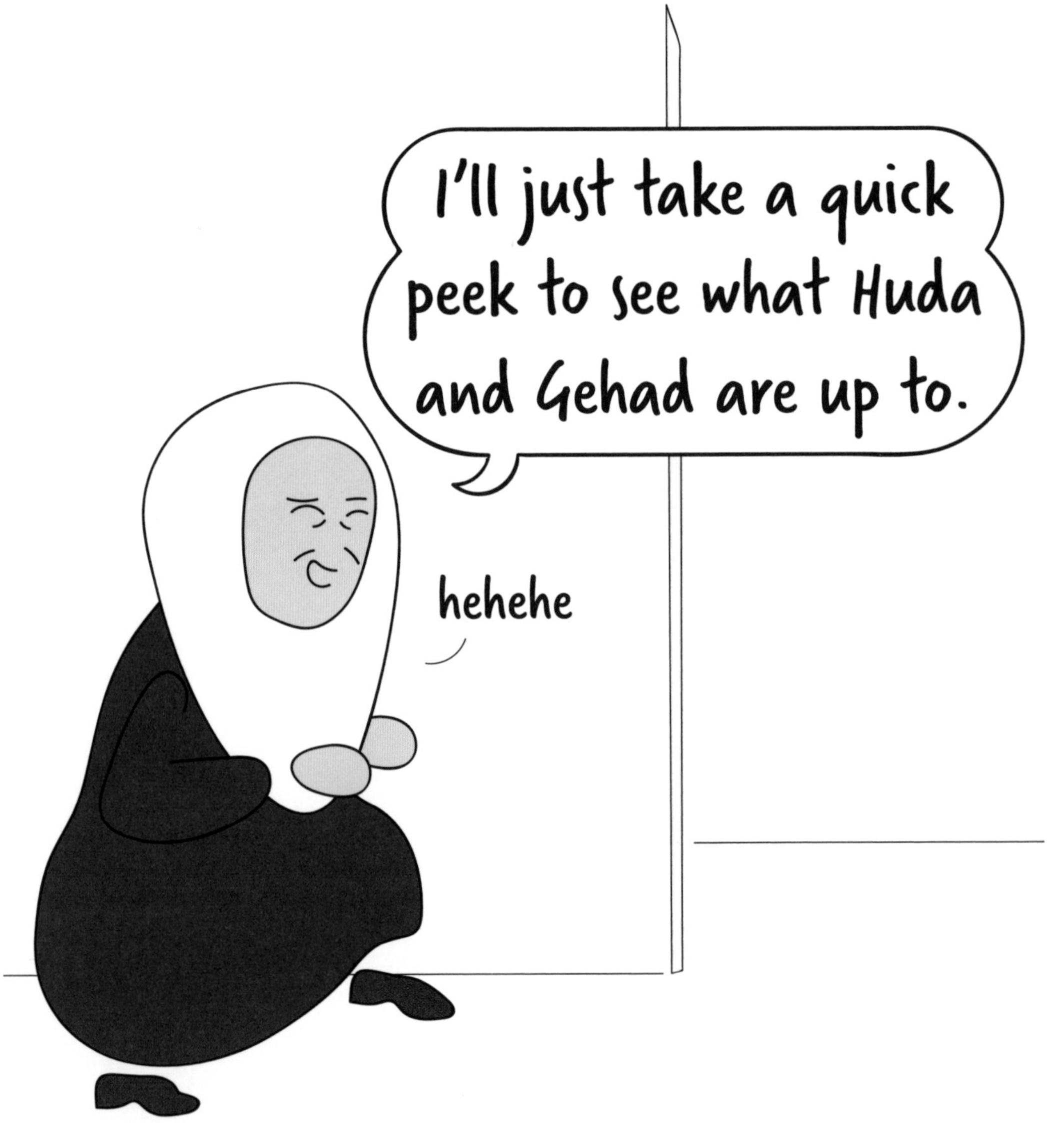
I'll just take a quick peek to see what Huda and Gehad are up to.
hehehe

We hit it off right away.

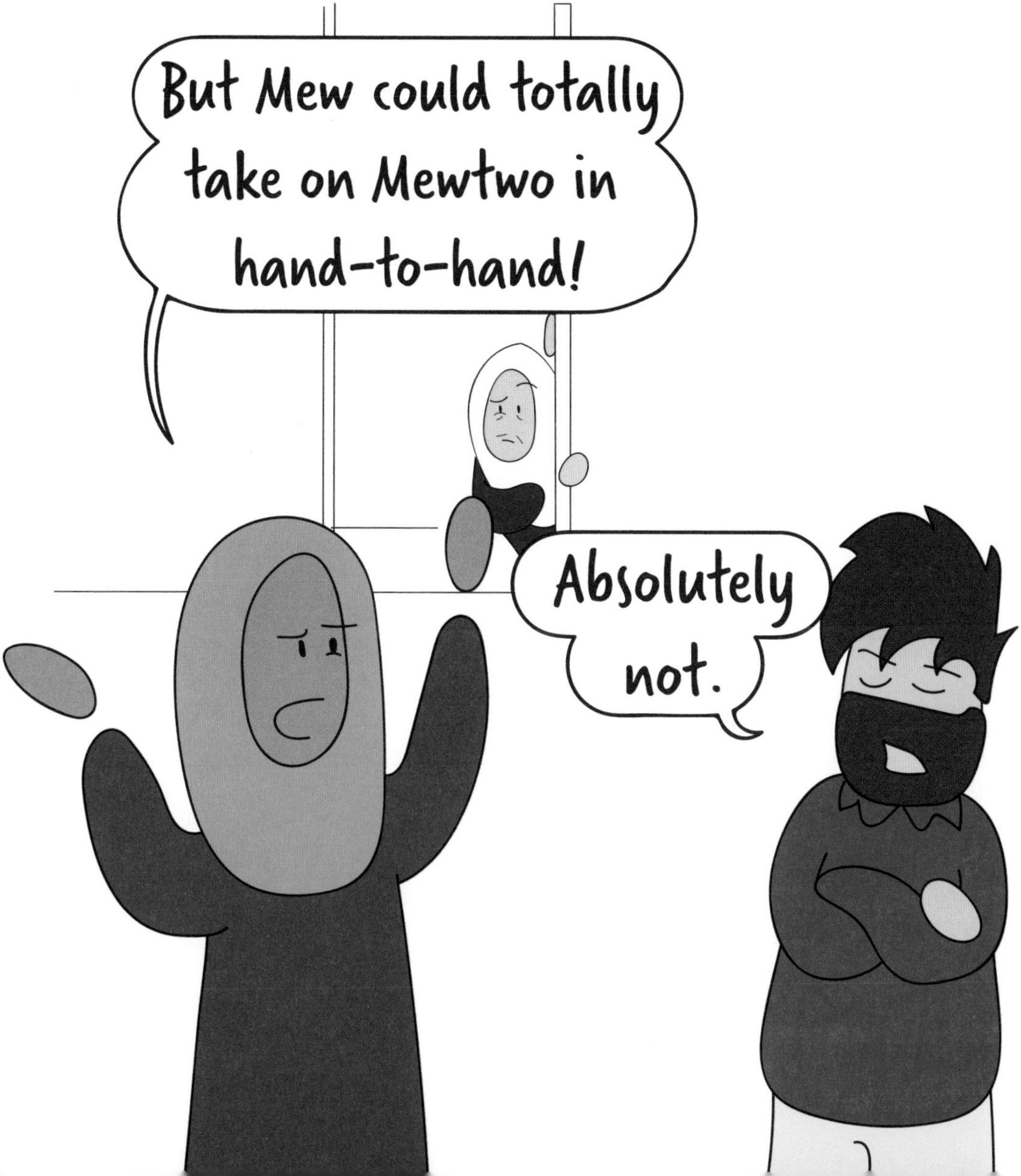

But Mew could totally take on Mewtwo in hand-to-hand!
Absolutely not.

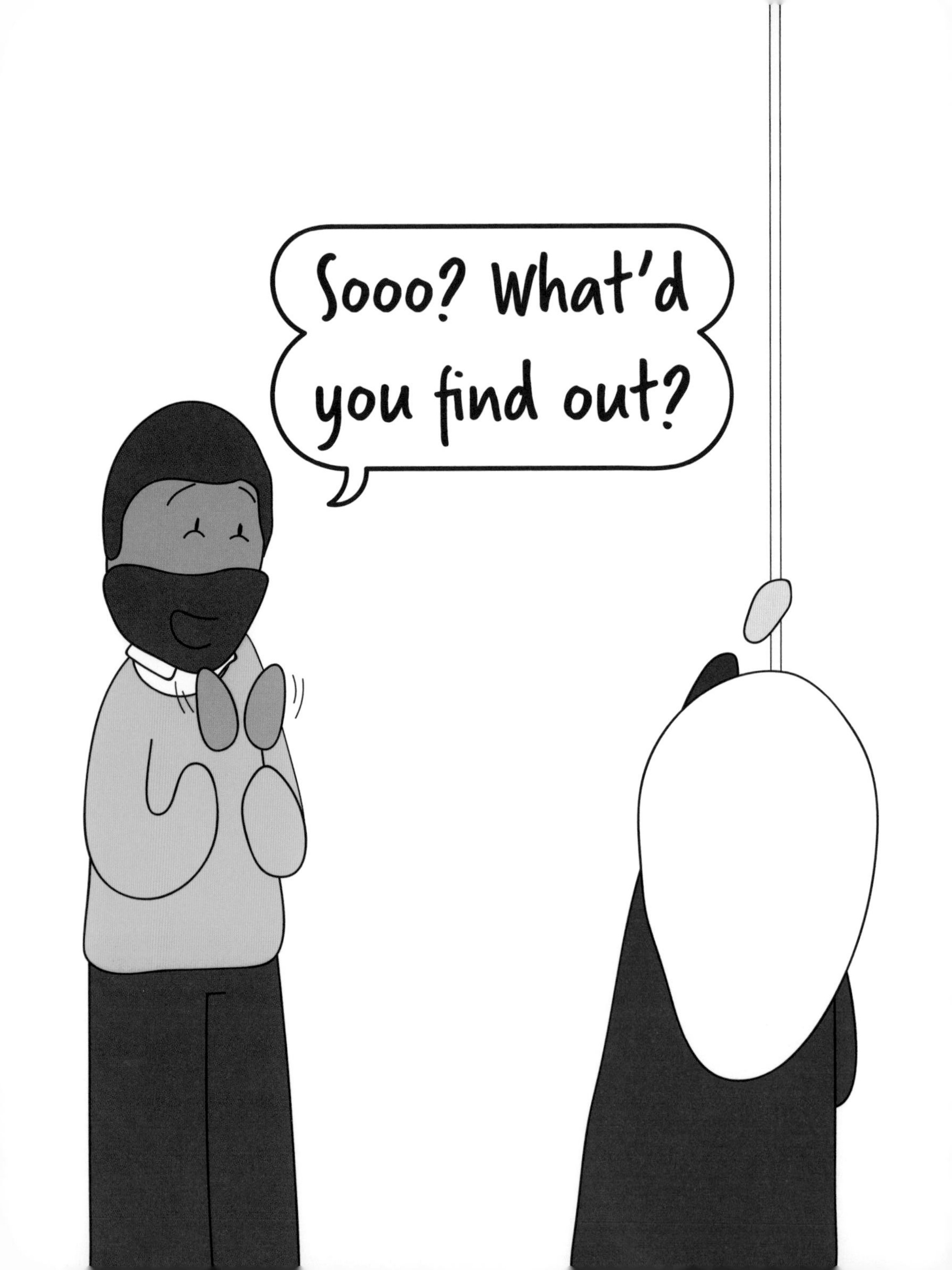
Sooo? What'd you find out?

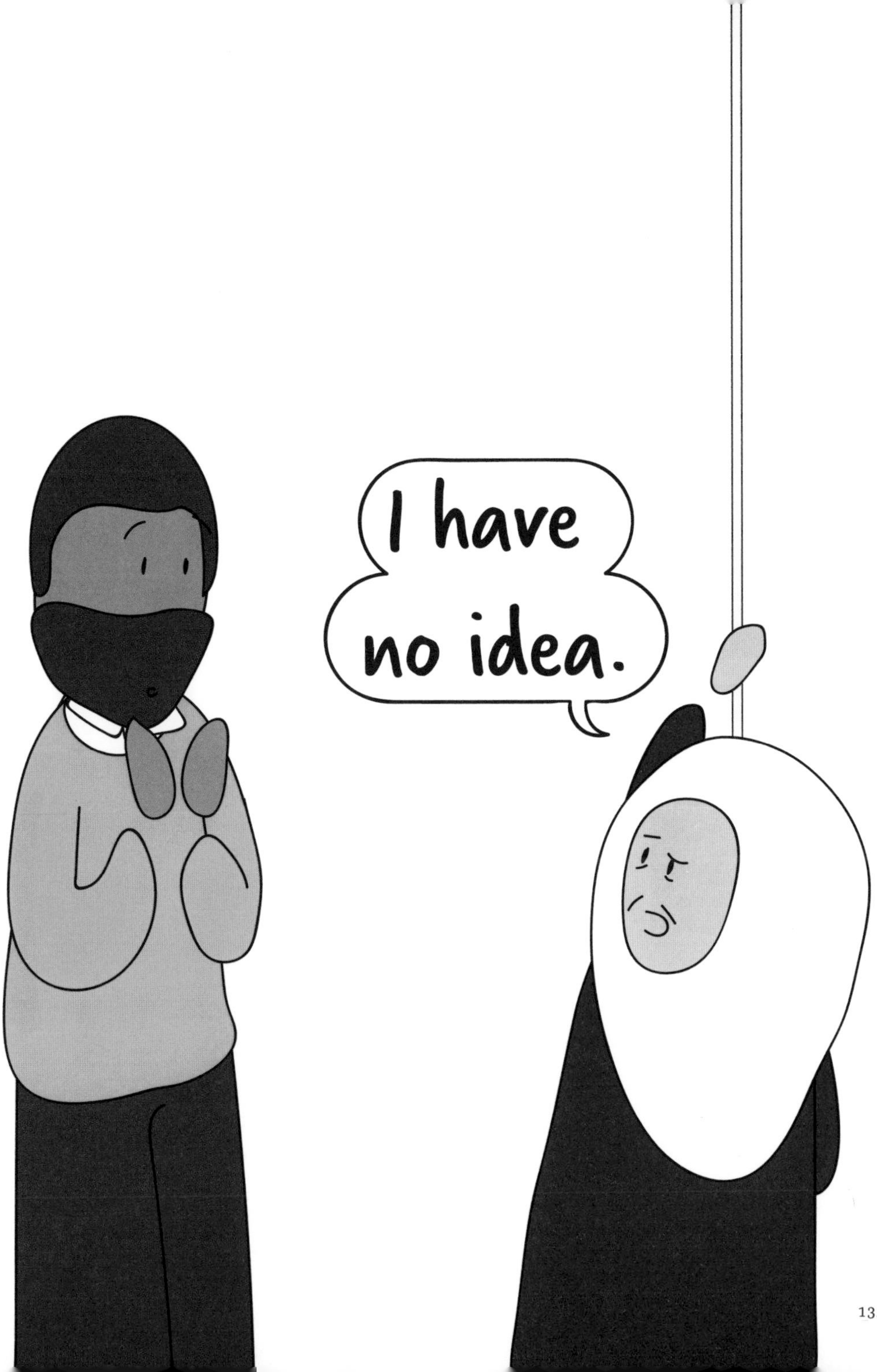
I have no idea.

My mom wasn't sure it would work out.

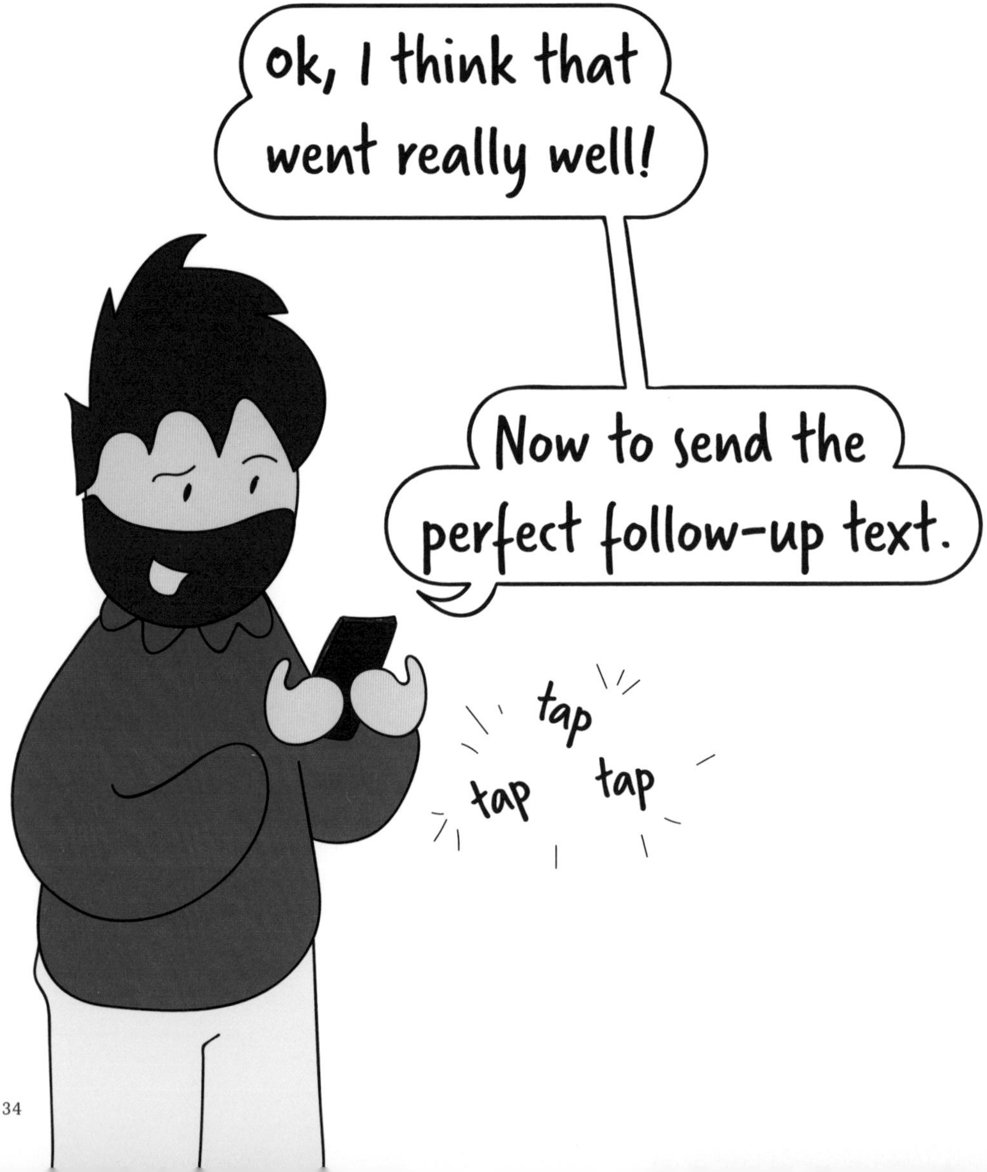
ok, I think that went really well!
Now to send the perfect follow-up text.
tap
tap
tap

Scratch that, she was positive it wouldn't work out.

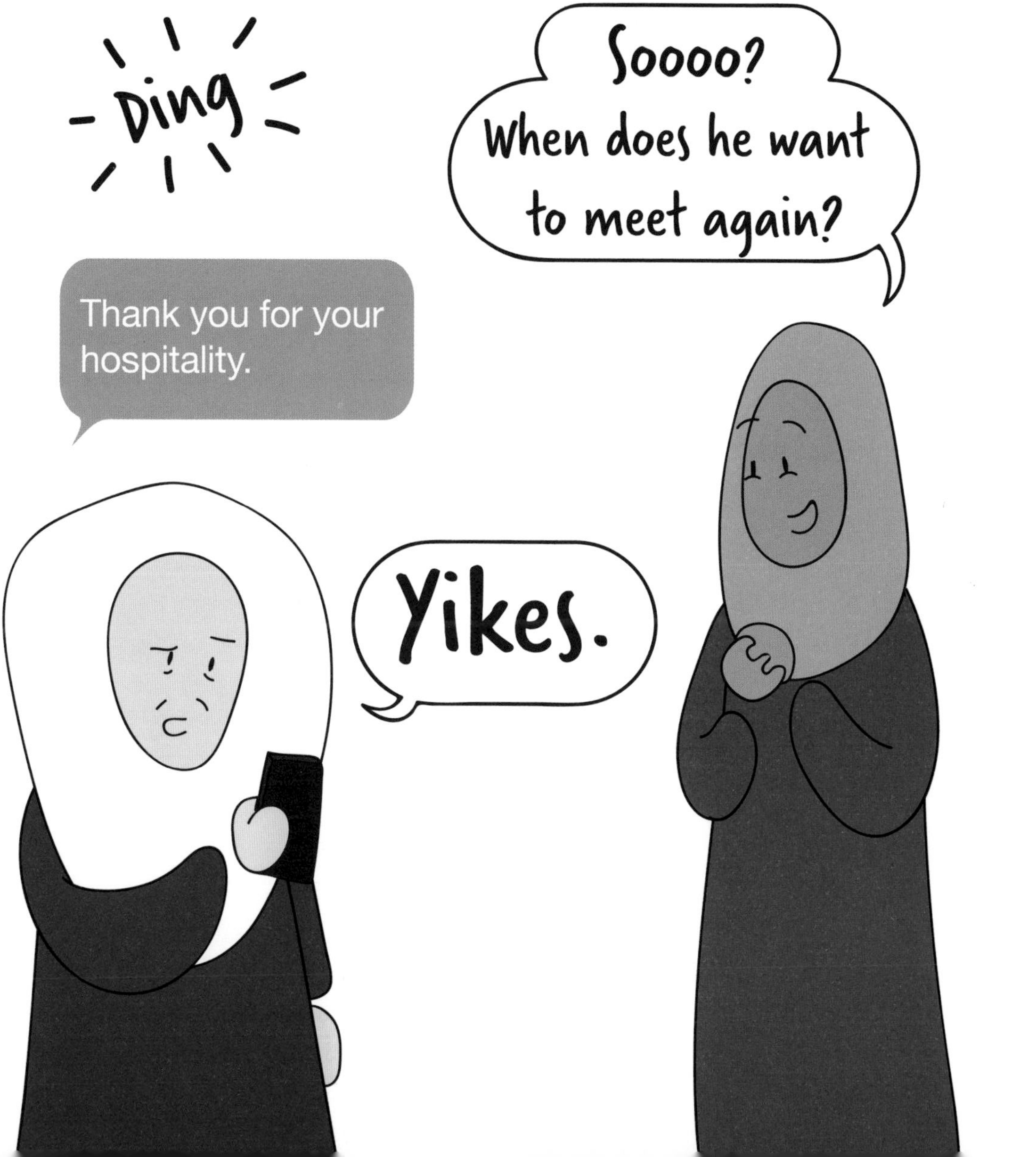
Ding
Thank you for your hospitality.
Soooo? When does he want to meet again?
Yikes.

Looks like he's trying to let you down gently.
B-But we had such chemistry.

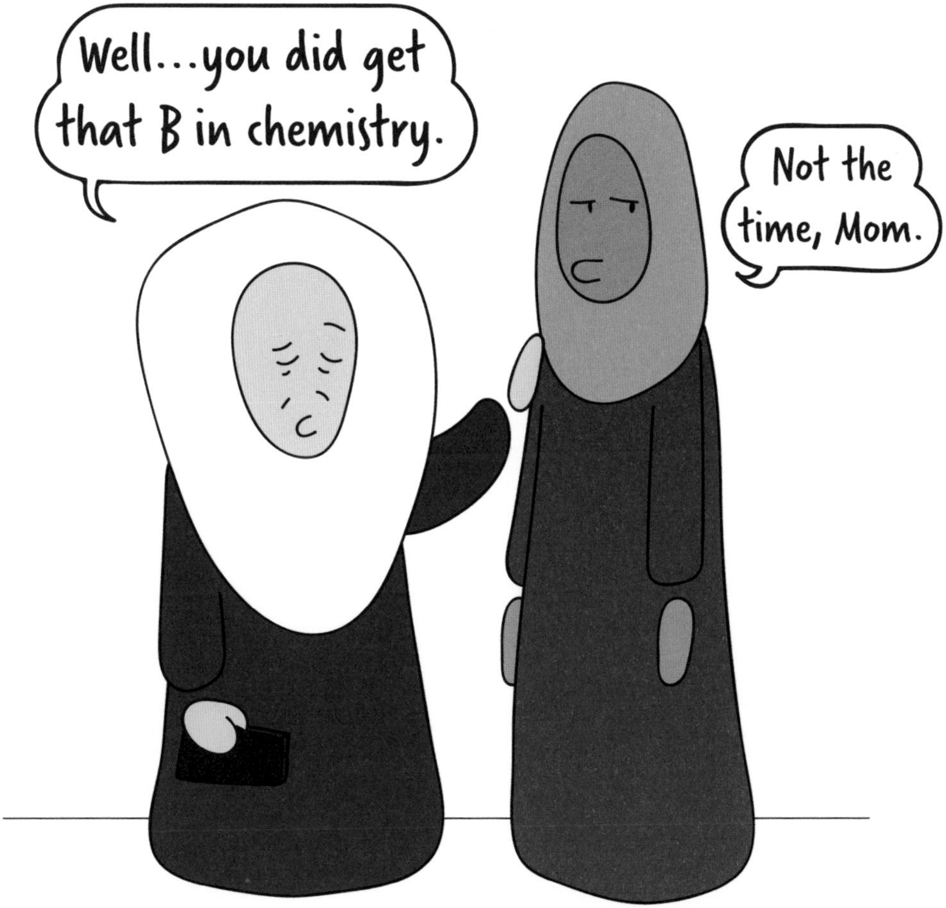
Well...you did get that B in chemistry.
Not the time, Mom.

I refused to believe it. The chemistry was there, I tell ya! So, I did what any self-respecting 25-year-old single woman of good family and education would do.

I just wanted to clarify, I had a wonderful time and would love to see Huda again soon!

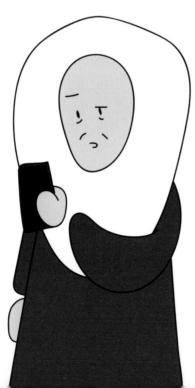

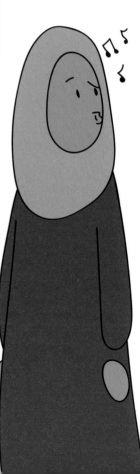

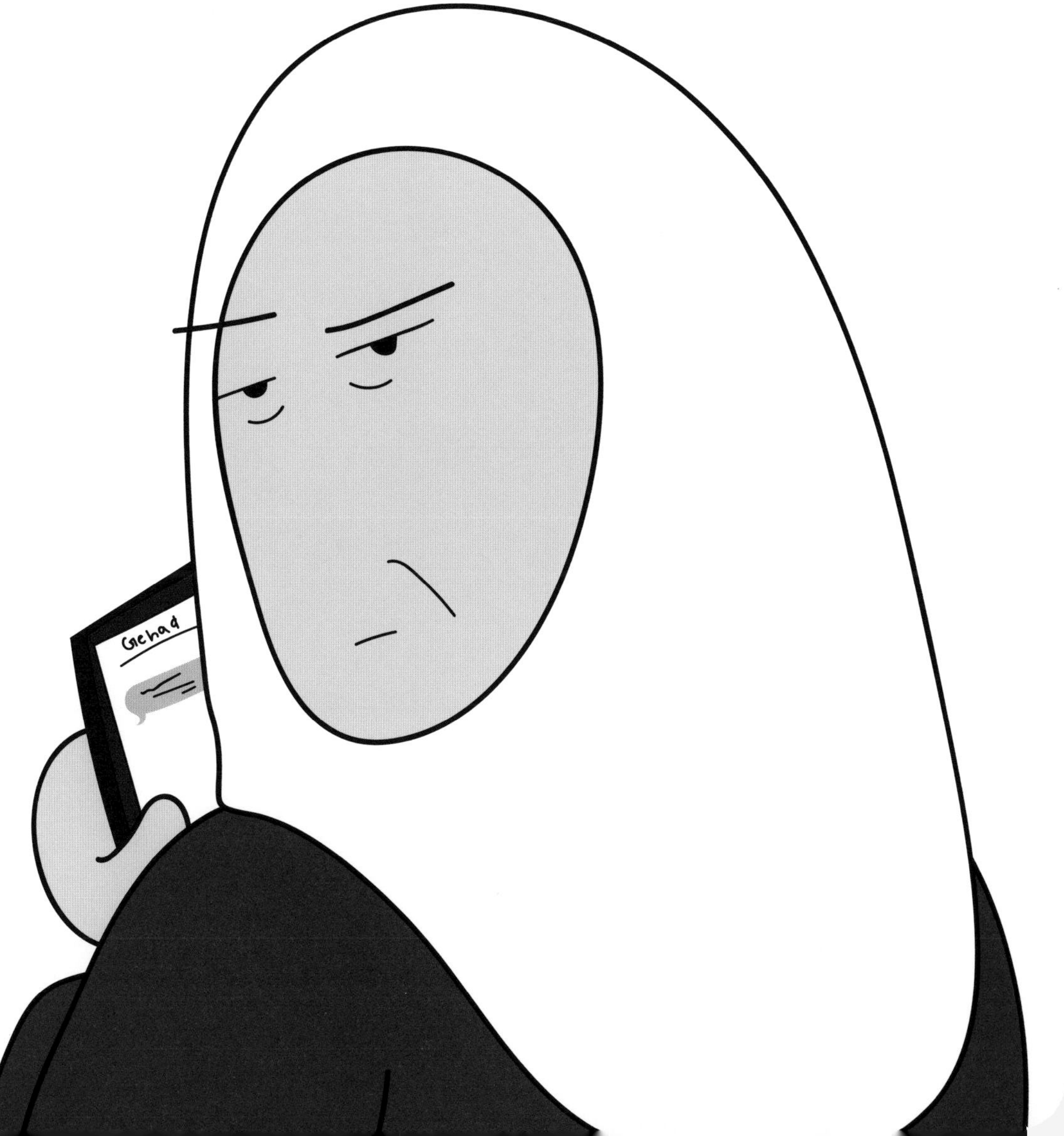
Gehad

I took matters into my own hands.

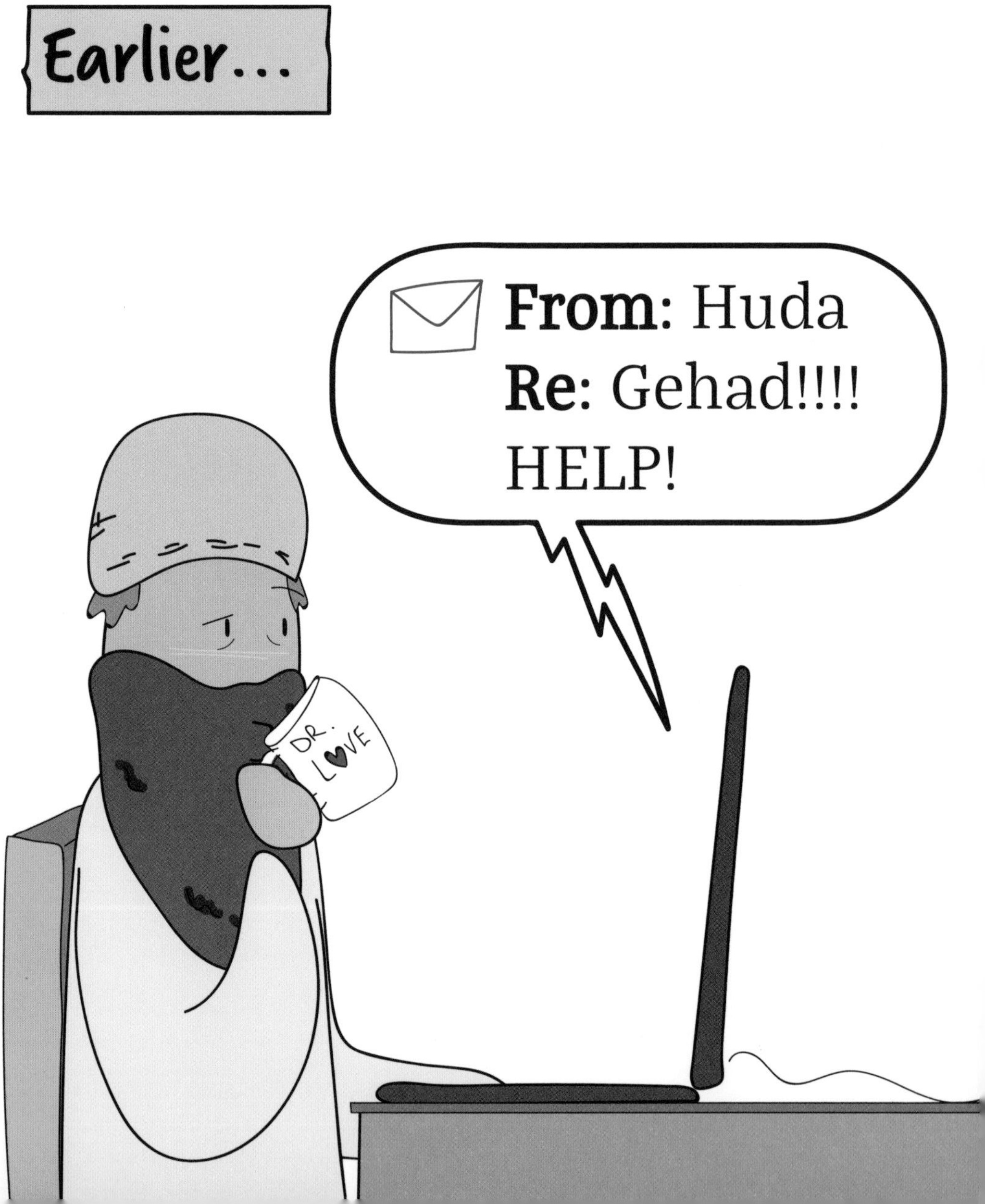
Earlier...
From: Huda
Re: Gehad!!!! HELP!
DR. LOVE

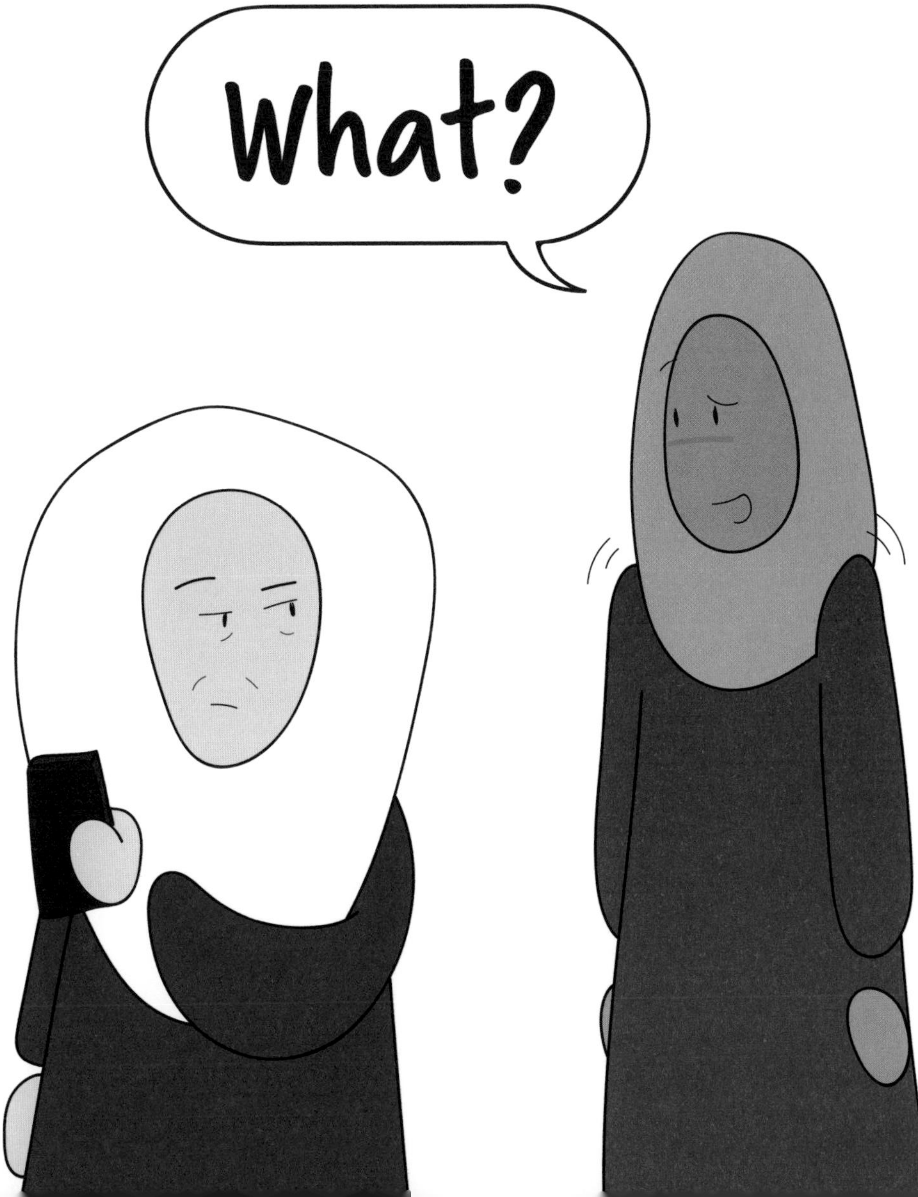
What?

Soul Meets

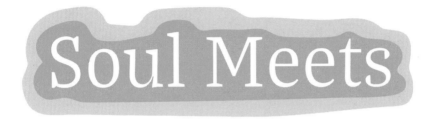

So we arranged times and dates to call and see each other.

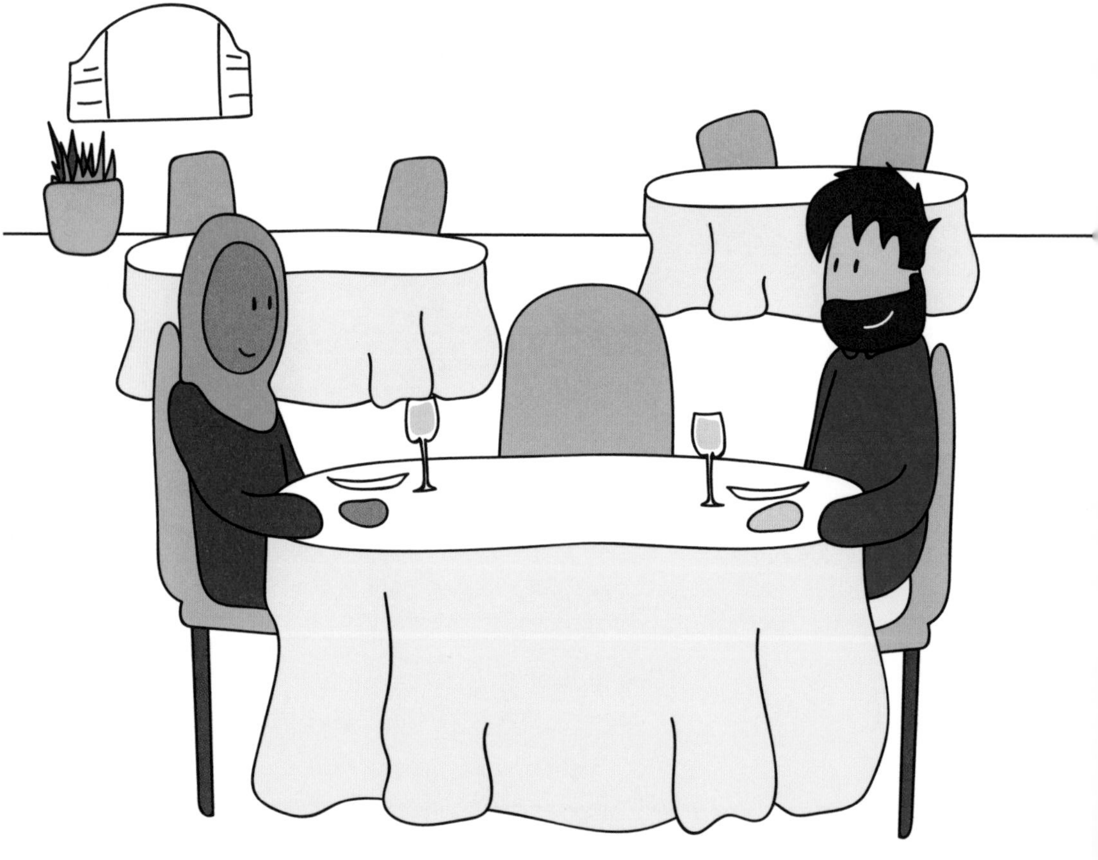

Chaperoned of course.

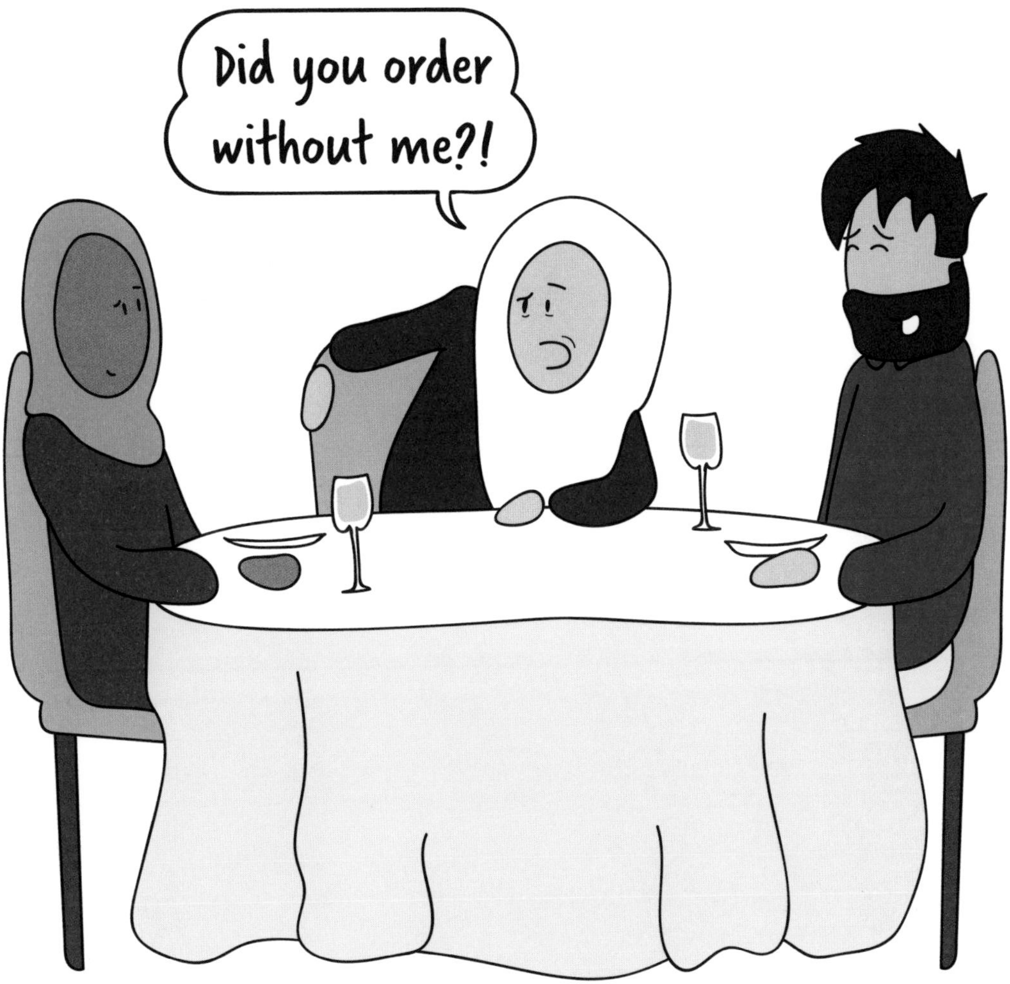
Did you order without me?!

We even had to CC my mom on emails.
("CC" stands for "Chaperone's Copy," after all.)

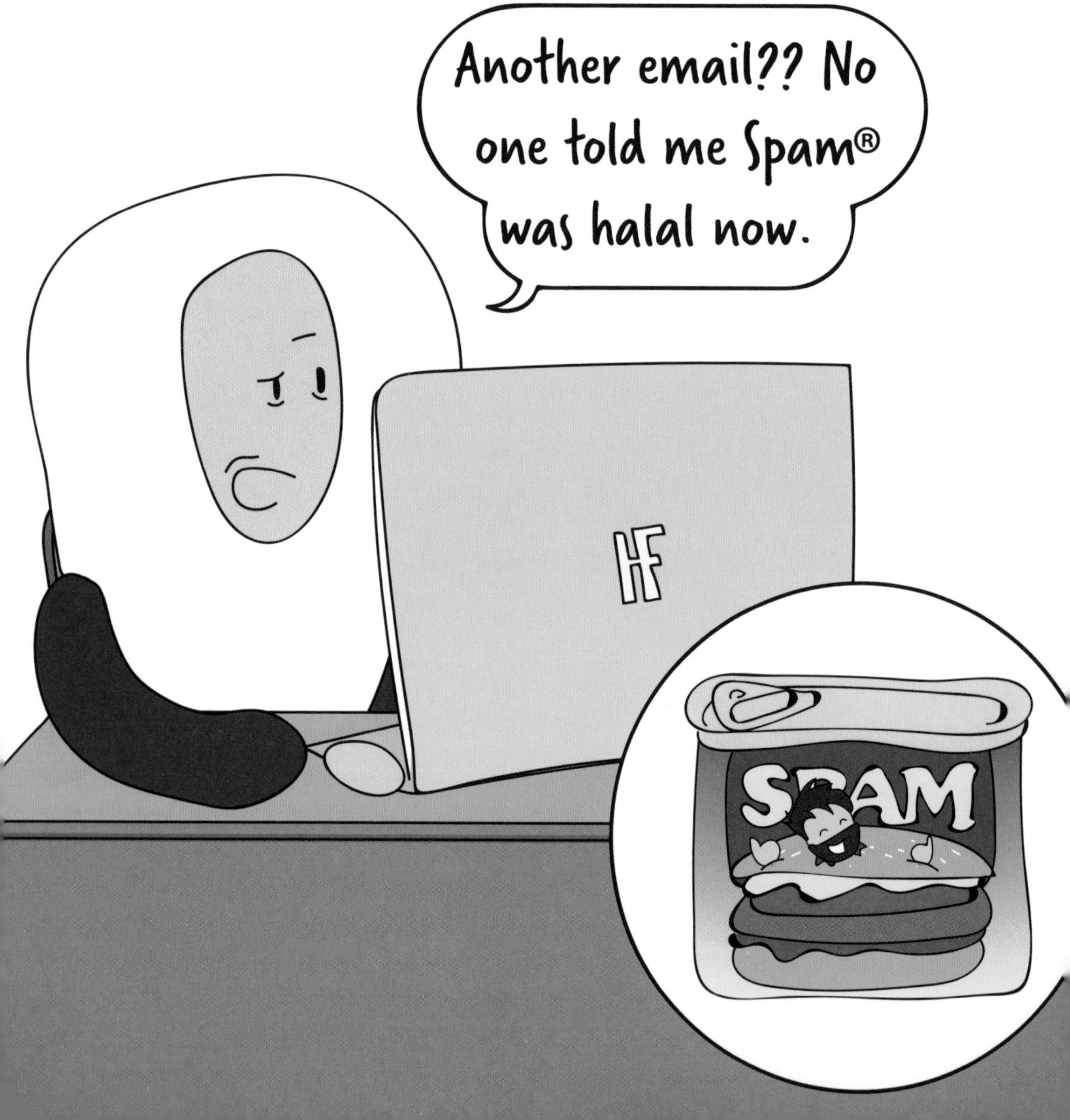
Another email?? No one told me Spam® was halal now.
HF
SPAM

It was great at first because our emails (read: love letters) were really long, and she never had time to read them.

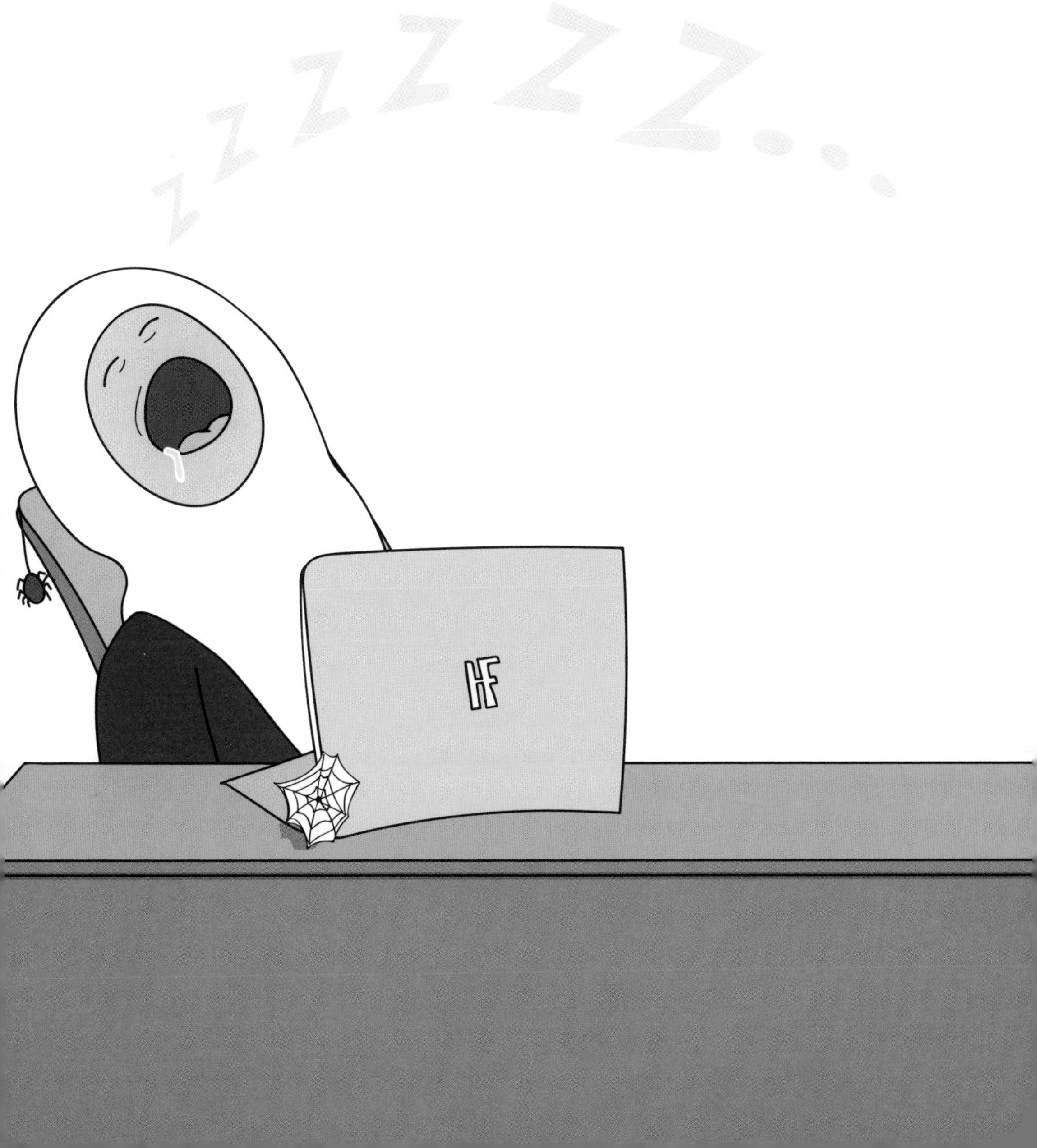

Then she assigned my hypervigilant little sister to be her designated email reader.

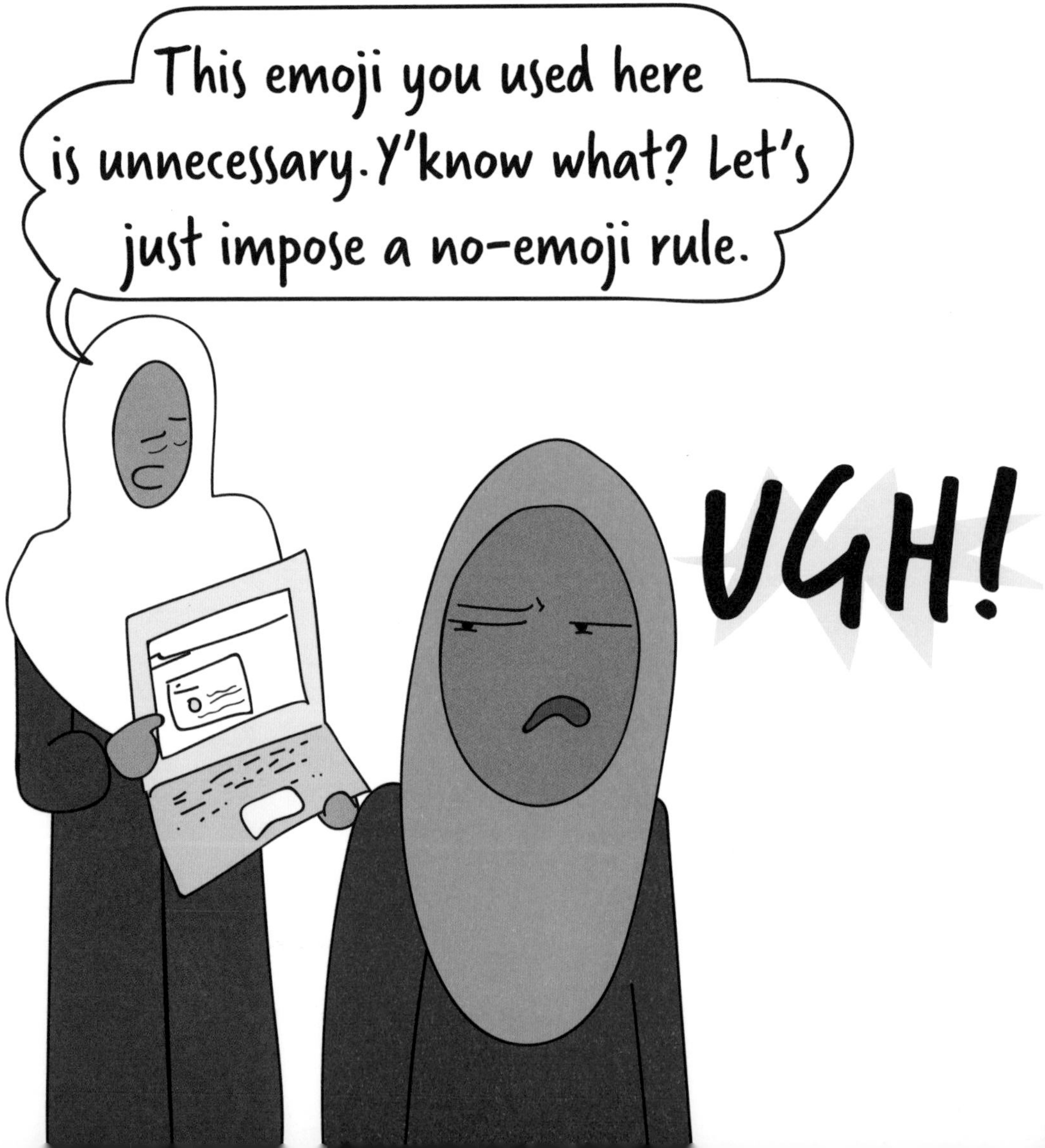
This emoji you used here is unnecessary. Y'know what? Let's just impose a no-emoji rule.
UGH!

Did you know that souls meet each other in a pre-earthly life? And when those souls meet each other again on Earth, it's as if they'd known each other forever. That's why you can meet someone for the first time and feel like you've known them your whole life.

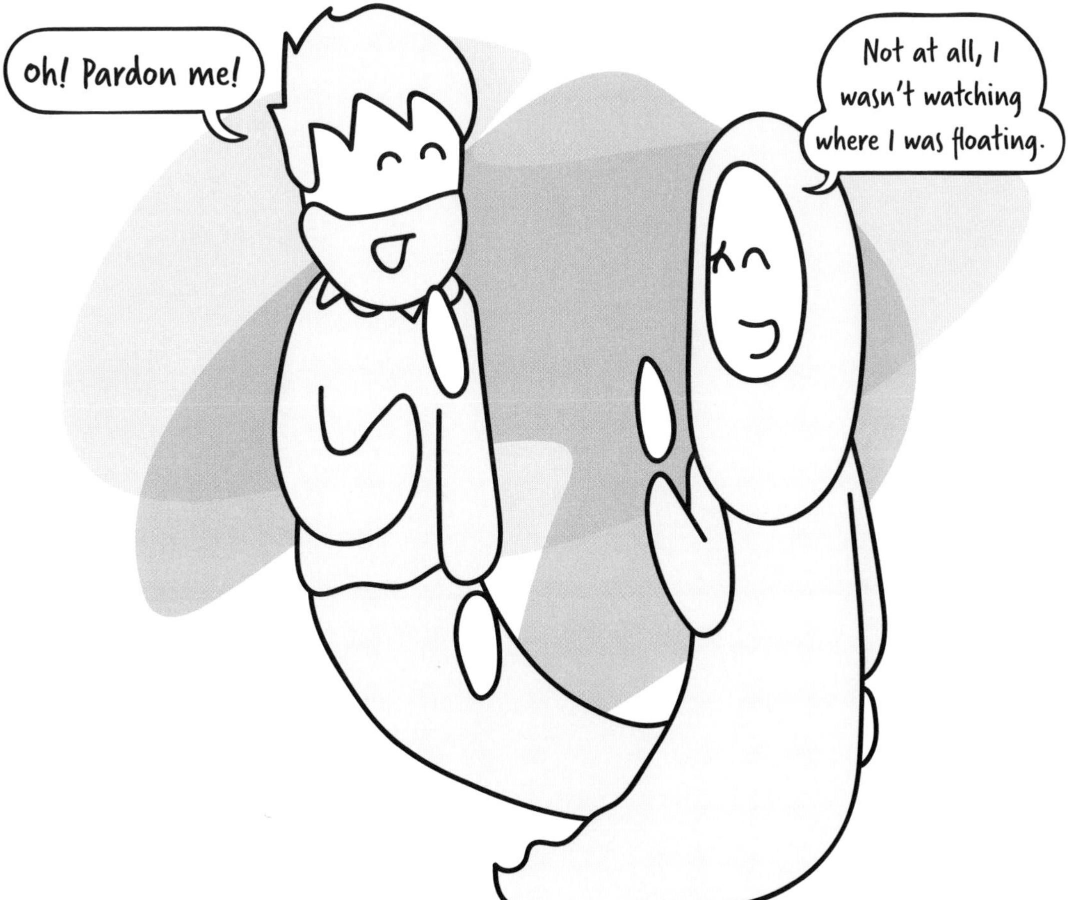
oh! Pardon me!
Not at all, I wasn't watching where I was floating.

With Gehad, I knew almost instantly that our souls had met before. It was undeniable.

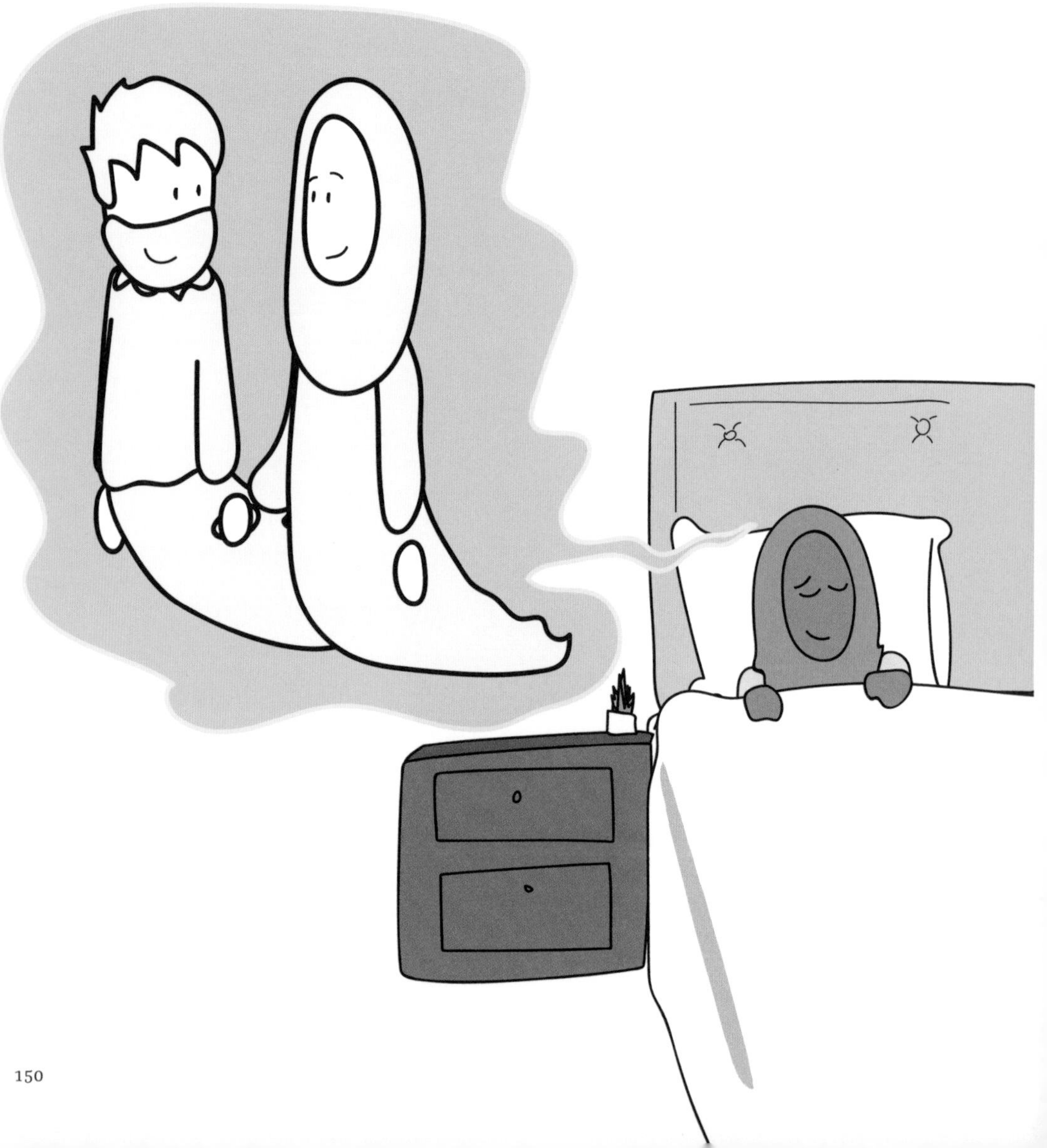

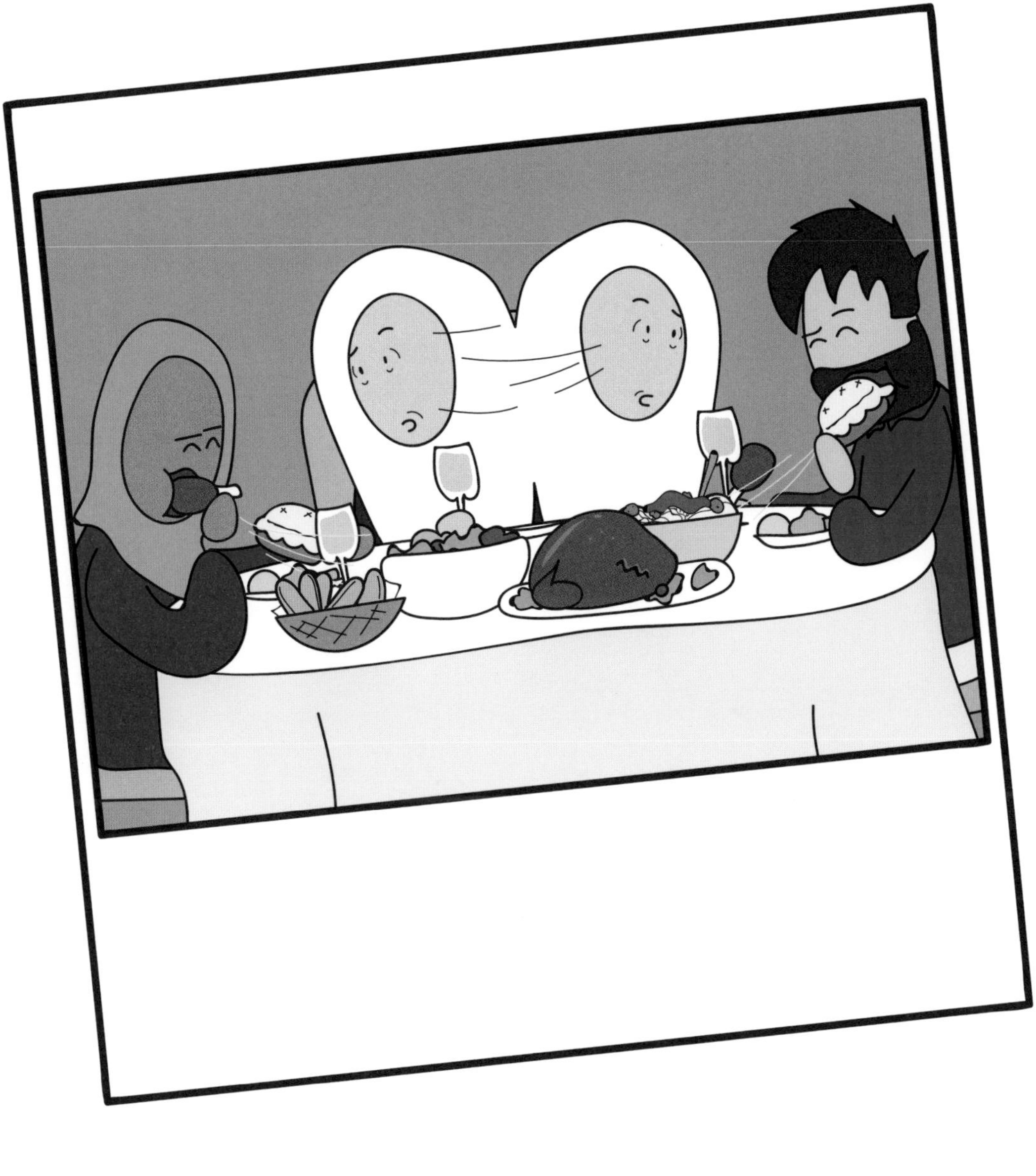

Finish this song: ♪ When there's trouble... ♪
♪ You call DW! ♪ Darkwing Duck! ♫

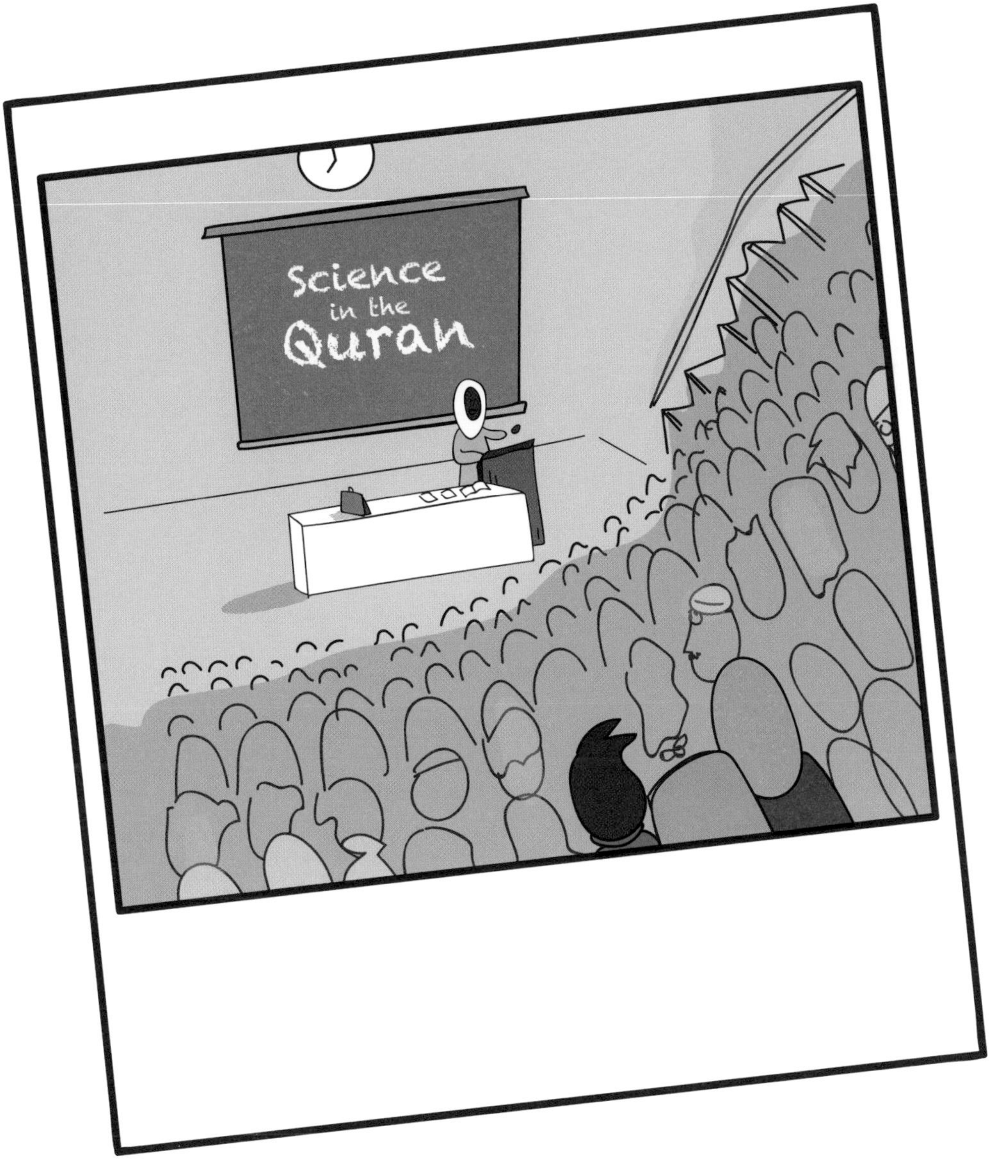
Science
in the
Quran

And I said, "I'd rather eat pumpkin-spiced hummus."
Can you even imagine?
ha ha ha ha

I met his parents.

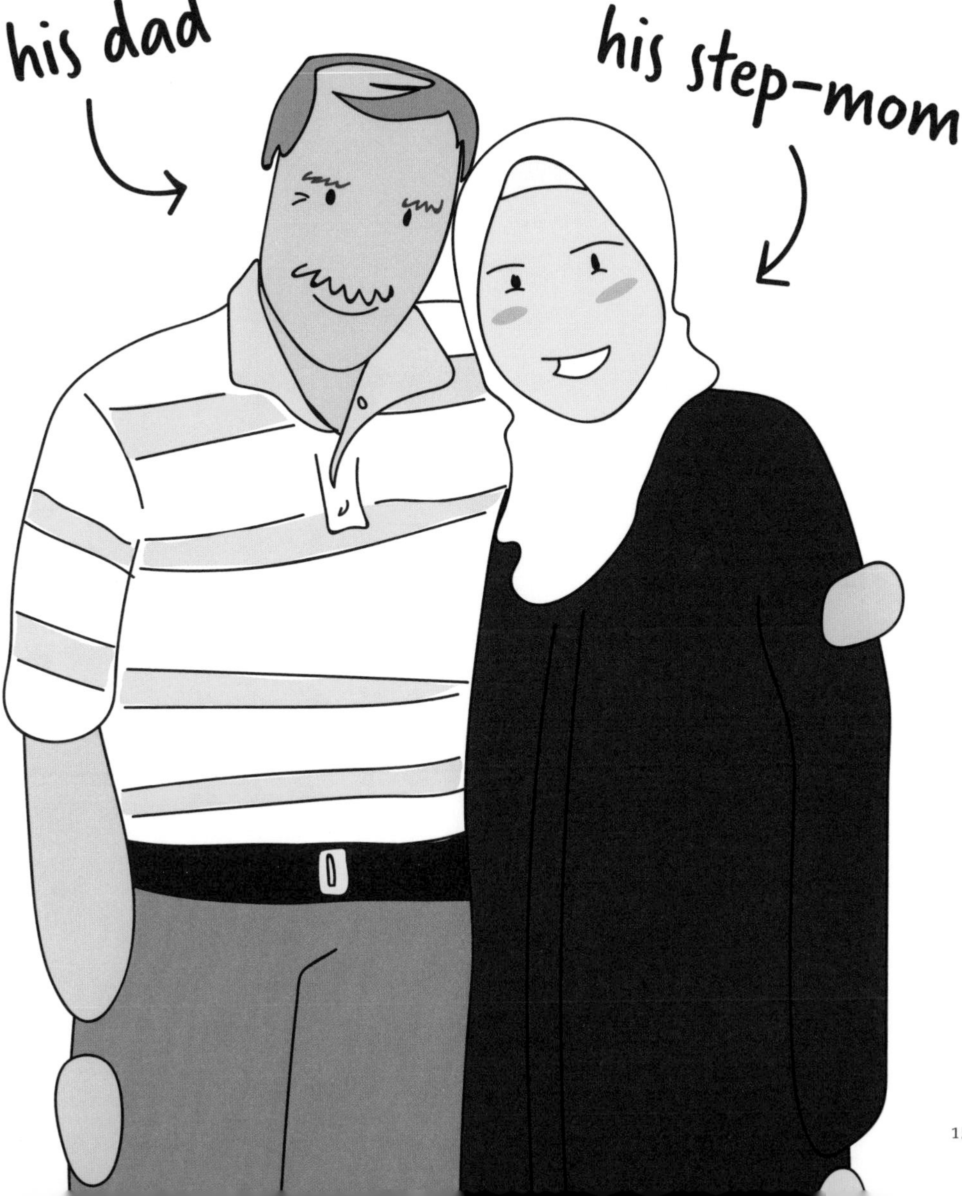
his dad
his step-mom

Both sets.

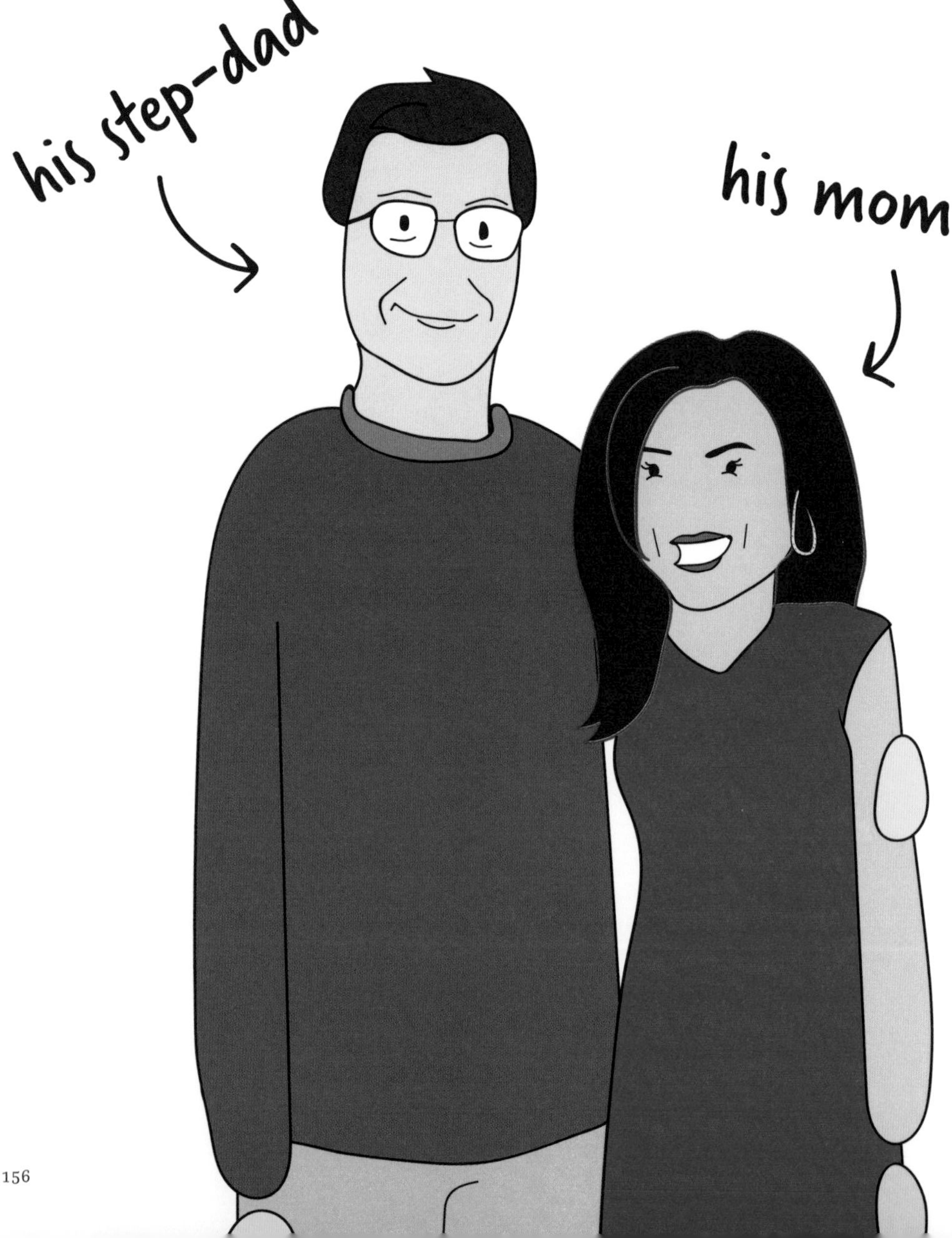
his step-dad
his mom

We exchanged traditional gifts.

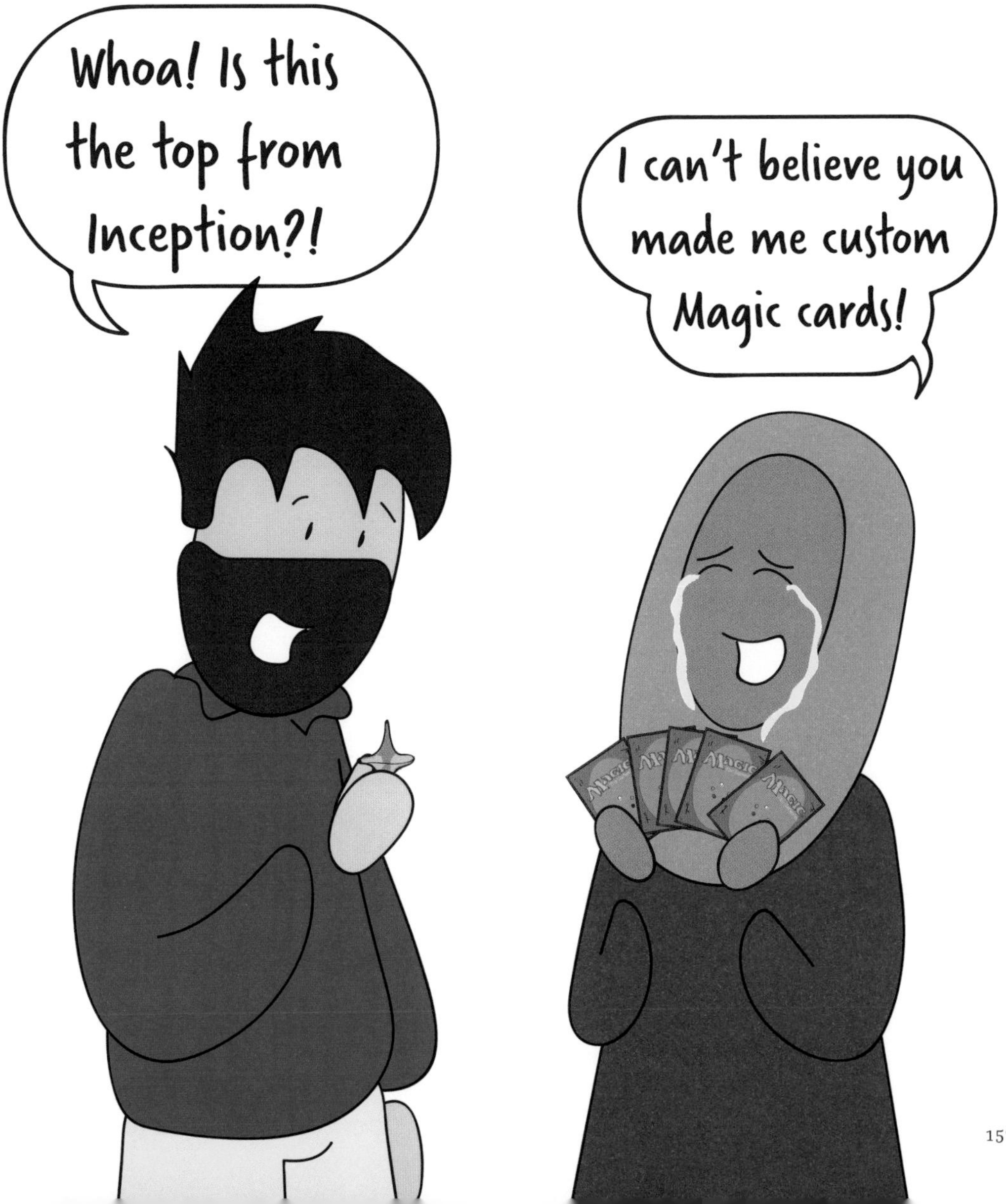
Whoa! Is this the top from Inception?!
I can't believe you made me custom Magic cards!

Went out on more chaperoned dates.

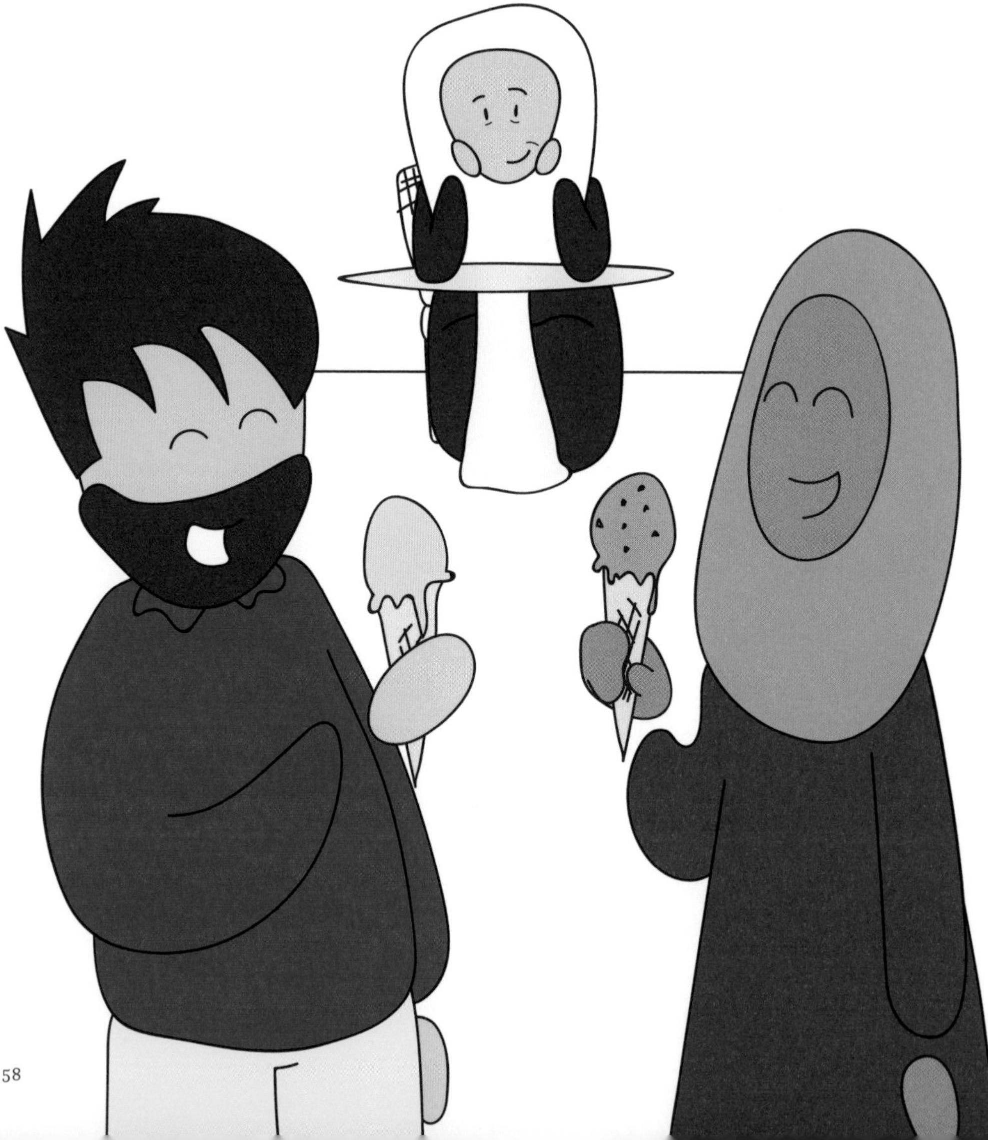

And finally arranged THE date.

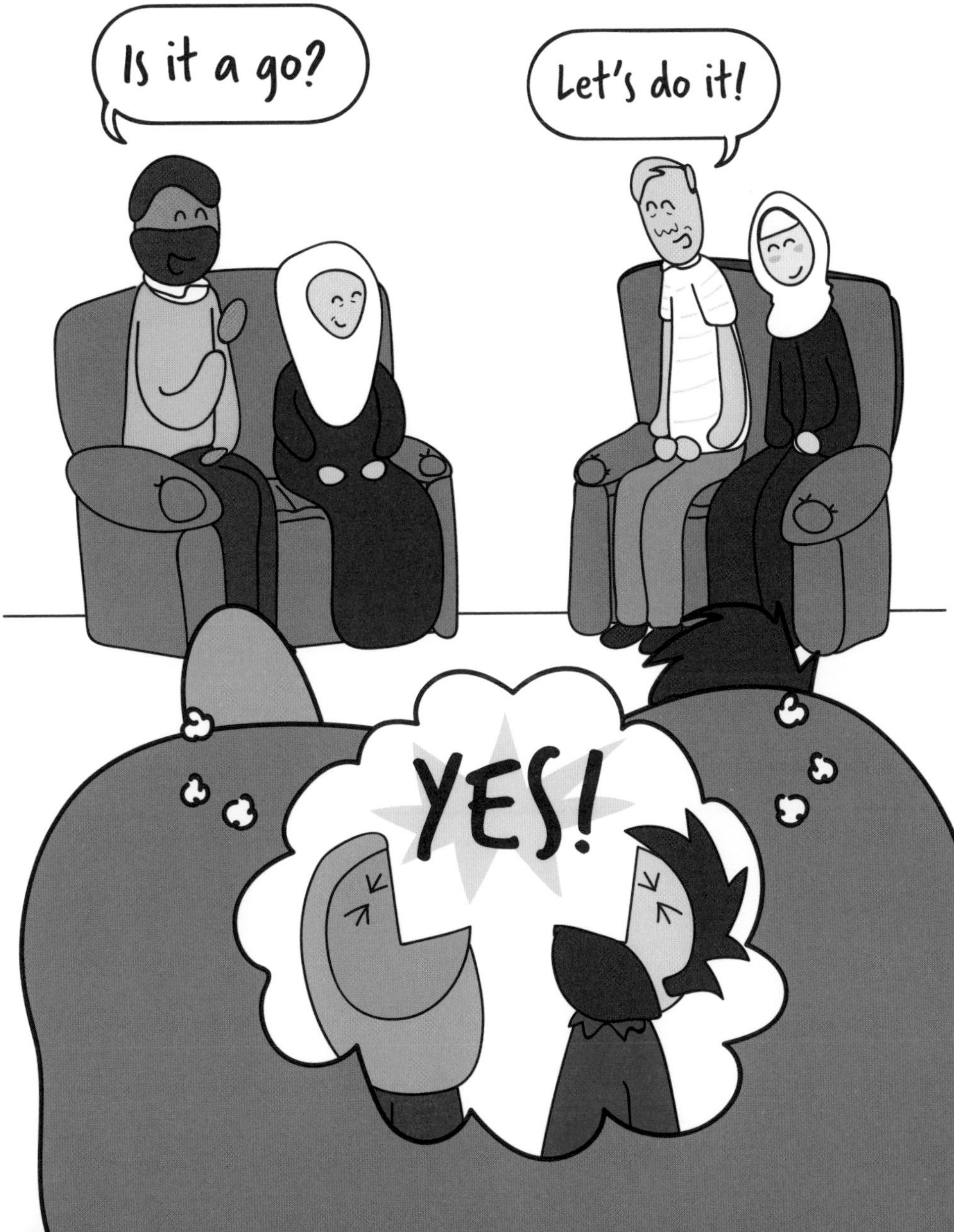
Is it a go?
Let's do it!
YES!

The Kitab and Walima

The kitab (also called a "nikah") is the first of the two parts of an Islamic wedding. It's the religious ceremony where the signing of the marriage contract happens and is usually followed by a dope party. *No actual dope present.*

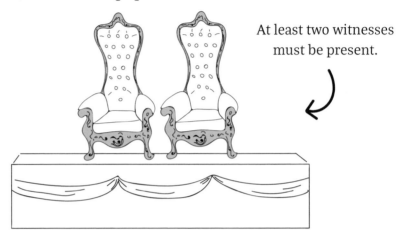

At least two witnesses must be present.

Then comes the walima. It's the second part of the Islamic wedding that could be held months after the kitab or literally the next day.

Early to my own wedding? Why do I keep doing this?!

I didn't care much for the actual wedding planning, so I let my mom take care of everything.

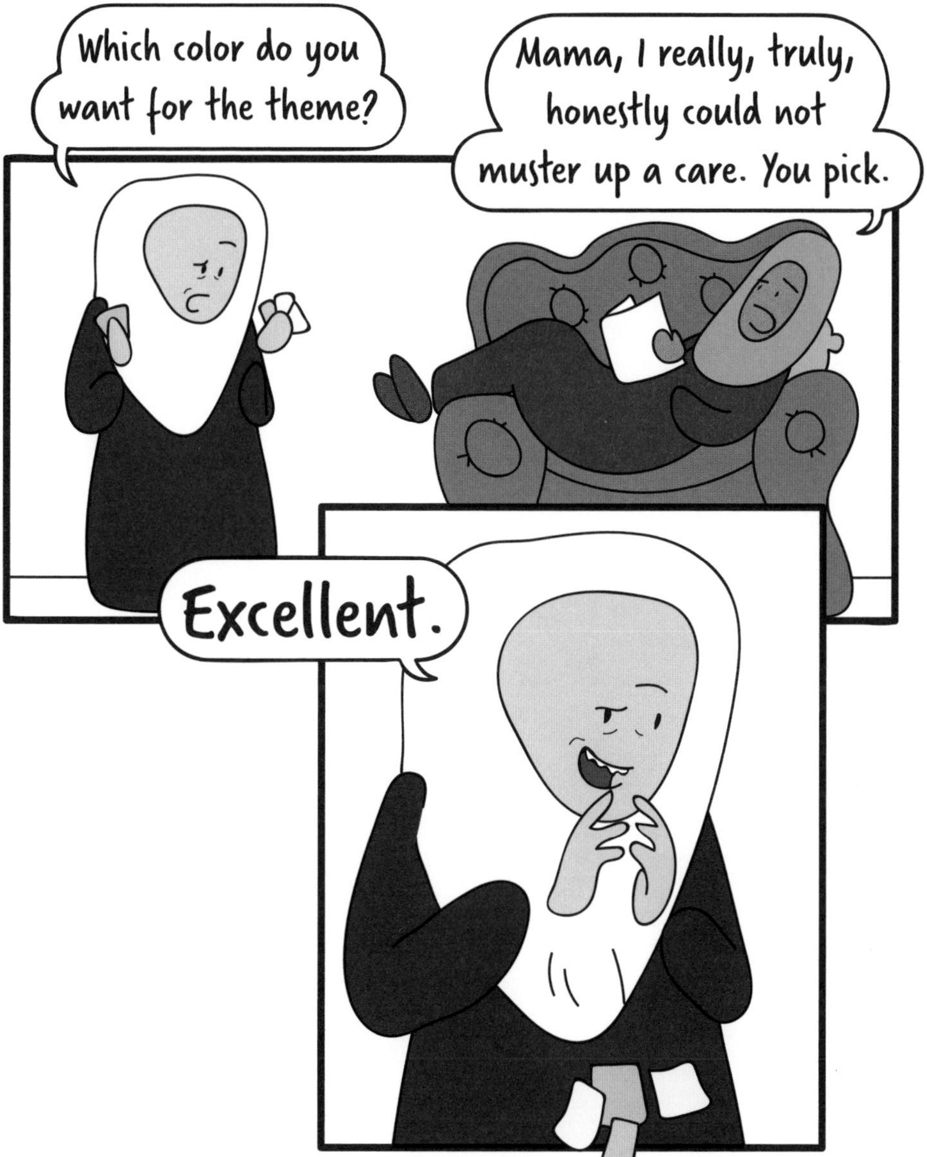
Which color do you want for the theme?
Mama, I really, truly, honestly could not muster up a care. You pick.
Excellent.

There was a bridal shower.

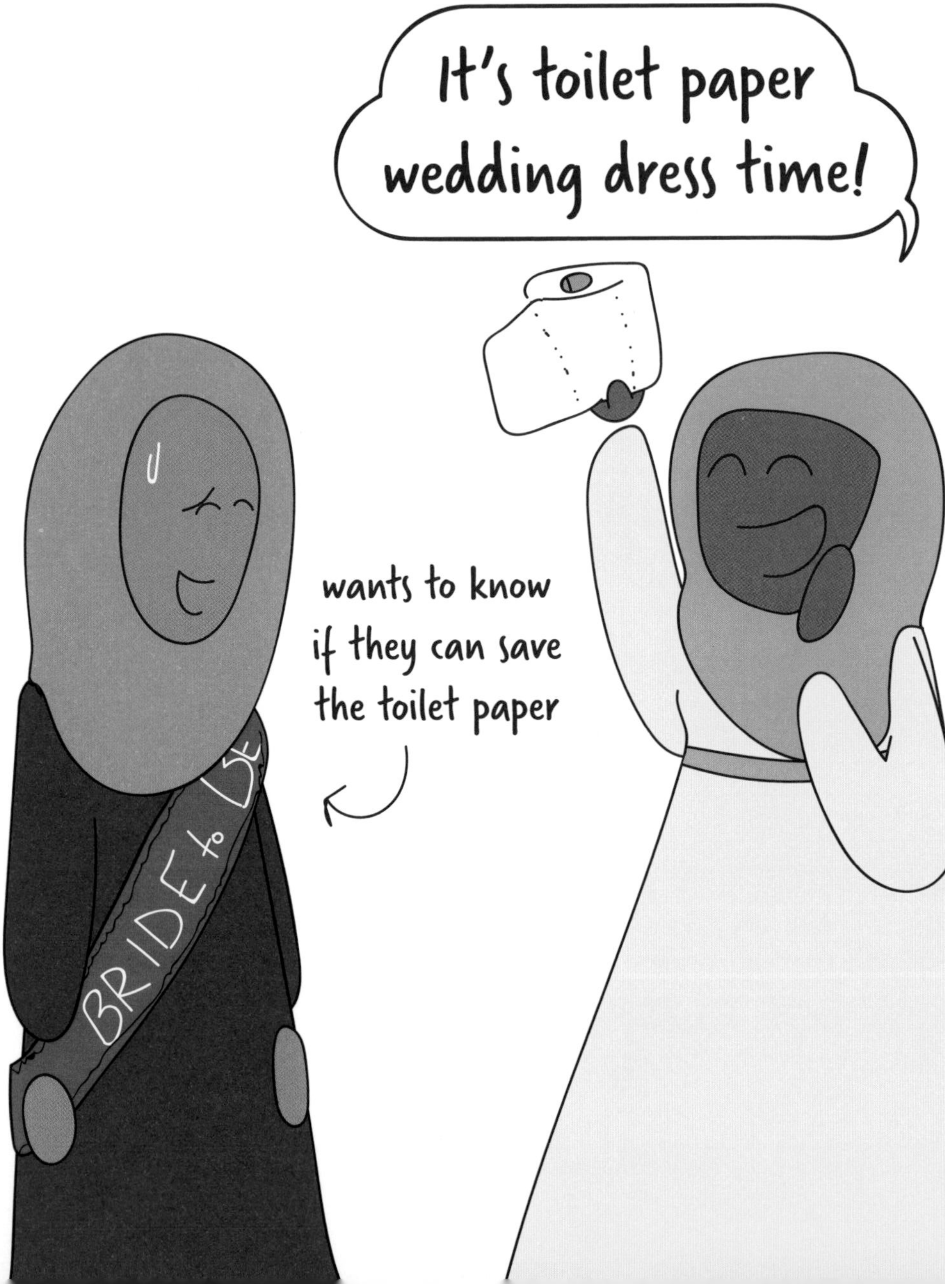
It's toilet paper wedding dress time!
wants to know if they can save the toilet paper
BRIDE to BE

And a surprise bachelorette party.

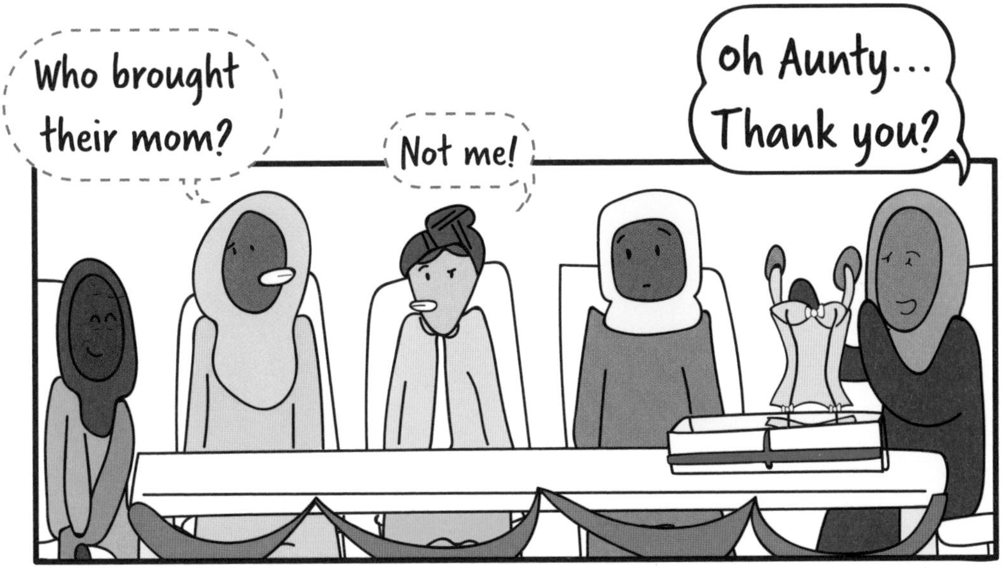
Who brought their mom?
Not me!
Oh Aunty... Thank you?

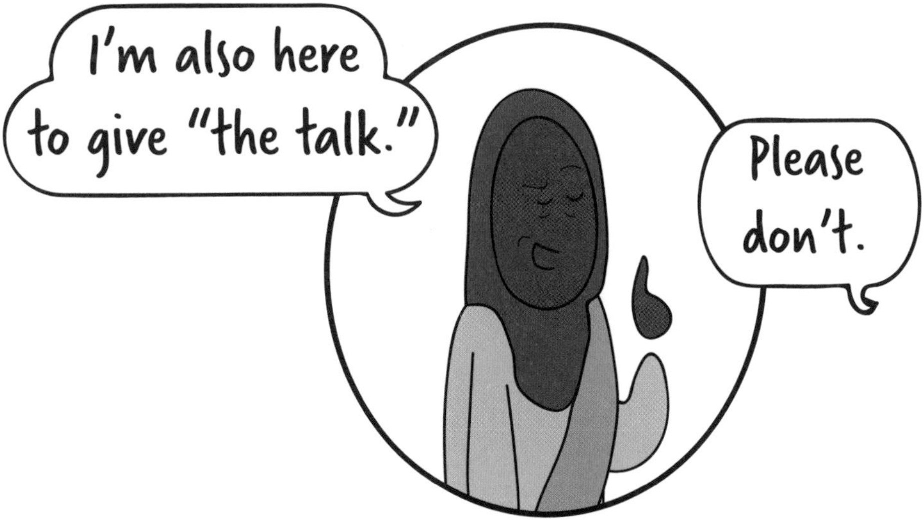
I'm also here to give "the talk."
Please don't.

The kitab itself was a lot of fun. The men partied in one hall and the women in another. The women dressed up, let their hair down, and danced to their hearts' content. Usually, the "shy, demure bride" would make a grand entrance to the sound of loud and shrill ululations (or zagharit) by every lady who knew how.

Lelelelelelelelelelelelelelelelelelelelelelel

lelelelelelel elelel eeeeeeeeeeeeees

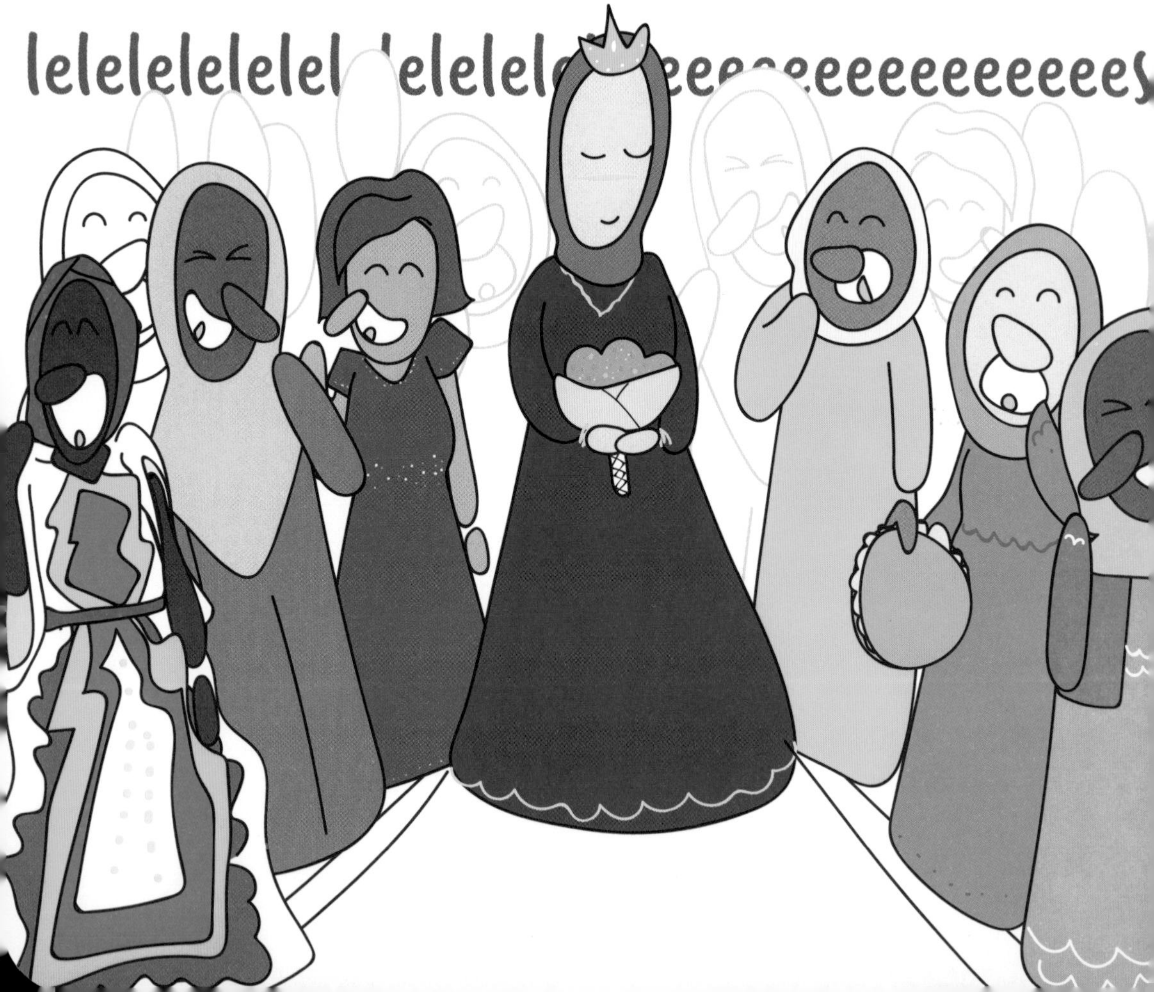

But not me. Much to the embarrassment of my mother, I walked in doing my own zaghrouta.

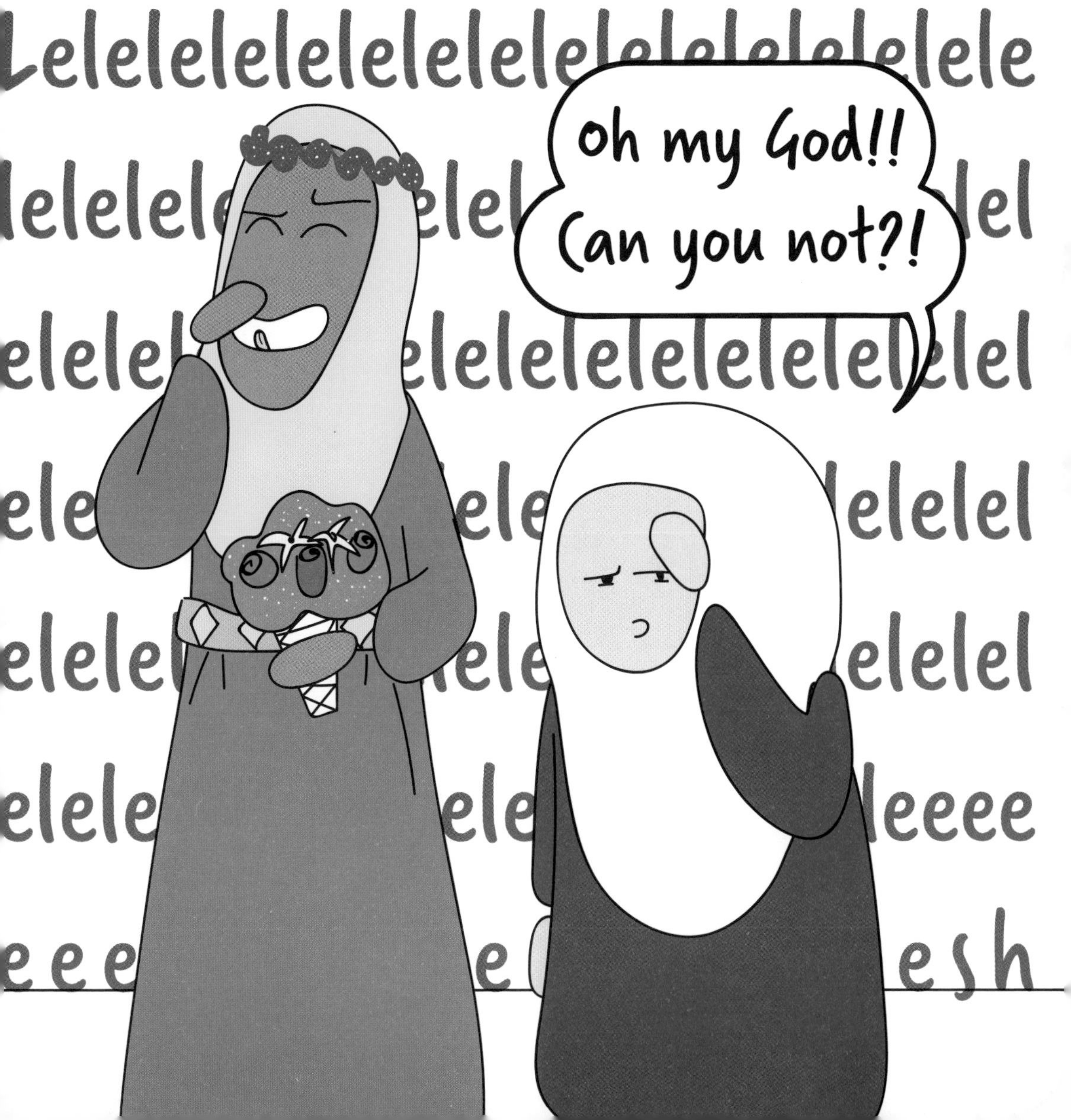
oh my God!! Can you not?!

Gehad and I signed the contract (cue more zagharit).

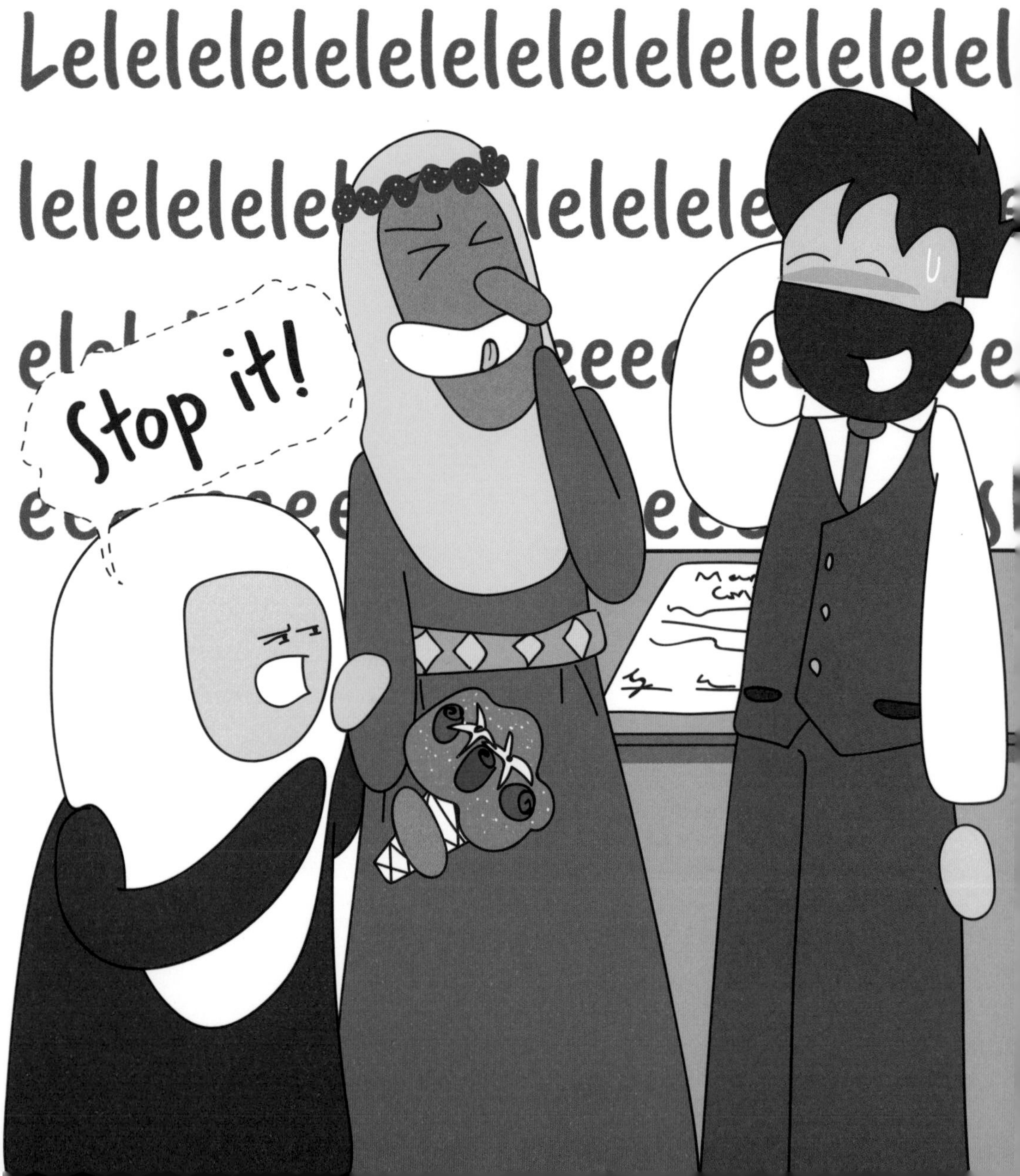
Lelelelelelelelelelelelelelelelelel
Stop it!

The walima happened three months later.

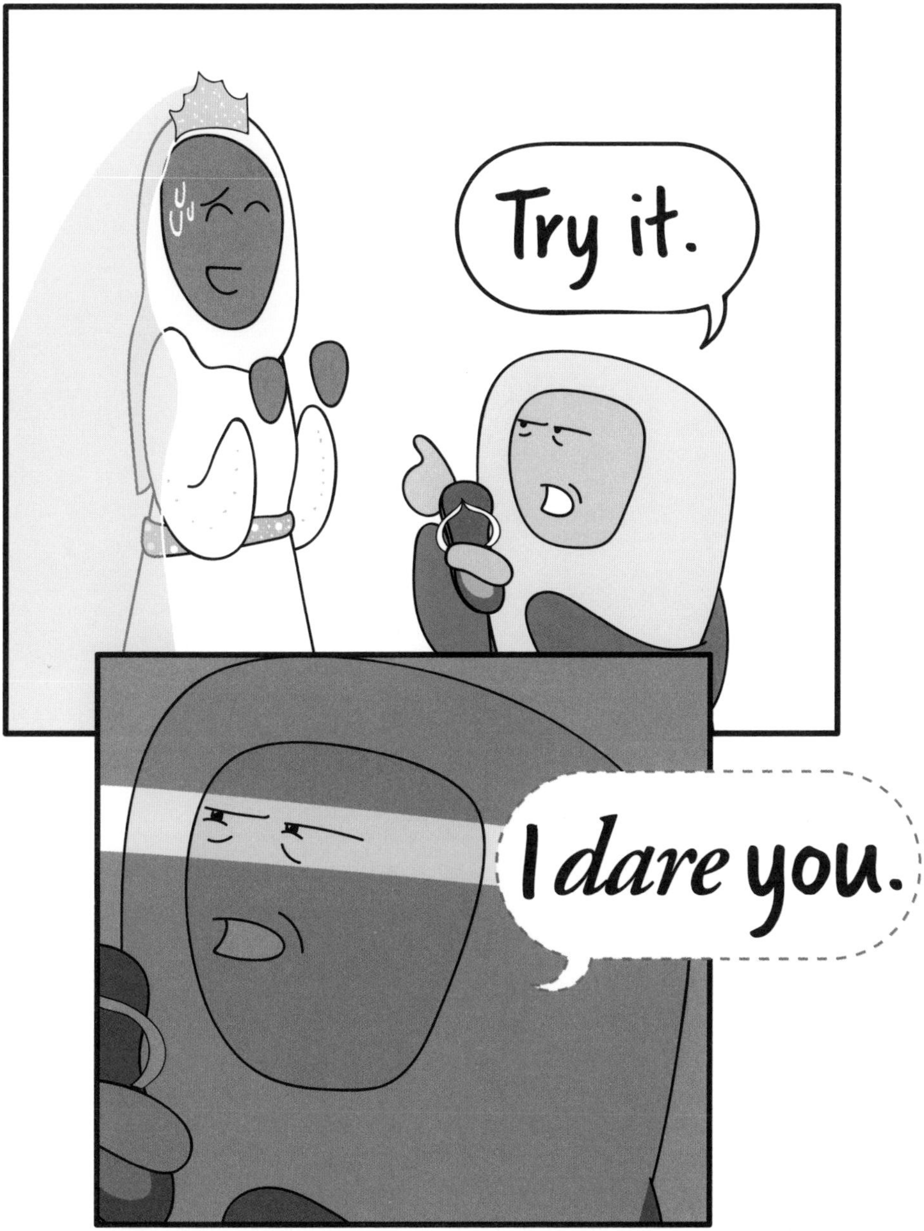
Try it.
I dare you.

A few weeks shy of turning 26, and there I was dancing at my wedding, defying all aunty odds, in my white gown and all.

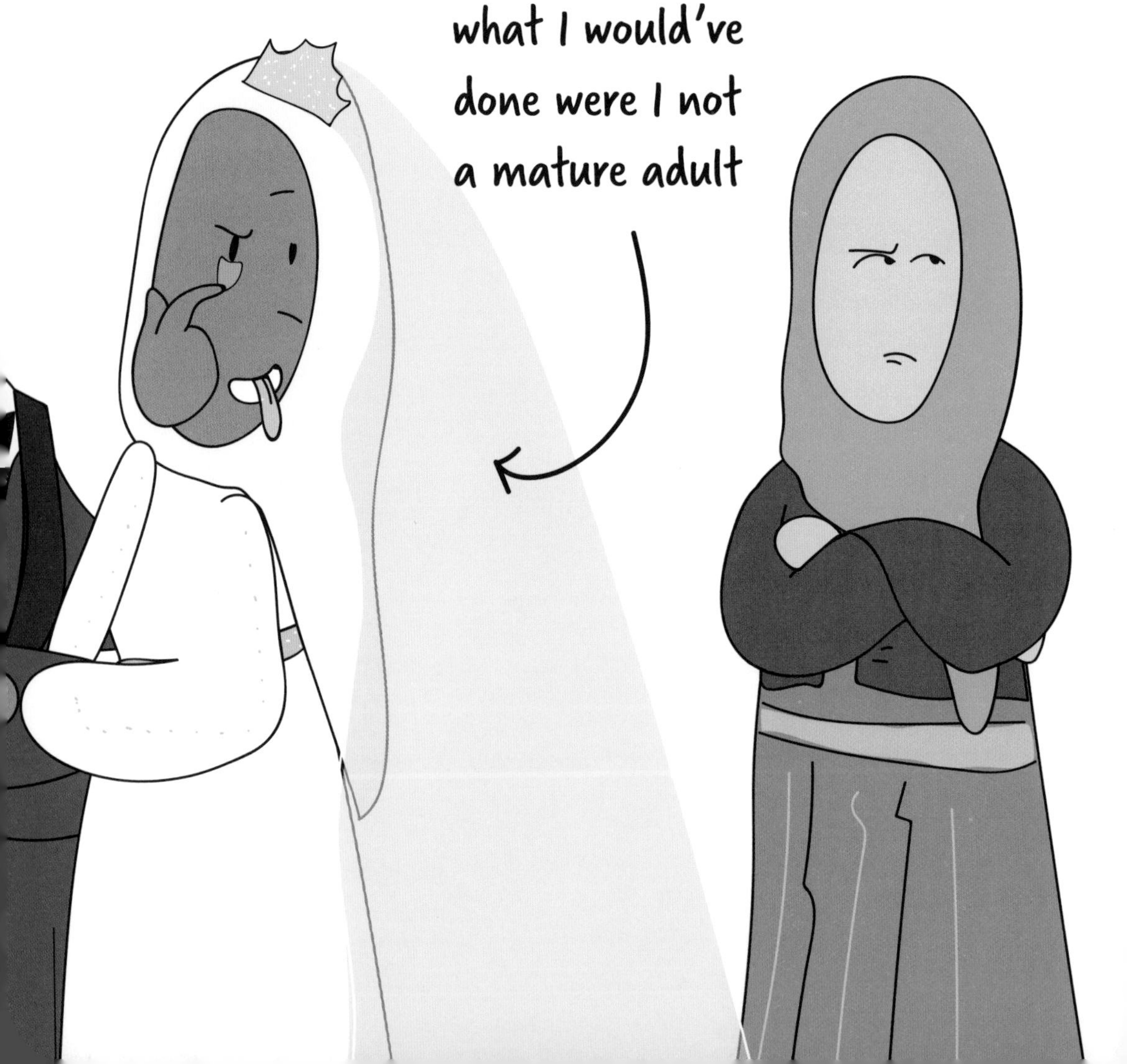
what I would've done were I not a mature adult

I don't really remember much about that day, and it certainly didn't help that our photographer was still new to the craft.

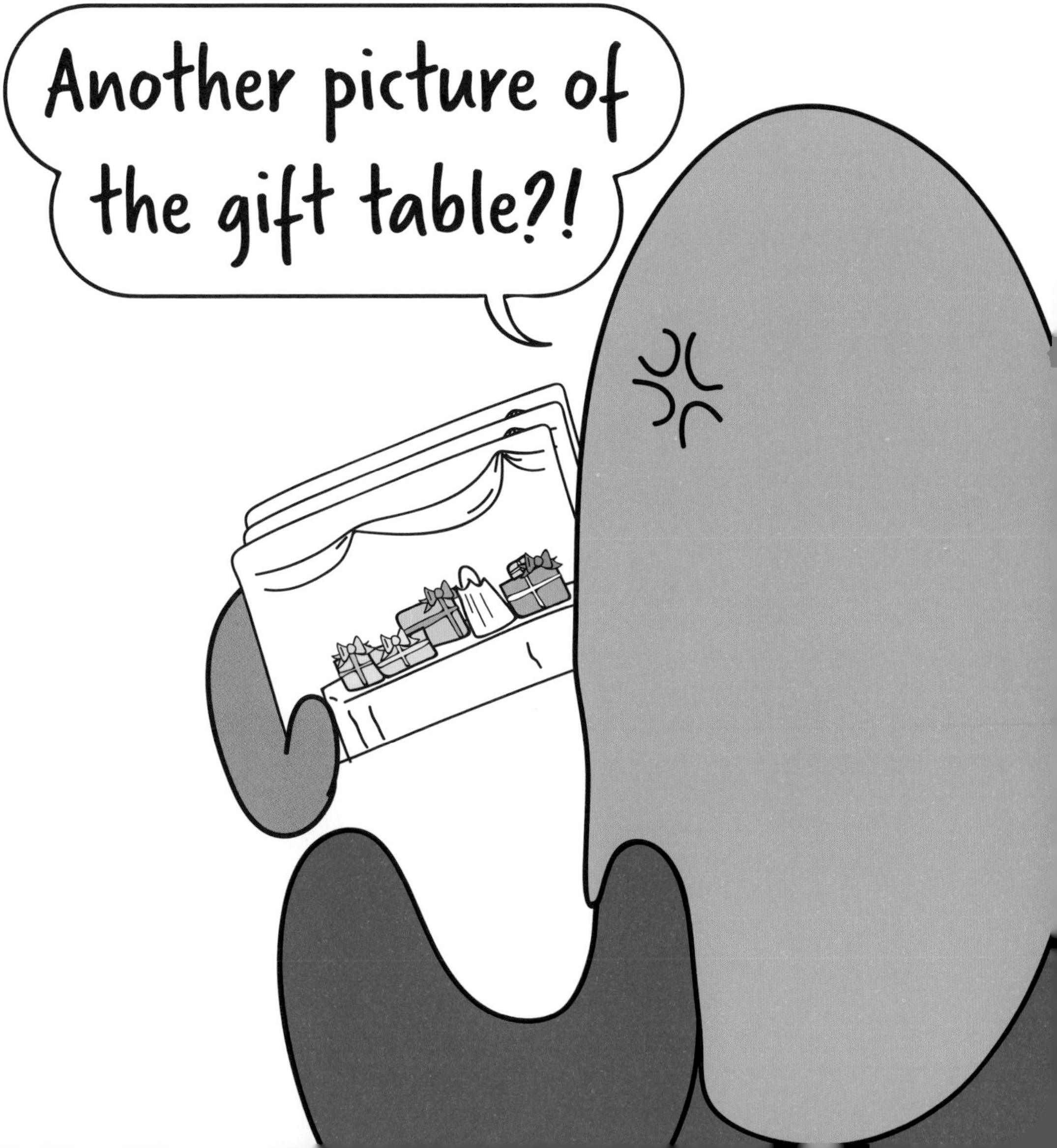
Another picture of the gift table?!

But I don't mind. What I do remember is that I couldn't wait to start the next chapter of my life with a man who was worth waiting for.

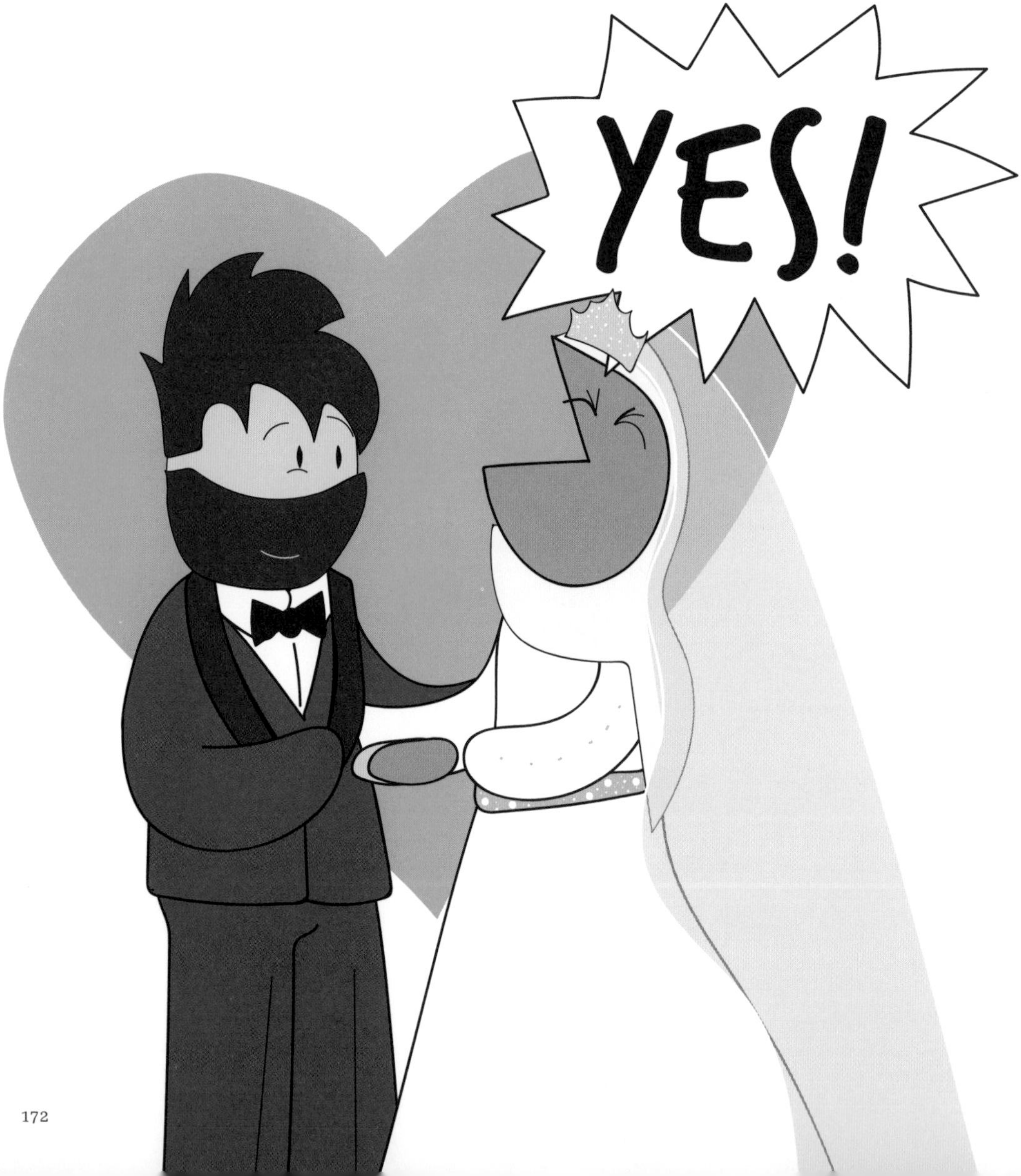
YES!

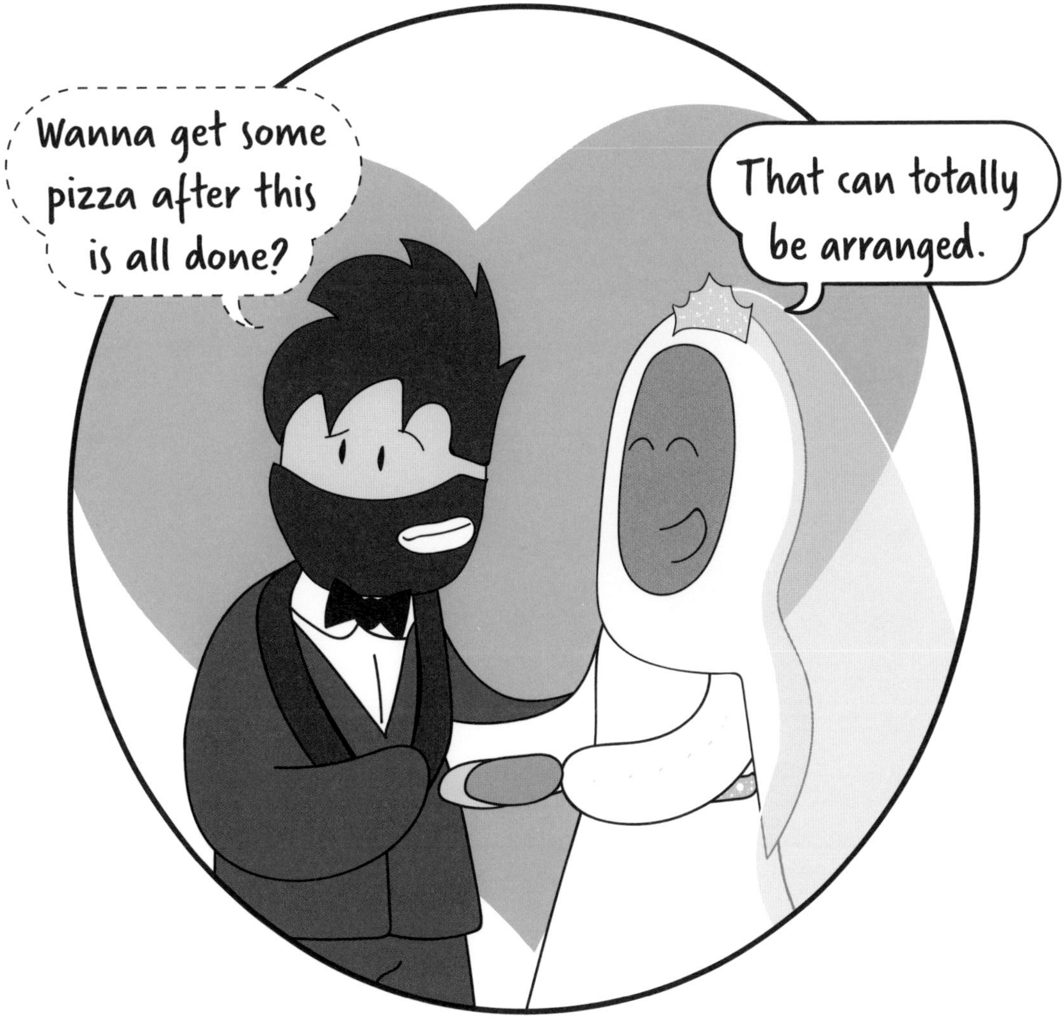
Wanna get some pizza after this is all done?
That can totally be arranged.

ACKNOWLEDGMENTS

Thank you, Immi, for your patience with me during my "boy-crazy phase." I know I didn't make it easy. Thank you for your support, for your love, for your duas, for never giving up on me, and for trusting me enough to trust myself.

To my sisters, you are my role models and constant inspirations. Also, the fact that there are five of us and five Bennet sisters always made me smile (P.S., I'm obviously Elizabeth).

To Sarah, thank you for being my wing woman at the conference and for still being one of my best friends today. You and I were "soul meets" before Gehad and I ever met.

To Rahaf, Nabil, Maha, and Samir. Most people pray to get a set of great in-laws. I was blessed with two. Thank you for being my home away from home and for welcoming me to the family with such open arms.

To my suitor (yes, you). Shelby Lorman said it best: ya didn't get me here, but I wouldn't be here without you, so thanks.

To my editor, Patty Rice. Thank you for seeing my potential and for loving this story as much as I do!

To my agent, Kathleen! I don't even know where to begin. Thank you for being my hype woman, for the pep talks, for believing in me and my worth, and for having my back in every way!

To Gehad, thank you for laughing at my jokes, for making me feel less like a weirdo for bringing a legal pad to our first meeting (because you had one, too!), for being with me through ups and downs, for hyping me up, for ALWAYS believing in me, for getting frustrated with me for not believing in myself, and for being the smartest, kindest, most generous man I know.

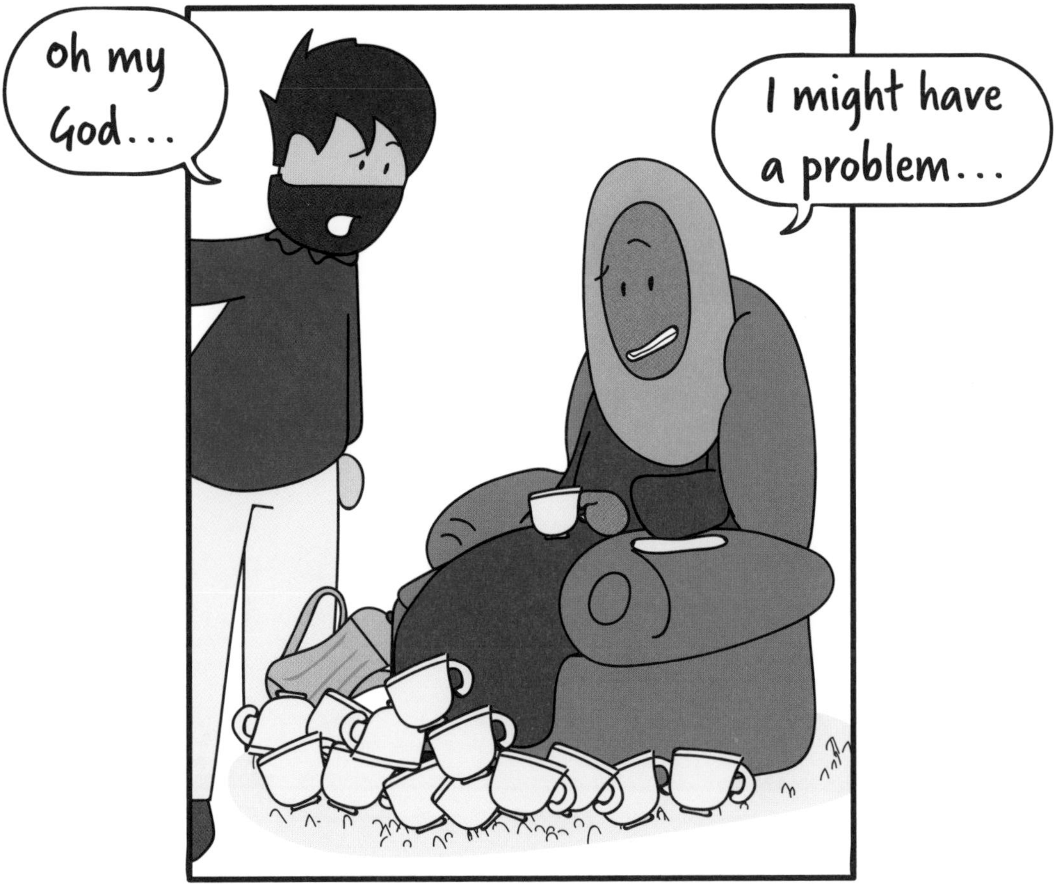
Oh my God...
I might have a problem...

ABOUT THE AUTHOR

Huda Fahmy grew up in Dearborn, Michigan, and has loved comics since she was a kid. She attended the University of Michigan, where she majored in English. She taught English to middle and high schoolers for eight years before she started writing about her experiences as a visibly Muslim woman in America and was encouraged by her older sister to turn these stories into comics. Huda, her husband, Gehad, and their son reside in Houston, Texas. She continues to identify as a hopeless romantic.

Andrews McMeel Publishing
a division of Andrews McMeel Universal
1130 Walnut Street, Kansas City, Missouri 64106

www.andrewsmcmeel.com

20 21 22 23 24 SDB 10 9 8 7 6 5 4 3 2 1

ISBN: 978-1-5248-5622-9

Library of Congress Control Number: 2019946558

Editor: Patty Rice
Art Director: Holly Swayne
Production Editor: Elizabeth A. Garcia
Production Manager: Tamara Haus

ATTENTION: SCHOOLS AND BUSINESSES
Andrews McMeel books are available at quantity discounts with bulk purchase
for educational, business, or sales promotional use. For information, please e-mail the
Andrews McMeel Publishing Special Sales Department:
specialsales@amuniversal.com.